UNIVERSITY CASEBOOK SERIES

2019 STATUTORY APPENDIX AND CASE SUPPLEMENT TO

COX AND BOK'S

LABOR LAW

CASES AND MATERIALS

SIXTEENTH EDITION

ROBERT A. GORMAN
Kenneth W. Gemmill Professor of Law Emeritus
University of Pennsylvania

MATTHEW W. FINKIN
Swanlund Chair and Center for Advanced Study Professor of Law
University of Illinois

TIMOTHY P. GLYNN
Senior Associate Dean and Andrea J. Catania Endowed Professor of Law
Seton Hall University School of Law

SUPPLEMENT

by

MATTHEW W. FINKIN
TIMOTHY P. GLYNN

FOUNDATION
PRESS

University Casebook Series is a trademark registered in the U.S. Patent and Trademark Office.

© 2016–2018 LEG, Inc. d/b/a West Academic
© 2019 LEG, Inc. d/b/a West Academic
    444 Cedar Street, Suite 700
    St. Paul, MN 55101
    1-877-888-1330

Printed in the United States of America

ISBN: 978-1-68467-147-2

TABLE OF CONTENTS

TABLE OF CASES

The principal cases are in bold type.

UNIVERSITY CASEBOOK SERIES®

2019 STATUTORY APPENDIX AND CASE SUPPLEMENT TO

COX AND BOK'S

LABOR LAW

CASES AND MATERIALS

SIXTEENTH EDITION

SHERMAN ACT

26 Stat. 209 (1890), as amended, 15 U.S.C. §§ 1 et seq. (1988).

Sec. 1. Every contract, combination in the form of a trust or otherwise, or conspiracy, in restraint of trade or commerce among the several States, or with foreign nations, is hereby declared to be illegal. Every person who shall make any such contract or engage in any such combination or conspiracy, shall be deemed guilty of a misdemeanor, and, on conviction thereof, shall be punished by fine not exceeding five thousand dollars, or by imprisonment not exceeding one year, or by both said punishments, in the discretion of the court.

Sec. 2. Every person who shall monopolize, or attempt to monopolize, or combine or conspire with any other person or persons, to monopolize any part of the trade or commerce among the several States, or with foreign nations, shall be deemed guilty of a misdemeanor, and, on conviction thereof, shall be punished by fine not exceeding five thousand dollars, or by imprisonment not exceeding one year, or by both said punishments, in the discretion of the court.

Sec. 3. Every contract, combination in form of trust or otherwise, or conspiracy, in restraint of trade or commerce in any territory of the United States or of the District of Columbia, or in restraint of trade or commerce between any such territory and another, or between any such territory or territories and any State or States or the District of Columbia, or with foreign nations, or between the District of Columbia and any State or States or foreign nations, is hereby declared illegal. Every person who shall make any such contract or engage in any such combination or conspiracy, shall be deemed guilty of a misdemeanor, and, on conviction thereof, shall be punished by fine not exceeding five thousand dollars, or by imprisonment not exceeding one year, or by both said punishments, in the discretion of the court.

Sec. 4. The several circuit courts of the United States are hereby invested with jurisdiction to prevent and restrain violations of this act; and it shall be the duty of the several district attorneys of the United States, in their respective districts, under the direction of the Attorney General, to institute proceedings in equity to prevent and restrain such violations. Such proceedings may be by way of petition setting forth the case and praying that such violation shall be enjoined or otherwise prohibited. When the parties complained of shall have been duly notified of such petition the court shall proceed, as soon as may be, to the hearing and determination of the case; and pending such petition and before final decree, the court may at any time make such temporary restraining order or prohibition as shall be deemed just in the premises.

Sec. 5. Whenever it shall appear to the court before which any proceeding under section 4 of this act may be pending, that the ends of justice require that other parties should be brought before the court, the court may cause them to be summoned, whether they reside in the district in which the court is held or not; and subpoenas to that end may be served in any district by the marshal thereof.

Sec. 6. Any property owned under any contract or by any combination, or pursuant to any conspiracy (and being the subject thereof) mentioned in section 1 of this act, and being in the course of transportation from one State to another, or to a foreign country, shall be forfeited to the United States, and may be seized and condemned by like proceedings as those provided by law for the forfeiture, seizure, and condemnation of property imported into the United States contrary to law.

Sec. 7. Any person who shall be injured in his business or property by any other person or corporation by reason of anything forbidden or declared to be unlawful by this act, may sue therefor in any Circuit Court of the United States in the district in which the defendant resides or is found, without respect to the amount in controversy, and shall recover three-fold the damages sustained, and the costs of suit, including a reasonable attorney's fee.

Sec. 8. That the word "person," or "persons" wherever used in this act shall be deemed to include corporations and associations existing under or authorized by the laws of either the United States, the laws of any State or the laws of any foreign country.

CLAYTON ACT

38 Stat. 730 (1914), as amended, 15 U.S.C. §§ 12 et seq. (1988).

Be it enacted by the Senate and House of Representatives of the United States of America in Congress assembled, That "anti-trust laws," as used herein, includes the Act entitled "An Act to protect trade and commerce against unlawful restraints and monopolies", approved July second, eighteen hundred and ninety [Sherman Act, supra.] * * *

* * *

Sec. 6. That the labor of a human being is not a commodity or article of commerce. Nothing contained in the anti-trust laws shall be construed to forbid the existence and operation of labor, agricultural, or horticultural organizations, instituted for the purposes of mutual help, and not having capital stock or conducted for profit, or to forbid or restrain individual members of such organizations from lawfully carrying out the legitimate objects thereof; nor shall such organizations, or the members thereof, be held or construed to be illegal combinations or conspiracies in restraint of trade, under the anti-trust laws.

* * *

Sec. 16. That any person, firm, corporation, or association shall be entitled to sue for and have injunctive relief, in any court of the United States having jurisdiction over the parties, against threatened loss or damage by a violation of the anti-trust laws, including sections two, three, seven and eight of this Act, when and under the same conditions and principles as injunctive relief against threatened conduct that will cause loss or damage is granted by courts of equity, under the rules governing such proceedings, and upon the execution of proper bond against damages for an injunction improvidently granted and a showing that the danger of irreparable loss or damage is immediate, a preliminary injunction may issue: *Provided,* That nothing herein contained shall be construed to entitle any person, firm, corporation, or association, except the United States, to bring suit in equity for injunctive relief against any common carrier subject to the provisions of the Act to regulate commerce, approved February fourth, eighteen hundred and eighty-seven, in respect of any matter subject to the regulation, supervision, or other jurisdiction of the Interstate Commerce Commission.

* * *

Sec. 20. That no restraining order or injunction shall be granted by any court of the United States, or a judge or the judges thereof, in any case between an employer and employees, or between employers and employees, or between employees, or between persons employed and persons seeking employment, involving, or growing out of, a dispute concerning terms or conditions of employment, unless necessary to prevent irreparable injury to property, or to a property right, of the party making the application, for which injury there is no adequate remedy at law, and such property or property right must be described with particularity in the application, which must be in writing and sworn to by the applicant or by his agent or attorney.

And no such restraining order or injunction shall prohibit any person or persons, whether singly or in concert, from terminating any relation of employment, or from ceasing to perform any work or labor, or from recommending, advising, or persuading others by peaceful means so to do; or from attending at any place where any such person or persons may lawfully be, for the purpose of peacefully obtaining or communicating information, or from peacefully persuading any person to work or to abstain from working; or from ceasing to patronize or to employ any party to such dispute, or from recommending, advising, or persuading others by peaceful and lawful means so to do; or from paying or giving to, or withholding from, any person engaged in such dispute, any strike benefits or other moneys or things of value; or from peaceably assembling in a lawful manner, and for lawful purposes; or from doing any act or thing which might lawfully be done in the absence of such dispute by any party thereto; nor shall any of the acts specified in this paragraph be considered or held to be violations of any law of the United States.

* * *

Norris-LaGuardia Act

47 Stat. 70 (1932), 29 U.S.C. §§ 101–15 (1988).

Sec. 1. No court of the United States, as herein defined, shall have jurisdiction to issue any restraining order or temporary or permanent injunction in a case involving or growing out of a labor dispute, except in a strict conformity with the provisions of this Act; nor shall any such restraining order or temporary or permanent injunction be issued contrary to the public policy declared in this Act.

Sec. 2. In the interpretation of this Act and in determining the jurisdiction and authority of the courts of the United States, as such jurisdiction and authority are herein defined and limited, the public policy of the United States is hereby declared as follows:

Whereas under prevailing economic conditions, developed with the aid of governmental authority for owners of property to organize in the corporate and other forms of ownership association, the individual unorganized worker is commonly helpless to exercise actual liberty of contract and to protect his freedom of labor, and thereby to obtain acceptable terms and conditions of employment, wherefore, though he should be free to decline to associate with his fellows, it is necessary that he have full freedom of association, self-organization, and designation of representatives of his own choosing, to negotiate the terms and conditions of his employment, and that he shall be free from the interference, restraint, or coercion of employers of labor, or their agents, in the designation of such representatives or in self-organization or in other concerted activities for the purpose of collective bargaining or other mutual aid or protection; therefore, the following definitions of, and limitations upon, the jurisdiction and authority of the courts of the United States are hereby enacted.

Sec. 3. Any undertaking or promise, such as is described in this section, or any other undertaking or promise in conflict with the public policy declared in section 2 of this Act, is hereby declared to be contrary to the public policy of the United States, shall not be enforceable in any court of the United States and shall not afford any basis for the granting of legal or equitable relief by any such court, including specifically the following:

Every undertaking or promise hereafter made, whether written or oral, express or implied, constituting or contained in any contract or agreement of hiring or employment between any individual, firm, company, association, or corporation, and any employee or prospective employee of the same whereby

(a) Either party to such contract or agreement undertakes or promises not to join, become, or remain a member of any labor organization or of any employer organization; or

(b) Either party to such contract or agreement undertakes or promises that he will withdraw from an employment relation in the event that he joins, becomes, or remains a member of any labor organization or of any employer organization.

Sec. 4. No court of the United States shall have jurisdiction to issue any restraining order or temporary or permanent injunction in any case involving or growing out of any labor dispute to prohibit any person or persons participating or interested in such dispute (as these terms are herein defined) from doing, whether singly or in concert, any of the following acts:

(a) Ceasing or refusing to perform any work or to remain in any relation of employment;

(b) Becoming or remaining a member of any labor organization or of any employer organization, regardless of any such undertaking or promise as is described in section 3 of this Act;

(c) Paying or giving to, or withholding from, any person participating or interested in such labor dispute, any strike or unemployment benefits or insurance, or other moneys or things of value;

(d) By all lawful means aiding any person participating or interested in any labor dispute who is being proceeded against in, or is prosecuting, any action or suit in any court of the United States or of any State;

(e) Giving publicity to the existence of, or the facts involved in, any labor dispute, whether by advertising, speaking, patrolling, or by any other method not involving fraud or violence;

(f) Assembling peaceably to act or to organize to act in promotion of their interests in a labor dispute;

(g) Advising or notifying any person of an intention to do any of the Acts heretofore specified;

(h) Agreeing with other persons to do or not to do any of the acts heretofore specified; and

(i) Advising, urging, or otherwise causing or inducing without fraud or violence the acts heretofore specified, regardless of any such undertaking or promise as is described in section 3 of this Act.

Sec. 5. No court of the United States shall have jurisdiction to issue a restraining order or temporary or permanent injunction upon the ground that any of the persons participating or interested in a labor dispute constitute or are engaged in an unlawful combination or conspiracy because of the doing in concert of the acts enumerated in section 4 of this Act.

Sec. 6. No officer or member of any association or organization, and no association or organization participating or interested in a labor dispute, shall be held responsible or liable in any court of the United

States for the unlawful acts of individual officers, members, or agents, except upon clear proof of actual participation in, or actual authorization of, such acts, or of ratification of such acts after actual knowledge thereof.

Sec. 7. No court of the United States shall have jurisdiction to issue a temporary or permanent injunction in any case involving or growing out of a labor dispute, as herein defined, except after hearing the testimony of witnesses in open court (with opportunity for cross-examination) in support of the allegations of a complaint made under oath, and testimony in opposition thereto, if offered, and except after findings of fact by the court, to the effect—

(a) That unlawful acts have been threatened and will be committed unless restrained or have been committed and will be continued unless restrained, but no injunction or temporary restraining order shall be issued on account of any threat or unlawful act excepting against the person or persons, association, or organization making the threat or committing the unlawful act or actually authorizing or ratifying the same after actual knowledge thereof;

(b) That substantial and irreparable injury to complainant's property will follow:

(c) That as to each item of relief granted greater injury will be inflicted upon complainant by the denial of relief than will be inflicted upon defendants by the granting of relief;

(d) That complainant has no adequate remedy at law; and

(e) That the public officers charged with the duty to protect complainant's property are unable or unwilling to furnish adequate protection.

Such hearing shall be held after due and personal notice thereof has been given, in such manner as the court shall direct, to all known persons against whom relief is sought, and also to the chief of those public officials of the county and city within which the unlawful acts have been threatened or committed charged with the duty to protect complainant's property: *Provided, however*, That if a complainant shall also allege that, unless a temporary restraining order shall be issued without notice, a substantial and irreparable injury to complainant's property will be unavoidable, such a temporary restraining order may be issued upon testimony under oath, sufficient, if sustained, to justify the court in issuing a temporary injunction upon a hearing after notice. Such a temporary restraining order shall be effective for no longer than five days and shall become void at the expiration of said five days. No temporary restraining order or temporary injunction shall be issued except on condition that complainant shall first file an undertaking with adequate security in an amount to be fixed by the court sufficient to recompense those enjoined for any loss, expense, or damage caused by the improvident or erroneous issuance of such order or injunction, including all reasonable costs (together with a reasonable attorney's fee) and expense of defense against the order or against the granting of any injunctive relief sought in the same proceeding and subsequently denied by the court.

The undertaking herein mentioned shall be understood to signify an agreement entered into by the complainant and the surety upon which a decree may be rendered in the same suit or proceeding against said complainant and surety, upon a hearing to assess damages of which hearing complainant and surety shall have reasonable notice, the said complainant and surety submitting themselves to the jurisdiction of the court for that purpose. But nothing herein contained shall deprive any party having a claim or cause of action under or upon such undertaking from electing to pursue his ordinary remedy by suit at law or in equity.

Sec. 8. No restraining order or injunctive relief shall be granted to any complainant who has failed to comply with any obligation imposed by law which is involved in the labor dispute in question, or who has failed to make every reasonable effort to settle such dispute either by negotiation or with the aid of any available governmental machinery of mediation or voluntary arbitration.

Sec. 9. No restraining order or temporary or permanent injunction shall be granted in a case involving or growing out of a labor dispute, except on the basis of findings of fact made and filed by the court in the record of the case prior to the issuance of such restraining order or injunction; and every restraining order or injunction granted in a case involving or growing out of a labor dispute shall include only a prohibition of such specific act or acts as may be expressly complained of in the bill of complaint or petition filed in such case and as shall be expressly included in said findings of fact made and filed by the court as provided herein.

Sec. 10. Whenever any court of the United States shall issue or deny any temporary injunction in a case involving or growing out of a labor dispute, the court shall, upon the request of any party to the proceedings and on his filing the usual bond for costs, forthwith certify as in ordinary cases the record of the case to the circuit court of appeals for its review. Upon the filing of such record in the circuit court of appeals, the appeal shall be heard and the temporary injunctive order affirmed, modified, or set aside with the greatest possible expedition, giving the proceedings precedence over all other matters except older matters of the same character.

Sec. 11.* In all cases arising under this Act in which a person shall be charged with contempt in a court of the United States (as herein defined), the accused shall enjoy the right to a speedy and public trial by an impartial jury of the State and district wherein the contempt shall

---

* Sections 11 and 12 were repealed in 1948, 62 Stat. 862. The text of Section 11 is now in 18 U.S.C. § 3692 (1982); Rule 42 of the Federal Rules of Criminal Procedure now governs the matters formerly treated in Section 12.

have been committed: *Provided*, That this right shall not apply to contempts committed in the presence of the court or so near thereto as to interfere directly with the administration of justice or to apply to the misbehavior, misconduct, or disobedience of any officer of the court in respect to the writs, orders, or process of the court.

Sec. 12.* The defendant in any proceeding for contempt of court may file with the court a demand for the retirement of the judge sitting in the proceeding, if the contempt arises from an attack upon the character or conduct of such judge and if the attack occurred elsewhere than in the presence of the court or so near thereto as to interfere directly with the administration of justice. Upon the filing of any such demand the judge shall thereupon proceed no further, but another judge shall be designated in the same manner as is provided by law. The demand shall be filed prior to the hearing in the contempt proceeding.

Sec. 13. When used in this Act, and for the purposes of this Act—

(a) A case shall be held to involve or to grow out of a labor dispute when the case involves persons who are engaged in the same industry, trade, craft, or occupation; or have direct or indirect interests therein; or who are employees of the same employer; or who are members of the same or an affiliated organization of employers or employees; whether such dispute is (1) between one or more employers or associations of employers and one or more employees or associations of employees; (2) between one or more employers or associations of employers and one or more employers or associations of employers; or (3) between one or more employees or associations of employees and one or more employees or associations of employees; or when the case involves any conflicting or competing interests in a "labor dispute" (as hereinafter defined) of "persons participating or interested" therein (as hereinafter defined).

(b) A person or association shall be held to be a person participating or interested in a labor dispute if relief is sought against him or it, and if he or it is engaged in the same industry, trade, craft, or occupation in which such dispute occurs, or has a direct or indirect interest therein, or is a member, officer, or agent of any association composed in whole or in part of employers or employees engaged in such industry, trade, craft, or occupation.

(c) The term "labor dispute" includes any controversy concerning terms or conditions of employment, or concerning the association or representation of persons in negotiating, fixing, maintaining, changing, or seeking to arrange terms or conditions of employment, regardless of whether or not the disputants stand in the proximate relation of employer and employee.

(d) The term "court of the United States" means any court of the United States whose jurisdiction has been or may be conferred or defined or limited by Act of Congress, including the courts of the District of Columbia.

Sec. 14. If any provision of this Act or the application thereof to any person or circumstance is held unconstitutional or otherwise invalid, the remaining provisions of the Act and the application of such provisions to other persons or circumstances shall not be affected thereby.

Sec. 15. All Acts and parts of Acts in conflict with the provisions of this Act are hereby repealed.

RAILWAY LABOR ACT

44 Stat., Part II, 577 (1926), as amended;
45 U.S.C. §§ 151–88 (1988).

TITLE I

Sec. 1. When used in this Act and for the purposes of this Act—

First. The term "carrier" includes any express company, sleeping-car company, carrier by railroad, subject to the Interstate Commerce Act, and any company which is directly or indirectly owned or controlled by or under common control with any carrier by railroad and which operates any equipment or facilities or performs any service (other than trucking service) in connection with the transportation, receipt, delivery, elevation, transfer in transit, refrigeration or icing, storage, and handling of property transported by railroad, and any receiver, trustee, or other individual or body, judicial or otherwise, when in the possession of the business of any such "carrier": *Provided, however*, That the term "carrier" shall not include any street, interurban, or suburban electric railway, unless such railway is operating as a part of a general steam-railroad system of transportation, but shall not exclude any part of the general steam-railroad system of transportation now or hereafter operated by any other motive power. The Interstate Commerce Commission is authorized and directed upon request of the Mediation Board or upon complaint of any party interested to determine after hearing whether any line operated by electric power falls within the terms of this proviso. The term "carrier" shall not include any company by reason of its being engaged in the mining of coal, the supplying of coal to a carrier where delivery is not beyond the mine tipple, and the operation of equipment or facilities therefor, or in any of such activities.

Second. The term "Adjustment Board" means the National Railroad Adjustment Board created by this Act.

Third. The term "Mediation Board" means the National Mediation Board created by this Act.

Fourth. The term "commerce" means commerce among the several States or between any State, Territory, or the District of Columbia and any foreign nation, or between any Territory or the District of Columbia and any State, or between any Territory and any other Territory, or between any Territory and the District of Columbia, or within any Territory or the District of Columbia, or between points in the same State but through any other State or any Territory or the District of Columbia or any foreign nation.

Fifth. The term "employee" as used herein includes every person in the service of a carrier (subject to its continuing authority to supervise and direct the manner of rendition of his service) who performs any work defined as that of an employee or subordinate official in the orders of the

Interstate Commerce Commission now in effect, and as the same may be amended or interpreted by orders hereafter entered by the Commission pursuant to the authority which is conferred upon it to enter orders amending or interpreting such existing orders: *Provided, however,* That no occupational classification made by order of the Interstate Commerce Commission shall be construed to define the crafts according to which railway employees may be organized by their voluntary action, nor shall the jurisdiction or powers of such employee organizations be regarded as in any way limited or defined by the provisions of this Act or by the orders of the Commission. The term "employee" shall not include any individual while such individual is engaged in the physical operations consisting of the mining of coal, the preparation of coal, the handling (other than movement by rail with standard railroad locomotives) of coal not beyond the mine tipple, or the loading of coal at the tipple.

Sixth. The term "representative" means any person or persons, labor union, organization, or corporation designated either by a carrier or group of carriers or by its or their employees, to act for it or them.

Seventh. The term "district court" includes the United States District Court for the District of Columbia; and the term "circuit court of appeals" includes the United States Court of Appeals for the District of Columbia.

This Act may be cited as the "Railway Labor Act."

Sec. 2.   The purposes of the Act are:

(1) To avoid any interruption to commerce or to the operation of any carrier engaged therein; (2) to forbid any limitation upon freedom of association among employees or any denial, as a condition of employment or otherwise, of the right of employees to join a labor organization; (3) to provide for the complete independence of carriers and of employees in the matter of self-organization; (4) to provide for the prompt and orderly settlement of all disputes concerning rates of pay, rules, or working conditions; (5) to provide for the prompt and orderly settlement of all disputes growing out of grievances or out of the interpretation or application of agreements covering rates of pay, rules, or working conditions.

First. It shall be the duty of all carriers, their officers, agents, and employees to exert every reasonable effort to make and maintain agreements concerning rates of pay, rules, and working conditions, and to settle all disputes, whether arising out of the application of such agreements or otherwise, in order to avoid any interruption to commerce or to the operation of any carrier growing out of any dispute between the carrier and the employees thereof.

Second. All disputes between a carrier or carriers and its or their employees shall be considered, and, if possible, decided, with all expedition, in conference between representatives designated and authorized so to confer, respectively, by the carrier or carriers and by the employees thereof interested in the dispute.

Third. Representatives, for the purposes of this Act, shall be designated by the respective parties without interference, influence, or coercion by either party over the designation of representatives by the other; and neither party shall in any way interfere with, influence, or coerce the other in its choice of representatives. Representatives of employees for the purposes of this Act need not be persons in the employ of the carrier, and no carrier shall, by interference, influence, or coercion seek in any manner to prevent the designation by its employees as their representatives of those who or which are not employees of the carrier.

Fourth. Employees shall have the right to organize and bargain collectively through representatives of their own choosing. The majority of any craft or class of employees shall have the right to determine who shall be the representative of the craft or class for the purposes of this Act. No carrier, its officers or agents, shall deny or in any way question the right of its employees to join, organize, or assist in organizing the labor organization of their choice, and it shall be unlawful for any carrier to interfere in any way with the organization of its employees, or to use the funds of the carrier in maintaining or assisting or contributing to any labor organization, labor representative, or other agency of collective bargaining, or in performing any work therefor, or to influence or coerce employees in an effort to induce them to join or remain or not to join or remain members of any labor organization or to deduct from the wages of employees any dues, fees, assessments, or other contributions payable to labor organizations, or to collect or to assist in the collection of any such dues, fees, assessments, or other contributions: *Provided*, That nothing in this Act shall be construed to prohibit a carrier from permitting an employee, individually, or local representatives of employees from conferring with management during working hours without loss of time, or to prohibit a carrier from furnishing free transportation to its employees while engaged in the business of a labor organization.

Fifth. No carrier, its officers, or agents shall require any person seeking employment to sign any contract or agreement promising to join or not to join a labor organization; and if any such contract has been enforced prior to the effective date of this Act, then such carrier shall notify the employees by an appropriate order that such contract has been discarded and is no longer binding on them in any way.

Sixth. In case of a dispute between a carrier or carriers and its or their employees, arising out of grievances or out of the interpretation or application of agreements concerning rates of pay, rules, or working conditions, it shall be the duty of the designated representative or representatives of such carrier or carriers and of such employees, within ten days after the receipt of notice of a desire on the part of either party to confer in respect to such dispute, to specify a time and place at which such conference shall be held: *Provided*, (1) That the place so specified shall be situated upon the line of the carrier involved or as otherwise mutually agreed upon; and (2) that the time so specified shall allow the designated conferees reasonable opportunity to reach such place of conference, but shall not exceed twenty days from the receipt of such notice: *And provided further*, That nothing in this Act shall be construed to supersede the provisions of any agreement (as to conferences) then in effect between the parties.

Seventh. No carrier, its officers, or agents shall change the rates of pay, rules, or working conditions of its employees, as a class as embodied in agreements except in the manner prescribed in such agreements or in section 6 of this Act.

Eighth. Every carrier shall notify its employees by printed notices in such form and posted at such times and places as shall be specified by the Mediation Board that all disputes between the carrier and its employees will be handled in accordance with the requirements of this Act, and in such notices there shall be printed verbatim, in large type, the third, fourth, and fifth paragraphs of this section. The provisions of said paragraphs are hereby made a part of the contract of employment between the carrier and each employee, and shall be held binding upon the parties, regardless of any other express or implied agreements between them.

Ninth. If any dispute shall arise among a carrier's employees as to who are the representatives of such employees designated and authorized in accordance with the requirements of this Act, it shall be the duty of the Mediation Board, upon request of either party to the dispute, to investigate such dispute and to certify to both parties, in writing, within thirty days after the receipt of the invocation of its services, the name or names of the individuals or organizations that have been designated and authorized to represent the employees involved in the dispute, and certify the same to the carrier. Upon receipt of such certification the carrier shall treat with the representative so certified as the representative of the craft or class for the purposes of this Act. In such an investigation, the Mediation Board shall be authorized to take a secret ballot of the employees involved, or to utilize any other appropriate method of ascertaining the names of their duly designated and authorized representatives in such manner as shall insure the choice of representatives by the employees without interference, influence, or coercion exercised by the carrier. In the conduct of any election for the purposes herein indicated the Board shall designate who may participate in the election and establish the rules to govern the election, or may appoint a committee of three neutral persons who after hearing shall within ten days designate the employees who may participate in the election. The Board shall have access to and have power to make copies of the books and records of the carriers to obtain and utilize such information as may be deemed necessary by it to carry out the purposes and provisions of this paragraph.

Tenth. The willful failure or refusal of any carrier, its officers, or agents to comply with the terms of the third, fourth, fifth, seventh, or eighth paragraph of this section shall be a misdemeanor, and upon conviction thereof the carrier, officer, or agent offending shall be subject to a fine of not less than $1,000 nor more than $20,000 or imprisonment for not more than six months, or both fine and imprisonment, for each offense, and each day during which such carrier, officer, or agent shall willfully fail or refuse to comply with the terms of the said paragraphs of this section shall constitute a separate offense. It shall be the duty of any United States attorney to whom any duly designated representative of a carrier's employees may apply to institute in the proper court and to prosecute under the direction of the Attorney General of the United States, all necessary proceedings for the enforcement of the provisions of this section, and for the punishment of all violations thereof and the costs and expenses of such prosecution shall be paid out of the appropriation for the expenses of the courts of the United States: *Provided*, That nothing in this Act shall be construed to require an individual employee to render labor or service without his consent, nor shall anything in this Act be construed to make the quitting of his labor by an individual employee an illegal act; nor shall any court issue any process to compel the performance by an individual employee of such labor or service, without his consent.

Eleventh. Notwithstanding any other provisions of this chapter, or of any other statute or law of the United States, or Territory thereof, or of any State, any carrier or carriers as defined in this chapter and a labor organization or labor organizations duly designated and authorized to represent employees in accordance with the requirements of this chapter shall be permitted—

(a) to make agreements, requiring, as a condition of continued employment, that within sixty days following the beginning of such employment, or the effective date of such agreements, whichever is the later, all employees shall become members of the labor organization representing their craft or class: *Provided*, That no such agreement shall require such condition of employment with respect to employees to whom membership is not available upon the same terms and conditions as are generally applicable to any other member or with respect to employees to whom membership was denied or terminated for any reason other than the failure of the employee to tender the periodic dues, initiation fees, and assessments (not including fines and penalties) uniformly required as a condition of acquiring or retaining membership.

(b) to make agreements providing for the deduction by such carrier or carriers from the wages of its or their employees in a craft or class and payment to the labor organization representing the craft or class of such employees, of any periodic dues, initiation fees, and assessments (not including fines and penalties) uniformly required as a condition of acquiring or retaining membership: *Provided*, That no such agreement shall be effective with respect to any individual employee until he shall have furnished the employer with a written assignment to the labor organization of such membership dues, initiation fees, and assessments, which shall be revocable in writing after the expiration of one year or upon the termination date of the applicable collective agreement, whichever occurs sooner.

* * *

Sec. 3.   First. There is hereby established a Board, to be known as the "National Railroad Adjustment Board", the members of which shall be selected within thirty days after June 21, 1934, and it is hereby provided—

(a) That the said Adjustment Board shall consist of thirty-four members, seventeen of whom shall be selected by the carriers and seventeen by such labor organizations of the employees, national in scope, as have been or may be organized in accordance with the provisions of section 2 of this Act.

(b) The carriers, acting each through its board of directors or its receiver or receivers, trustee or trustees, or through an officer or officers designated for that purpose by such board, trustee or trustees, or receiver or receivers, shall prescribe the rules under which its representatives shall be selected and shall select the representatives of the carriers on the Adjustment Board and designate the division on which each such representative shall serve, but no carrier or system of carriers shall have more than one voting representative on any division of the Board.

(c) Except as provided in the second paragraph of subsection (h) of this section, the national labor organizations as defined in paragraph (a) of this section, acting each through the chief executive or other medium designated by the organization or association thereof, shall prescribe the rules under which the labor members of the Adjustment Board shall be selected and shall select such members and designate the division on which each member shall serve; but no labor organization shall have more than one voting representative on any division of the Board.

* * *

(h) The said Adjustment Board shall be composed of four divisions, whose proceedings shall be independent of one another, and the said divisions as well as the number of their members shall be as follows:

First division: To have jurisdiction over disputes involving train- and yard-service employees of carriers; that is, engineers, firemen, hostlers, and outside hostler helpers, conductors, trainmen, and yard-service employees. This division shall consist of eight members, four of whom shall be selected and designated by the carriers and four of whom shall be selected and designated by the labor organizations * * *.

Second division: To have jurisdiction over disputes involving machinists, boilermakers, blacksmiths, sheet-metal workers, electrical workers, car men, the helpers and apprentices of all the foregoing, coach cleaners, power-house employees, and railroad-shop laborers. This division shall consist of ten members, five of whom shall be selected by the carriers and five by the national labor organizations of the employees.

Third division: To have jurisdiction over disputes involving station, tower, and telegraph employees, train dispatchers, maintenance-of-way men, clerical employees, freight handlers, express, station, and store employees, signal men, sleeping-car conductors, sleeping-car porters, and maids and dining-car employees. This division shall consist of ten members, five of whom shall be selected by the carriers and five by the national labor organizations of employees.

Fourth division: To have jurisdiction over disputes involving employees of carriers directly or indirectly engaged in transportation of passengers or property by water, and all other employees of carriers over which jurisdiction is not given to the first, second, and third divisions. This division shall consist of six members, three of whom shall be selected by the carriers and three by the national labor organizations of the employees.

(i) The disputes between an employee or group of employees and a carrier or carriers growing out of grievances or out of the interpretation or application of agreements concerning rates of pay, rules, or working conditions, including cases pending and unadjusted on the date of approval of this Act, shall be handled in the usual manner up to and including the chief operating officer of the carrier designated to handle such disputes; but, failing to reach an adjustment in this manner, the disputes may be referred by petition of the parties or by either party to the appropriate division of the Adjustment Board with a full statement of the facts and all supporting data bearing upon the disputes.

(j) Parties may be heard either in person, by counsel, or by other representatives, as they may respectively elect, and the several divisions of the Adjustment Board shall give due notice of all hearings to the employee or employees and the carrier or carriers involved in any disputes submitted to them.

(k) Any division of the Adjustment Board shall have authority to empower two or more of its members to conduct hearings and make findings upon disputes, when properly submitted, at any place designated by the division: *Provided, however*, That except as provided in paragraph (h) of this section, final awards as to any such dispute must be made by the entire division as hereinafter provided.

* * *

(m) The awards of the several divisions of the Adjustment Board shall be stated in writing. A copy of the awards shall be furnished to the respective parties to the controversy, and the awards shall be final and binding upon both parties to the dispute. In case a dispute arises involving an interpretation of the award the division of the Board upon request of either party shall interpret the award in the light of the dispute.

(n) A majority vote of all members of the division of the Adjustment Board eligible to vote shall be competent to make an award with respect to any dispute submitted to it.

(o) In case of an award by any division of the Adjustment Board in favor of petitioner, the division of the Board shall make an order, directed to the carrier, to make the award effective and, if the award includes a requirement for the payment of money, to pay the employee the sum to which he is entitled under the award on or before a day named. In the event any division determines that an award favorable to the petitioner should not be made in any dispute referred to it, the division shall make an order to the petitioner stating such determination.

(p) If a carrier does not comply with an order of a division of the Adjustment Board within the time limit in such order, the petitioner, or any person for whose benefit such order was made, may file in the District Court of the United States for the district in which he resides or in which is located the principal operating office of the carrier, or through which the carrier operates, a petition setting forth briefly the causes for which he claims relief, and the order of the division of the Adjustment Board in the premises. Such suit in the District Court of the United States shall proceed in all respects as other civil suits, except that on the trial of such suit the findings and order of the division of the Adjustment Board shall be conclusive on the parties, and except that the petitioner shall not be liable for costs in the district court nor for costs at any subsequent stage of the proceedings, unless they accrue upon his appeal, and such costs shall be paid out of the appropriation for the expenses of the courts of the United States. If the petitioner shall finally prevail he shall be allowed a reasonable attorney's fee, to be taxed and collected as a part of the costs of the suit. The district courts are empowered, under the rules of the court governing actions at law, to make such order and enter such judgment, by writ of mandamus or otherwise, as may be appropriate to enforce or set aside the order of the division of the Adjustment Board: *Provided, however,* That such order may not be set aside except for failure of the division to comply with the requirements of this chapter, for failure of the order to conform, or confine itself, to matters within the scope of the division's jurisdiction, or for fraud or corruption by a member of the division making the order.

(q) If any employee or group of employees, or any carrier, is aggrieved by the failure of any division of the Adjustment Board to make an award in a dispute referred to it, or is aggrieved by any of the terms of an award or by the failure of the division to include certain terms in such award, then such employee or group of employees or carrier may file in any United States district court in which a petition under paragraph

(p) could be filed, a petition for review of the division's order. A copy of the petition shall be forthwith transmitted by the clerk of the court to the Adjustment Board. The Adjustment Board shall file in the court the record of the proceedings on which it based its action. The court shall have jurisdiction to affirm the order of the division, or to set it aside, in whole or in part, or it may remand the proceeding to the division for such further action as it may direct. On such review, the findings and order of the division shall be conclusive on the parties, except that the order of the division may be set aside, in whole or in part, or remanded to the division, for failure of the division to comply with the requirements of this chapter, for failure of the order to conform, or confine itself, to matters within the scope of the division's jurisdiction, or for fraud or corruption by a member of the division making the order. The judgment of the court shall be subject to review as provided in sections 1291 and 1254 of title 28, United States Code.

(r) All actions at law based upon the provisions of this section shall be begun within two years from the time the cause of action accrues under the award of the division of the Adjustment Board, and not after.

* * *

Second. Nothing in this section shall be construed to prevent any individual carrier, system, or group of carriers and any class or classes of its or their employees, all acting through their representatives, selected in accordance with the provisions of this Act, from mutually agreeing to the establishment of system, group, or regional boards of adjustment for the purpose of adjusting and deciding disputes of the character specified in this section. In the event that either party to such a system, group, or regional board of adjustment is dissatisfied with such arrangement, it may upon ninety days' notice to the other party elect to come under the jurisdiction of the Adjustment Board.

* * *

Sec. 4. First. * * * There is hereby established, as an independent agency in the executive branch of the Government, a board to be known as the "National Mediation Board," to be composed of three members appointed by the President, by and with the advice and consent of the Senate, not more than two of whom shall be of the same political party. Each member of the Mediation Board in office on January 1, 1965, shall be deemed to have been appointed for a term of office which shall expire on July 1 of the year his term would have otherwise expired. The terms of office of all successors shall expire three years after the expiration of the terms for which their predecessors were appointed; but any member appointed to fill a vacancy occurring prior to the expiration of the term of which his predecessor was appointed shall be appointed only for the unexpired term of his predecessor. * * *

A member of the Board may be removed by the President for inefficiency, neglect of duty, malfeasance in office, or ineligibility, but for no other cause.

* * *

Sec. 5. First. The parties, or either party, to a dispute between an employee or group of employees and a carrier may invoke the services of the Mediation Board in any of the following cases:

(a) A dispute concerning changes in rates of pay, rules, or working conditions not adjusted by the parties in conference.

(b) Any other dispute not referable to the National Railroad Adjustment Board and not adjusted in conference between the parties or where conferences are refused.

The Mediation Board may proffer its services in case any labor emergency is found by it to exist at any time.

In either event the said Board shall promptly put itself in communication with the parties to such controversy, and shall use its best efforts, by mediation, to bring them to agreement. If such efforts to bring about an amicable settlement through mediation shall be unsuccessful, the said Board shall at once endeavor as its final required action (except as provided in paragraph third of this section and in section 10 of this Act) to induce the parties to submit their controversy to arbitration, in accordance with the provisions of this Act.

If arbitration at the request of the Board shall be refused by one or both parties, the Board shall at once notify both parties in writing that its mediatory efforts have failed and for thirty days thereafter, unless in the intervening period the parties agree to arbitration, or an emergency board shall be created under section 10 of this Act, no change shall be made in the rates of pay, rules, or working conditions or establish practices in effect prior to the time the dispute arose.

* * *

Sec. 6. Carriers and representatives of the employees shall give at least thirty days' written notice of an intended change in agreements affecting rates of pay, rules, or working conditions, and the time and place for the beginning of conference between the representatives of the parties interested in such intended changes shall be agreed upon within ten days after the receipt of said notice, and said time shall be within the thirty days provided in the notice. In every case where such notice of intended change has been given, or conferences are being held with reference thereto, or the services of the Mediation Board have been requested by either party, or said Board has proffered its services, rates of pay, rules, or working conditions shall not be altered by the carrier until the controversy has been finally acted upon as required by section 5 of this Act, by the Mediation Board, unless a period of ten days has elapsed after termination of conferences without request for or proffer of the services of the Mediation Board.

Sec. 7. First. Whenever a controversy shall arise between a carrier or carriers and its or their employees which is not settled either in conference between representatives of the parties or by the appropriate adjustment board or through mediation, in the manner provided in the preceding sections, such controversy may, by agreement of the parties to such controversy, be submitted to the arbitration of a board of three (or, if the parties to the controversy so stipulate, of six) persons: *Provided, however,* That the failure or refusal of either party to submit a controversy to arbitration shall not be construed as a violation of any legal obligation imposed upon such party by the terms of this Act or otherwise.

Second. Such board of arbitration shall be chosen in the following manner:

(a) In the case of a board of three, the carrier or carriers and the representatives of the employees, parties respectively to the agreement to arbitrate, shall each name one arbitrator; the two arbitrators thus chosen shall select a third arbitrator. If the arbitrators chosen by the parties shall fail to name the third arbitrator within five days after their first meeting, such third arbitrator shall be named by the Mediation Board.

(b) In the case of a board of six, the carrier or carriers and the representatives of the employees, parties respectively to the agreement to arbitrate, shall each name two arbitrators; the four arbitrators thus chosen shall, by a majority vote, select the remaining two arbitrators. If the arbitrators chosen by the parties shall fail to name the two arbitrators within fifteen days after their first meeting, the said two arbitrators, or as many of them as have not been named, shall be named by the Mediation Board.

Third. (a) When the arbitrators selected by the respective parties have agreed upon the remaining arbitrator or arbitrators, they shall notify the Mediation Board, and, in the event of their failure to agree upon any or upon all of the necessary arbitrators within the period fixed by this Act, they shall, at the expiration of such period, notify the Mediation Board of the arbitrators selected, if any, or of their failure to make or complete such selection.

(b) The board of arbitration shall organize and select its own chairman and make all necessary rules for conducting its hearings: *Provided, however,* That the board of arbitration shall be bound to give the parties to the controversy a full and fair hearing, which shall include an opportunity to present evidence in support of their claims, and an opportunity to present their case in person, by counsel, or by other representative as they may respectively elect.

* * *

Sec. 9.   First. The award of a board of arbitration, having been acknowledged as herein provided, shall be filed in the clerk's office of the district court designated in the agreement to arbitrate.

Second. An award acknowledged and filed as herein provided shall be conclusive on the parties as to the merits and facts of the controversy submitted to arbitration, and unless, within ten days after the filing of the award, a petition to impeach the award, on the grounds hereinafter set forth, shall be filed in the clerk's office of the court in which the award has been filed, the court shall enter judgment on the award, which judgment shall be final and conclusive on the parties.

Third. Such petition for the impeachment or contesting of any award so filed shall be entertained by the court only on one or more of the following grounds:

(a)   That the award plainly does not conform to the substantive requirements laid down by this Act for such awards, or that the proceedings were not substantially in conformity with this Act;

(b)   That the award does not conform, nor confine itself, to the stipulations of the agreement to arbitrate; or

(c)   That a member of the board of arbitration rendering the award was guilty of fraud or corruption; or that a party to the arbitration practiced fraud or corruption which fraud or corruption affected the result of the arbitration. *Provided, however*, That no court shall entertain any such petition on the ground that an award is invalid for uncertainty; in such case the proper remedy shall be a submission of such award to a reconvened board, or subcommittee thereof, for interpretation, as provided by this Act: *Provided further*, That an award contested as herein provided shall be construed liberally by the court, with a view to favoring its validity, and that no award shall be set aside for trivial irregularity or clerical error, going only to form and not to substance.

* * *

Sec. 10. If a dispute between a carrier and its employees be not adjusted under the foregoing provisions of this Act and should, in the judgment of the Mediation Board, threaten substantially to interrupt interstate commerce to a degree such as to deprive any section of the country of essential transportation service, the Mediation Board shall notify the President, who may thereupon, in his discretion, create a board to investigate and report respecting such dispute. Such board shall be composed of such number of persons as to the President may seem desirable: *Provided, however*, That no member appointed shall be pecuniarily or otherwise interested in any organization of employees or any carrier. The compensation of the members of any such board shall be fixed by the President. Such board shall be created separately in each instance and it shall investigate promptly the facts as to the dispute and make a report thereon to the President within thirty days from the date of its creation.

* * *

After the creation of such board, and for thirty days after such board has made its report to the President, no change, except by agreement, shall be made by the parties to the controversy in the conditions out of which the dispute arose.

* * *

TITLE II

Sec. 201. All of the provisions of title I of this Act, except the provisions of section 3 thereof, are extended to and shall cover every common carrier by air engaged in interstate or foreign commerce, and every carrier by air transporting mail for or under contract with the United States Government, and every air pilot or other person who performs any work as an employee or subordinate official of such carrier or carriers, subject to its or their continuing authority to supervise and direct the manner of rendition of his service.

Sec. 202. The duties, requirements, penalties, benefits, and privileges prescribed and established by the provisions of title I of this Act, except section 3 thereof, shall apply to said carriers by air and their employees in the same manner and to the same extent as though such carriers and their employees were specifically included within the definition of "carrier" and "employee", respectively, in section 1 thereof.

Sec. 203. The parties or either party to a dispute between an employee or a group of employees and a carrier or carriers by air may invoke the services of the National Mediation Board and the jurisdiction of said Mediation Board is extended to any of the following cases:

(a) A dispute concerning changes in rates of pay, rules, or working conditions not adjusted by the parties in conference.

(b) Any other dispute not referable to an adjustment board, as hereinafter provided, and not adjusted in conference between the parties, or where conferences are refused.

The National Mediation Board may proffer its services in case any labor emergency is found by it to exist at any time.

The services of the Mediation Board may be invoked in a case under this title in the same manner and to the same extent as are the disputes covered by section 5 of title I of this Act.

Sec. 204. The disputes between an employee or group of employees and a carrier or carriers by air growing out of grievances, or out of interpretation or application of agreements concerning rates of pay, rules, or working conditions, including cases pending and unadjusted on the date of approval of this Act before the National Labor Relations Board, shall be handled in the usual manner up to and including the chief operating officer of the carrier designated to handle such disputes; but, failing to reach an adjustment in this manner, the disputes may be referred by petition of the parties or by either party to an appropriate adjustment board, as hereinafter provided, with a full statement of the facts and supporting data bearing upon the disputes.

It shall be the duty of every carrier and of its employees, acting through their representatives, selected in accordance with the provisions of this title, to establish a board of adjustment of jurisdiction not exceeding the jurisdiction which may be lawfully exercised by system, group, or regional boards of adjustment, under the authority of section 3, Title I, of this Act.

Such boards of adjustment may be established by agreement between employees and carriers either on any individual carrier, or system, or group of carriers by air and any class or classes of its or their employees; or pending the establishment of a permanent National Board of Adjustment as hereinafter provided. Nothing in this Act shall prevent said carriers by air, or any class or classes of their employees, both acting through their representatives selected in accordance with provisions of this title, from mutually agreeing to the establishment of a National Board of Adjustment of temporary duration and of similarly limited jurisdiction.

* * *

NATIONAL LABOR RELATIONS ACT*

49 Stat. 449 (1935), as amended; 29 U.S.C. §§ 151–69 (1988).

FINDINGS AND POLICIES

Sec. 1. The denial by **some** employers of the right of employees to organize and the refusal by **some** employers to accept the procedure of collective bargaining lead to strikes and other forms of industrial strife or unrest, which have the intent or the necessary effect of burdening or obstructing commerce by (a) impairing the efficiency, safety, or operation of the instrumentalities of commerce; (b) occurring in the current of commerce; (c) materially affecting, restraining, or controlling the flow of raw materials or manufactured or processed goods from or into the channels of commerce, or the prices of such materials or goods in commerce; or (d) causing diminution of employment and wages in such volume as substantially to impair or disrupt the market for goods flowing from or into the channels of commerce.

The inequality of bargaining power between employees who do not possess full freedom of association or actual liberty of contract, and employers who are organized in the corporate or other forms of ownership association substantially burdens and affects the flow of commerce, and tends to aggravate recurrent business depressions, by depressing wage rates and the purchasing power of wage earners in industry and by preventing the stabilization of competitive wage rates and working conditions within and between industries.

Experience has proved that protection by law of the right of employees to organize and bargain collectively safeguards commerce from injury, impairment, or interruption, and promotes the flow of commerce by removing certain recognized sources of industrial strife and unrest, by encouraging practices fundamental to the friendly adjustment of industrial disputes arising out of differences as to wages, hours, or other working conditions, and by restoring equality of bargaining power between employers and employees.

Experience has further demonstrated that certain practices by some labor organizations, their officers, and members have the intent or the necessary effect of burdening or obstructing commerce by preventing the free flow of goods in such commerce through strikes and other forms of industrial unrest or through concerted activities which impair the interest of the public in the free flow of such commerce. The elimination of such practices is

---

* The text of the original Wagner Act of 1935 is printed in roman type; the Taft-Hartley amendments of 1947 are in boldface type; the Landrum-Griffin amendments of 1959 are in italics; the 1974 amendments are underscored. Deleted matter is in brackets; bracketed matter in regular roman type was deleted in 1947, and bracketed matter in boldface type was deleted in 1959. Other amendments and deletions are specifically noted.

a necessary condition to the assurance of the rights herein guaranteed.

It is hereby declared to be the policy of the United States to eliminate the causes of certain substantial obstructions to the free flow of commerce and to mitigate and eliminate these obstructions when they have occurred by encouraging the practice and procedure of collective bargaining and by protecting the exercise by workers of full freedom of association, self-organization, and designation of representatives of their own choosing, for the purpose of negotiating the terms and conditions of their employment or other mutual aid or protection.

DEFINITIONS

Sec. 2. When used in this Act—

(1) The term "person" includes one or more individuals, labor organizations, partnerships, associations, corporations, legal representatives, trustees, trustees in bankruptcy, or receivers.

(2) The term "employer" includes any person acting [in the interest of] **as an agent** of an employer, directly or indirectly, but shall not include the United States **or any wholly owned Government corporation, or any Federal Reserve Bank,** or any State or political subdivision thereof, [**or any corporation or association operating a hospital, if no part of the net earnings inures to the benefit of any private shareholder or individual,**]* or any person subject to the Railway Labor Act, as amended from time to time, or any labor organization (other than when acting as an employer), or anyone acting in the capacity of officer or agent of such labor organization.

(3) The term "employee" shall include any employee, and shall not be limited to the employees of a particular employer, unless the Act explicitly states otherwise, and shall include any individual whose work has ceased as a consequence of, or in connection with, any current labor dispute or because of any unfair labor practice, and who has not obtained any other regular and substantially equivalent employment, but shall not include any individual employed as an agricultural laborer, or in the domestic service of any family or person at his home, or any individual employed by his parent or spouse, **or any individual having the status of an independent contractor, or any individual employed as a supervisor, or any individual employed by an employer subject to the Railway Labor Act, as amended from time to time, or by any other person who is not an employer as herein defined.**

(4) The term "representatives" includes any individual or labor organization.

(5) The term "labor organization" means any organization of any kind, or any agency or employee representation committee or plan, in which employees participate and which exists for the purpose, in whole

---

* The bracketed matter was deleted in 1974, by 88 Stat. 395 (1974).

or in part, of dealing with employers concerning grievances, labor disputes, wages, rates of pay, hours of employment, or conditions of work.

(6) The term "commerce" means trade, traffic, commerce, transportation, or communication among the several States, or between the District of Columbia or any Territory of the United States and any State or other Territory, or between any foreign country and any State, Territory, or the District of Columbia, or within the District of Columbia or any Territory, or between points in the same State but through any other State or any Territory or the District of Columbia or any foreign country.

(7) The term "affecting commerce" means in commerce, or burdening or obstructing commerce or the free flow of commerce, or having led or tending to lead to a labor dispute burdening or obstructing commerce or the free flow of commerce.

(8) The term "unfair labor practice" means any unfair labor practice listed in section 8.

(9) The term "labor dispute" includes any controversy concerning terms, tenure or conditions of employment, or concerning the association or representation of persons in negotiating, fixing, maintaining, changing, or seeking to arrange terms or conditions of employment, regardless of whether the disputants stand in the proximate relation of employer and employee.

(10) The term "National Labor Relations Board" means the National Labor Relations Board provided for in section 3 of this Act.

(11) The term "supervisor" means any individual having authority, in the interest of the employer, to hire, transfer, suspend, lay off, recall, promote, discharge, assign, reward, or discipline other employees, or responsibly to direct them, or to adjust their grievances, or effectively to recommend such action, if in connection with the foregoing the exercise of such authority is not of a merely routine or clerical nature, but requires the use of independent judgment.

(12) The term "professional employee" means—

(a) any employee engaged in work (i) predominantly intellectual and varied in character as opposed to routine mental, manual, mechanical, or physical work; (ii) involving the consistent exercise of discretion and judgment in its performance; (iii) of such a character that the output produced or the result accomplished cannot be standardized in relation to a given period of time; (iv) requiring knowledge of an advanced type in a field of science or learning customarily acquired by a prolonged course of specialized intellectual instruction and study in an institution of higher learning or a hospital, as distinguished from a general academic education or from an apprenticeship or from

training in the performance of routine mental, manual, or physical processes; or

(b) any employee, who (i) has completed the courses of specialized intellectual instruction and study described in clause (iv) of paragraph (a), and (ii) is performing related work under the supervision of a professional person to qualify himself to become a professional employee as defined in paragraph (a).

(13) In determining whether any person is acting as an "agent" of another person so as to make such other person responsible for his acts, the question of whether the specific acts performed were actually authorized or subsequently ratified shall not be controlling.

(14) The term "health care institution" shall include any hospital, convalescent hospital, health maintenance organization, health clinic, nursing home, extended care facility, or other institution devoted to the care of sick, infirm, or aged person.

NATIONAL LABOR RELATIONS BOARD

Sec. 3.* (a) The National Labor Relations Board (hereinafter called the "Board") created by this Act prior to its amendment by the Labor Management Relations Act, 1947, is continued as an agency of the United States, except that the Board shall consist of five instead of three members, appointed by the President by and with the advice and consent of the Senate. Of the two additional members so provided for, one shall be appointed for a term of five years and the other for a term of two years. Their successors, and the successors of the other members, shall be appointed for terms of five years each, excepting that any individual chosen to fill a vacancy shall be appointed only for the unexpired term of the member whom he shall succeed. The President shall designate one member to serve as Chairman of the Board. Any member of the Board may be removed by the President, upon notice and hearing, for neglect of duty or malfeasance in office, but for no other cause.

(b) The Board is authorized to delegate to any group of three or more members any or all of the powers which it may itself exercise. *The Board is also authorized to delegate to its regional directors its powers under section 9 to determine the unit appropriate for the purpose of collective bargaining, to investigate and provide for hearings, and determine whether a question of representation exists, and to direct an election or take a secret ballot under subsection (c) or (e) of section 9 and certify the results thereof, except that upon the filing of a request*

---

* The changes made in Sections 3 and 4 by the Taft-Hartley amendments were so extensive, that the typeface designations for these two sections show only the 1947 and 1959 amendments.

therefor with the Board by any interested person, the Board may review any action of a regional director delegated to him under this paragraph, but such a review shall not, unless specifically ordered by the Board, operate as a stay of any action taken by the regional director. **A vacancy in the Board shall not impair the right of the remaining members to exercise all of the powers of the Board, and three members of the Board shall, at all times, constitute a quorum of the Board, except that two members shall constitute a quorum of any group designated pursuant to the first sentence hereof. The Board shall have an official seal which shall be judicially noticed.**

(c)   The Board shall at the close of each fiscal year make a report in writing to Congress and to the President [stating in detail the cases it has heard, the decisions it has rendered, the names, salaries, and duties of all employees and officers in the employ or under the supervision of the Board, and an account of all moneys it has disbursed.]* summarizing significant case activities and operations for that fiscal year.

(d)   **There shall be a General Counsel of the Board who shall be appointed by the President, by and with the advice and consent of the Senate, for a term of four years. The General Counsel of the Board shall exercise general supervision over all attorneys employed by the Board (other than administrative law judges** and legal assistants to Board members) and over the officers and employees in the regional offices. He shall have final authority, on behalf of the Board, in respect of the investigation of charges and issuance of complaints under section 10, and in respect of the prosecution of such complaints before the Board, and shall have such other duties as the Board may prescribe or as may be provided by law.** *In case of a vacancy in the office of the General Counsel the President is authorized to designate the officer or employee who shall act as General Counsel during such vacancy, but no person or persons so designated shall so act (1) for more than forty days when the Congress is in session unless a nomination to fill such vacancy shall have been submitted to the Senate, or (2) after the adjournment sine die of the session of the Senate in which such nomination was submitted.*

Sec. 4.   (a) Each member of the Board and the General Counsel of the Board [shall receive a salary of $12,000 per annum,] shall be eligible for reappointment, and shall not engage in any other business, vocation, or employment. The Board shall appoint an executive secretary, and such attorneys, examiners, and regional directors, and such other employees as it may from time to time find necessary for the proper performance of its duties. The Board may not employ any attorneys for the purpose of reviewing transcripts of hearings or preparing drafts of

---

*   The bracketed matter was deleted in part in 1975 and in part in 1982, and the matter following was added in 1982.

**   The title "administrative law judge" was adopted in 5 U.S.C. § 3105, in 1972.

opinions except that any attorney employed for assignment as a legal assistant to any Board member may for such Board member review such transcripts and prepare such drafts. No administrative law judge's report shall be reviewed, either before or after its publication, by any person other than a member of the Board or his legal assistant, and no administrative law judge shall advise or consult with the Board with respect to exceptions taken to his findings, rulings, or recommendations. The Board may establish or utilize such regional, local, or other agencies, and utilize such voluntary and uncompensated services, as may from time to time be needed. Attorneys appointed under this section may, at the direction of the Board, appear for and represent the Board in any case in court. Nothing in this Act shall be construed to authorize the Board to appoint individuals for the purpose of conciliation or mediation, or for economic analysis.

(b) All of the expenses of the Board, including all necessary traveling and subsistence expenses outside the District of Columbia incurred by the members or employees of the Board under its orders, shall be allowed and paid on the presentation of itemized vouchers therefor approved by the Board or by any individual it designates for that purpose.

Sec. 5. The principal office of the Board shall be in the District of Columbia, but it may meet and exercise any or all of its powers at any other place. The Board may, by one or more of its members or by such agents or agencies as it may designate, prosecute any inquiry necessary to its functions in any part of the United States. A member who participates in such an inquiry shall not be disqualified from subsequently participating in a decision of the Board in the same case.

Sec. 6. The Board shall have authority from time to time to make, amend, and rescind, **in the manner prescribed by the Administrative Procedure Act,** such rules and regulations as may be necessary to carry out the provisions of this Act. [Such rules and regulations shall be effective upon publication in the manner which the Board shall prescribe.]

RIGHTS OF EMPLOYEES

Sec. 7. Employees shall have the right to self-organization, to form, join, or assist labor organizations, to bargain collectively through representatives of their own choosing, and to engage in other concerted activities for the purpose of collective bargaining or other mutual aid or protection, **and shall also have the right to refrain from any or all of such activities except to the extent that such right may be affected by an agreement requiring membership in a labor organization as a condition of employment as authorized in section 8(a)(3).**

UNFAIR LABOR PRACTICES

Sec. 8. (a) It shall be an unfair labor practice for an employer—

(1) to interfere with, restrain, or coerce employees in the exercise of the rights guaranteed in section 7;

(2) to dominate or interfere with the formation or administration of any labor organization or contribute financial or other support to it: *Provided,* That subject to rules and regulations made and published by the Board pursuant to section 6, an employer shall not be prohibited from permitting employees to confer with him during working hours without loss of time or pay;

(3) by discrimination in regard to hire or tenure of employment or any term or condition of employment to encourage or discourage membership in any labor organization: *Provided,* That nothing in this Act, or in any other statute of the United States, shall preclude an employer from making an agreement with a labor organization (not established, maintained, or assisted by any action defined in **section 8(a) of** this Act as an unfair labor practice) to require as a condition of employment membership therein **on or after the thirtieth day following the beginning of such employment or the effective date of such agreement, whichever is the later, (i)** if such labor organization is the representative of the employees as provided in section 9(a), in the appropriate collective-bargaining unit covered by such agreement when made, **[and has at the time the agreement was made or within the preceding twelve months received from the Board a notice of compliance with Section 9(f), (g), (h)], and (ii) unless following an election held as provided in section 9(e) within one year preceding the effective date of such agreement, the Board shall have certified that at least a majority of the employees eligible to vote in such election have voted to rescind the authority of such labor organization to make such an agreement:*** *Provided further,* **That no employer shall justify any discrimination against an employee for nonmembership in a labor organization (A) if he has reasonable grounds for believing that such membership was not available to the employee on the same terms and conditions generally applicable to other members, or (B) if he has reasonable grounds for believing that membership was denied or terminated for reasons other than the failure of the employee to tender the periodic dues and the initiation fees uniformly required as a condition of acquiring or retaining membership;**

(4) to discharge or otherwise discriminate against an employee because he has filed charges or given testimony under this Act;

---

*   The (ii) provision was added in 1951 by 65 Stat. 601.

(5) to refuse to bargain collectively with the representatives of his employees, subject to the provisions of section 9(a).

(b) **It shall be an unfair labor practice for a labor organization or its agents—**

(1) **to restrain or coerce (A) employees in the exercise of the rights guaranteed in section 7:** *Provided,* **That this paragraph shall not impair the right of a labor organization to prescribe its own rules with respect to the acquisition or retention of membership therein; or (B) an employer in the selection of his representatives for the purposes of collective bargaining or the adjustment of grievances;**

(2) **to cause or attempt to cause an employer to discriminate against an employee in violation of subsection (a)(3) or to discriminate against an employee with respect to whom membership in such organization has been denied or terminated on some ground other than his failure to tender the periodic dues and the initiation fees uniformly required as a condition of acquiring or retaining membership;**

(3) **to refuse to bargain collectively with an employer, provided it is the representative of his employees subject to the provisions of section 9(a);**

(4)*(i)* **to engage in, or to induce or encourage [the employees of any employer]** *any individual employed by any person engaged in commerce or in an industry affecting commerce* **to engage in, a strike or a [concerted] refusal in the course of [their]** *his* **employment to use, manufacture, process, transport, or otherwise handle or work on any goods, articles, materials, or commodities or to perform any services[,];** *or (ii) to threaten, coerce, or restrain any person engaged in commerce or in an industry affecting commerce,* **where** *in either case* **an object thereof is—**

(A) **forcing or requiring any employer or self-employed person to join any labor or employer organization [or any employer or other person to cease using, selling, handling, transporting, or otherwise dealing in the products of any other producer, processor, or manufacturer, or to cease doing business with any other person;]** *or to enter into any agreement which is prohibited by section 8(e);*

(B) *forcing or requiring any* **[any employer or other]** *person to cease using, selling, handling, transporting, or otherwise dealing in the products of any other producer, processor, or manufacturer, or to cease doing business with any other person, or* **forcing or requiring any other employer to recognize or bargain with a labor organization as the** representative of his employees unless such labor organization has been certified as the representative of such employees under the provisions of section 9[;]; *Provided, That nothing contained in this clause (B) shall be construed to make unlawful, where not otherwise unlawful, any primary strike or primary picketing;*

(C) forcing or requiring any employer to recognize or bargain with a particular labor organization as the representative of his employees if another labor organization has been certified as the representative of such employees under the provisions of section 9;

(D) forcing or requiring any employer to assign particular work to employees in a particular labor organization or in a particular trade, craft, or class rather than to employees in another labor organization or in another trade, craft, or class, unless such employer is failing to conform to an order or certification of the Board determining the bargaining representative for employees performing such work:

Provided, That nothing contained in this subsection (b) shall be construed to make unlawful a refusal by any person to enter upon the premises of any employer (other than his own employer), if the employees of such employer are engaged in a strike ratified or approved by a representative of such employees whom such employer is required to recognize under this Act: *Provided further, That for the purposes of this paragraph (4) only, nothing contained in such paragraph shall be construed to prohibit publicity, other than picketing, for the purpose of truthfully advising the public, including consumers and members of a labor organization, that a product or products are produced by an employer with whom the labor organization has a primary dispute and are distributed by another employer, as long as such publicity does not have an effect of inducing any individual employed by any person other than the primary employer in the course of his employment to refuse to pick up, deliver, or transport any goods, or not to perform any services, at the establishment of the employer engaged in such distribution:*

(5) to require of employees covered by an agreement authorized under subsection (a)(3) the payment, as a condition precedent to becoming a member of such organization, of a fee in an amount which the Board finds excessive or discriminatory under all the circumstances. In making such a finding, the Board shall consider, among other relevant factors, the practices and customs of labor organizations in the particular industry, and the wages currently paid to the employees affected; [and]

(6) to cause or attempt to cause an employer to pay or deliver or agree to pay or deliver any money or other thing of value, in the nature of an exaction, for services which are not performed or not to be performed[.]; *and*

(7)   to picket or cause to be picketed, or threaten to picket or cause to be picketed, any employer where an object thereof is forcing or requiring an employer to recognize or bargain with a labor organization as the representatives of his employees, or forcing or requiring the employees of an employer to accept or select such labor organization as their collective bargaining representative, unless such labor organization is currently certified as the representative of such employees:

(A) where the employer has lawfully recognized in accordance with this Act any other labor organization and a question concerning representation may not appropriately be raised under section 9(c) of this Act.

(B) where within the preceding twelve months a valid election under section 9(c) of this Act has been conducted, or

(C) where such picketing has been conducted without a petition under section 9(c) being filed within a reasonable period of time not to exceed thirty days from the commencement of such picketing: Provided, That when such a petition has been filed the Board shall forthwith, without regard to the provisions of section 9(c)(1) or the absence of a showing of a substantial interest on the part of the labor organization, direct an election in such unit as the Board finds to be appropriate and shall certify the results thereof: Provided further, That nothing in this subparagraph (C) shall be construed to prohibit any picketing or other publicity for the purpose of truthfully advising the public (including consumers) that an employer does not employ members of, or have a contract with, a labor organization, unless an effect of such picketing is to induce any individual employed by any other person in the course of his employment, not to pick up, deliver or transport any goods or not to perform any services.

Nothing in this paragraph (7) shall be construed to permit any act which would otherwise be an unfair labor practice under this section 8(b).

(c)   The expressing of any views, argument, or opinion, or the dissemination thereof, whether in written, printed, graphic, or visual form, shall not constitute or be evidence of an unfair labor practice under any of the provisions of this Act, if such expression contains no threat of reprisal or force or promise of benefit.

(d)   For the purposes of this section, to bargain collectively is the performance of the mutual obligation of the employer and the representative of the employees to meet at reasonable times and confer in good faith with respect to wages, hours, and other terms and conditions of employment, or the negotiation of an agreement, or any question arising thereunder, and the execution of a written contract incorporating any agreement reached if requested by either party, but such obligation does not compel either party to agree to a proposal or require the making of a concession: *Provided,* That where there is in effect a collective-bargaining contract covering employees in an industry affecting commerce, the duty to bargain collectively shall also mean that no party to such contract shall terminate or modify such contract, unless the party desiring such termination or modification—

(1) serves a written notice upon the other party to the contract of the proposed termination or modification sixty days prior to the expiration date thereof, or in the event such contract contains no expiration date, sixty days prior to the time it is proposed to make such termination or modification;

(2) offers to meet and confer with the other party for the purpose of negotiating a new contract or a contract containing the proposed modifications;

(3) notifies the Federal Mediation and Conciliation Service within thirty days after such notice of the existence of a dispute, and simultaneously therewith notifies any State or Territorial agency established to mediate and conciliate disputes within the State or Territory where the dispute occurred, provided no agreement has been reached by that time; and

(4) continues in full force and effect, without resorting to strike or lock-out, all the terms and conditions of the existing contract for a period of sixty days after such notice is given or until the expiration date of such contract, whichever occurs later:

The duties imposed upon employers, employees, and labor organizations by paragraphs (2), (3), and (4) shall become inapplicable upon an intervening certification of the Board, under which the labor organization or individual, which is a party to the contract, has been superseded as or ceased to be the representative of the employees subject to the provisions of section 9(a), and the duties so imposed shall not be construed as requiring either party to discuss or agree to any modification of the terms and conditions contained in a contract for a fixed period, if such modification is to become effective before such terms and conditions can be reopened under the provisions of the contract. Any employee who engages in a strike within [the sixty-day] any notice period specified in this subsection, or who engages in any strike within the appropriate period specified in subsection (g) of this section, **shall lose his status as an employee of the employer engaged in the particular labor dispute, for the purposes of sections 8, 9, and 10 of this Act, but such loss of status for such employee shall terminate if and when he is reemployed by such employer.** Whenever the collective bargaining involves employees of a health care institution, the provisions of this section 8(d) shall be modified as follows:

(A) The notice of section 8(d)(1) shall be ninety days; the notice of section 8(d)(3) shall be sixty days; and the contract period of section 8(d)(4) shall be ninety days.

(B) Where the bargaining is for an initial agreement following certification or recognition, at least thirty days' notice of the existence of a dispute shall be given by the labor organization to the agencies set forth in section 8(d)(3).

(C) After notice is given to the Federal Mediation and Conciliation Service under either clause (A) or (B) of this sentence, the Service shall promptly communicate with the parties and use its best efforts, by mediation and conciliation, to bring them to agreement. The parties shall participate fully and promptly in such meetings as may be undertaken by the Service for the purpose of aiding in a settlement of the dispute.

(e) It shall be an unfair labor practice for any labor organization and any employer to enter into any contract or agreement, express or implied, whereby such employer ceases or refrains or agrees to cease or refrain from handling, using, selling, transporting or otherwise dealing in any of the products of any other employer, or to cease doing business with any other person, and any contract or agreement entered into heretofore or hereafter containing such an agreement shall be to such extent unenforcible and void: Provided, That nothing in this subsection (e) shall apply to an agreement between a labor organization and an employer in the construction industry relating to the contracting or subcontracting of work to be done at the site of the construction, alteration, painting, or repair of a building, structure, or other work: Provided further, That for the purposes of this subsection (e) and section 8(b)(4)(B) the terms "any employer", "any person engaged in commerce or an industry affecting commerce", and "any person" when used in relation to the terms "any other producer, processor, or manufacturer", "any other employer", or "any other person" shall not include persons in the relation of a jobber, manufacturer, contractor, or subcontractor working on the goods or premises of the jobber or manufacturer or performing parts of an integrated process of production in the apparel and clothing industry: Provided further, That nothing in this Act shall prohibit the enforcement of any agreement which is within the foregoing exception.

(f)* It shall not be an unfair labor practice under subsections (a) and (b) of this section for an employer engaged primarily in the building and construction industry to make an agreement covering employees engaged (or who, upon their employment, will be engaged) in the building and construction industry with a labor organization of which building and construction employees are members (not established, maintained, or assisted by any action defined in section 8(a) of this Act as an unfair labor practice) because (1) the majority status of such labor organization has not been established under the provisions of section 9 of this Act prior to the making of such agreement, or (2) such agreement requires as a condition of employment, membership in such labor organization after the seventh day following the beginning of such employment or the effective date of the agreement, whichever is later, or (3) such agreement requires the employer to notify such labor organization of opportunities for employment with such employer, or gives such labor organization an opportunity to refer qualified applicants for such employment, or (4) such agreement specifies minimum training or experience qualifications for employment or provides for priority in opportunities for employment based upon length of service with such employer, in the industry or in the particular geographical area: Provided, That nothing in this subsection shall set aside the final proviso to section 8(a)(3) of this Act: Provided further, That any agreement which would be invalid, but for clause (1) of this subsection, shall not be a bar to a petition filed pursuant to section 9(c) or 9(e).

(g) A labor organization before engaging in any strike, picketing, or other concerted refusal to work at any health care institution shall, not less than ten days prior to such action, notify the institution in writing and the Federal Mediation and Conciliation Service of that intention, except that in the case of bargaining for an initial agreement following certification or recognition the notice required by this subsection shall not be given until the expiration of the period specified in clause (B) of the last sentence of section 8(d) of this Act. The notice shall state the date and time that such action will commence. The notice, once given, may be extended by the written agreement of both parties.

REPRESENTATIVES AND ELECTIONS

Sec. 9. (a) Representatives designated or selected for the purposes of collective bargaining by the majority of the employees in a unit appropriate for such purposes, shall be the exclusive representatives of all the employees in such unit for the purposes of collective bargaining in respect to rates of pay, wages, hours of employment, or other conditions of employment: *Provided,* That any individual employee or a

---

* Sec. 8(f) was inserted in the Act by subsec. (a) of Sec. 705 of Public Law 86–257. Sec. 705(b) provides:

Nothing contained in the amendment made by subsection (a) shall be construed as authorizing the execution or application of agreements requiring membership in a labor organization as a condition of employment in any State or Territory in which such execution or application is prohibited by State or Territorial law.

group of employees shall have the right at any time to present grievances to their employer **and to have such grievances adjusted, without the intervention of the bargaining representative, as long as the adjustment is not inconsistent with the terms of a collective-bargaining contract or agreement then in effect:** *Provided further*, **That the bargaining representative has been given opportunity to be present at such adjustment.**

(b)   The Board shall decide in each case whether, in order to assure to employees the fullest freedom in exercising the rights guaranteed by this Act, the unit appropriate for the purposes of collective bargaining shall be the employer unit, craft unit, plant unit, or subdivision thereof: *Provided*, **That the Board shall not (1) decide that any unit is appropriate for such purposes if such unit includes both professional employees and employees who are not professional employees unless a majority of such professional employees vote for inclusion in such unit; or (2) decide that any craft unit is inappropriate for such purposes on the ground that a different unit has been established by a prior Board determination, unless a majority of the employees in the proposed craft unit vote against separate representation or (3) decide that any unit is appropriate for such purposes if it includes, together with other employees, any individual employed as a guard to enforce against employees and other persons rules to protect property of the employer or to protect the safety of persons on the employer's premises; but no labor organization shall be certified as the representative of employees in a bargaining unit of guards if such organization admits to membership, or is affiliated directly or indirectly with an organization which admits to membership, employees other than guards.**

[(c)   Whenever a question affecting commerce arises concerning the representation of employees, the Board may investigate such controversy and certify to the parties, in writing, the name or names of the representatives that have been designated or selected. In any such investigation, the Board shall provide for an appropriate hearing upon due notice, either in conjunction with a proceeding under section 10 or otherwise, and may take a secret ballot of employees, or utilize any other suitable method to ascertain such representatives.]

(c)(1) Whenever a petition shall have been filed, in accordance with such regulations as may be prescribed by the Board—

  (A) by an employee or group of employees or any individual or labor organization acting in their behalf alleging that a substantial number of employees (i) wish to be represented for collective bargaining and that their employer declines to recognize their representative as the representative defined in section 9(a), or (ii) assert that the

individual or labor organization, which has been certified or is being currently recognized by their employer as the bargaining representative, is no longer a representative as defined in section 9(a); or

(B) by an employer, alleging that one or more individuals or labor organizations have presented to him a claim to be recognized as the representative defined in section 9(a);

the Board shall investigate such petition and if it has reasonable cause to believe that a question of representation affecting commerce exists shall provide for an appropriate hearing upon due notice. Such hearing may be conducted by an officer or employee of the regional office, who shall not make any recommendations with respect thereto. If the Board finds upon the record of such hearing that such a question of representation exists, it shall direct an election by secret ballot and shall certify the results thereof.

(2) In determining whether or not a question of representation affecting commerce exists, the same regulations and rules of decision shall apply irrespective of the identity of the persons filing the petition or the kind of relief sought and in no case shall the Board deny a labor organization a place on the ballot by reason of an order with respect to such labor organization or its predecessor not issued in conformity with section 10(c).

(3) No election shall be directed in any bargaining unit or any subdivision within which, in the preceding twelve-month period, a valid election shall have been held. Employees [on strike] *engaged in an economic strike* who are not entitled to reinstatement shall [not] be eligible to vote *under such regulations as the Board shall find are consistent with the purposes and provisions of this Act in any election conducted within twelve months after the commencement of the strike.* In any election where none of the choices on the ballot receives a majority, a run-off shall be conducted, the ballot providing for a selection between the two choices receiving the largest and second largest number of valid votes cast in the election.

(4) Nothing in this section shall be construed to prohibit the waiving of hearings by stipulation for the purpose of a consent election in conformity with regulations and rules of decision of the Board.

(5) In determining whether a unit is appropriate for the purposes specified in subsection (b) the extent to which the employees have organized shall not be controlling.

(d) Whenever an order of the Board made pursuant to section 10(c) is based in whole or in part upon facts certified following an investigation pursuant to subsection (c) of this section and there is a petition for the enforcement or review of such order, such certification and the record of such investigation shall be included in the transcript of the entire record required to be filed under section 10(e) or 10(f), and thereupon the decree of the court enforcing, modifying, or setting aside in whole or in part the order of the Board shall be made and entered upon the pleadings, testimony, and proceedings set forth in such transcript.

(e)*(1) Upon the filing with the Board, by 30 per centum or more of the employees in a bargaining unit covered by an agreement between their employer and a labor organization made pursuant to section 8(a)(3), of a petition alleging they desire that such authority be rescinded, the Board shall take a secret ballot of the employees in such unit, and shall certify the results thereof to such labor organization and to the employer.

(2) No election shall be conducted pursuant to this subsection in any bargaining unit or any subdivision within which, in the preceding twelve-month period, a valid election shall have been held.

[Subsections (f), (g) and (h) were deleted by the Labor-Management Reporting and Disclosure Act.]

PREVENTION OF UNFAIR LABOR PRACTICES

Sec. 10. (a) The Board is empowered, as hereinafter provided, to prevent any person from engaging in any unfair labor practice (listed in section 8) affecting commerce. This power shall not be affected by any other means of adjustment or prevention that has been or may be established by agreement, law, or otherwise: ***Provided*, That the Board is empowered by agreement with any agency of any State or Territory to cede to such agency jurisdiction over any cases in any industry (other than mining, manufacturing, communications, and transportation except where predominantly local in character) even though such cases may involve labor disputes affecting commerce, unless the provision of the State of Territorial statute applicable to the determination of such cases by such agency is inconsistent with the corresponding provision of this Act or has received a construction inconsistent therewith.**

(b) Whenever it is charged that any person has engaged in or is engaging in any such unfair labor practice, the Board, or any agent or agency designated by the Board for such purposes, shall have power to

---

* As enacted in 1947, Section 9(e) had three subsections. In 1951, the first subsection was deleted and the two remaining subsections were renumbered (1) and (2). 65 Stat. 601. The deleted subsection required, as a condition to the inclusion of a union-shop provision in a collective agreement, that a majority of employees authorize such inclusion in a Board-conducted election.

issue and cause to be served upon such person a complaint stating the charges in that respect, and containing a notice of hearing before the Board or a member thereof, or before a designated agent or agency, at a place therein fixed, not less than five days after the serving of said complaint: *Provided*, **That no complaint shall issue based upon any unfair labor practice occurring more than six months prior to the filing of the charge with the Board and the service of a copy thereof upon the person against whom such charge is made, unless the person aggrieved thereby was prevented from filing such charge by reason of service in the armed forces, in which event the six-month period shall be computed from the day of his discharge.** Any such complaint may be amended by the member, agent, or agency conducting the hearing or the Board in its discretion at any time prior to the issuance of an order based thereon. The person so complained of shall have the right to file an answer to the original or amended complaint and to appear in person or otherwise and give testimony at the place and time fixed in the complaint. In the discretion of the member, agent, or agency conducting the hearing or the Board, any other person may be allowed to intervene in the said proceeding and to present testimony. [In any such proceeding the rules of evidence prevailing in courts of law or equity shall not be controlling.] **Any such proceeding shall, so far as practicable, be conducted in accordance with the rules of evidence applicable in the district courts of the United States under the rules of civil procedure for the district courts of the United States, adopted by the Supreme Court of the United States pursuant to section 2072 of Title 28.**

(c)   The testimony taken by such member, agent, or agency or the Board shall be reduced to writing and filed with the Board. Thereafter, in its discretion, the Board upon notice may take further testimony or hear argument. If upon [all] **the preponderance of** the testimony taken the Board shall be of the opinion that any person named in the complaint has engaged in or is engaging in any such unfair labor practice, then the Board shall state its findings of fact and shall issue and cause to be served on such person an order requiring such person to cease and desist from such unfair labor practice, and to take such affirmative action including reinstatement of employees with or without back pay, as will effectuate the policies of this Act: *Provided*, **That where an order directs reinstatement of an employee, back pay may be required of the employer or labor organization, as the case may be, responsible for the discrimination suffered by him:** *And provided further*, **That in determining whether a complaint shall issue alleging a violation of section 8(a)(1) or section 8(a)(2), and in deciding such cases, the same regulations and rules of decision shall apply irrespective of whether or not the labor organization affected is affiliated with a labor organization national or international in scope.** Such order may further require such person to make reports from time to time showing the extent to which it has complied with the order.

If upon [all] **the preponderance of** the testimony taken the Board shall not be of the opinion that the person named in the complaint has engaged in or is engaging in any such unfair labor practice, then the Board shall state its findings of fact and shall issue an order dismissing the said complaint. **No order of the Board shall require the reinstatement of any individual as an employee who has been suspended or discharged, or the payment to him of any back pay, if such individual was suspended or discharged for cause. In case the evidence is presented before a member of the Board, or before an administrative law judge or judges* thereof, such member, or such judge or judges, as the case may be, shall issue and cause to be served on the parties to the proceeding a proposed report, together with a recommended order, which shall be filed with the Board, and if no exceptions are filed within twenty days after service thereof upon such parties, or within such further period as the Board may authorize, such recommended order shall become the order of the Board and become effective as therein prescribed.**

(d)   Until [**a transcript of**] the record in a case shall have been filed in a court, as hereinafter provided, the Board may at any time, upon reasonable notice and in such manner as it shall deem proper, modify or set aside, in whole or in part, any finding or order made or issued by it.

(e)   The Board shall have power to petition any [United States] court of appeals of the United States [(including the United States court of appeals for the District of Columbia)] or if all the courts of appeals to which application may be made are in vacation, any [United States] district court *of the United States*, within any circuit or district, respectively, wherein the unfair labor practice in question occurred or wherein such person resides or transacts business, for the enforcement of such order and for appropriate temporary relief or restraining order, and shall [certify and] file in the court [a transcript of] the [entire] record in the proceedings, [including the pleadings and testimony upon which such order was entered and the findings and order of the Board.] *as printed in section 2112 of Title 28.* Upon [such filing] *the filing of such petition*, the court shall cause notice thereof to be served upon such person, and thereupon shall have jurisdiction of the proceeding and of the question determined therein, and shall have power to grant such temporary relief or restraining order as it deems just and proper, and to make and enter [upon the pleadings, testimony, and proceedings set forth in such transcript] a decree enforcing, modifying, and enforcing as so modified, or setting aside in whole or in part the order of the Board. No objection that has not been urged before the Board, its member, agent, or agency, shall be considered by the court, unless the failure or neglect to urge such objection shall be excused because of extraordinary circumstances. The findings of the Board with respect to questions of fact

---

*   The title "administrative law judge" was adopted in 5 U.S.C. § 3105, in 1972.

if supported by **substantial** evidence **on the record considered as a whole** shall be conclusive. If either party shall apply to the court for leave to adduce additional evidence and shall show to the satisfaction of the court that such additional evidence is material and that there were reasonable grounds for the failure to adduce such evidence in the hearing before the Board, its member, agent, or agency, the court may order such additional evidence to be taken before the Board, its member, agent, or agency, and to be made a part of [the transcript] *record*. The Board may modify its findings as to the facts, or make new findings, by reason of additional evidence so taken and filed, and it shall file such modified or new findings, which findings with respect to questions of fact if supported by **substantial** evidence **on the record considered as a whole** shall be conclusive, and shall file its recommendations, if any, for the modification or setting aside of its original order. *Upon the filing of the record with it* the jurisdiction of the court shall be exclusive and its judgment and decree shall be final, except that the same shall be subject to review by the appropriate circuit court of appeals if application was made to the district court as hereinabove provided, and by the Supreme Court of the United States upon writ of certiorari or certification as provided in section 1254 of Title 28.

(f)   Any person aggrieved by a final order of the Board granting or denying in whole or in part the relief sought may obtain a review of such order in any United States court of appeals in the circuit wherein the unfair labor practice in question was alleged to have been engaged in or wherein such person resides or transacts business, or in the United States Court of Appeals for the District of Columbia, by filing in such court a written petition praying that the order of the Board be modified or set aside. A copy of such petition shall be forthwith [served upon the Board] *transmitted by the clerk of the court to the Board* and thereupon the aggrieved party shall file in the court [a transcript of] the [entire] record in the proceeding, certified by the Board, [including the pleading and testimony upon which the order complained of was entered, and the findings and order of the Board.] *as provided in section 2112 of Title 28.* Upon [such filing,] *the filing of such petition*, the court shall proceed in the same manner as in the case of an application by the Board under subsection (e) *of this section*, and shall have the same exclusive jurisdiction to grant to the Board such temporary relief or restraining order as it deems just and proper, and in like manner to make and enter a decree enforcing, modifying, and enforcing as so modified, or setting aside in whole or in part the order of the Board; the findings of the Board with respect to questions of fact if supported by **substantial** evidence **on the record considered as a whole** shall in like manner be conclusive.

(g)   The commencement of proceedings under subsection (e) or (f) of this section shall not, unless specifically ordered by the court, operate as a stay of the Board's order.

(h) When granting appropriate temporary relief or a restraining order, or making and entering a decree enforcing, modifying, and enforcing as so modified, or setting aside in whole or in part an order of the Board, as provided in this section, the jurisdiction of courts sitting in equity shall not be limited by sections 101 to 115 of title 29, United States Code.*

(i) [Repealed.]

(j) The Board shall have power, upon issuance of a complaint as provided in subsection (b) charging that any person has engaged in or is engaging in an unfair labor practice, to petition any United States district court within any district wherein the unfair labor practice in question is alleged to have occurred or wherein such person resides or transacts business, for appropriate temporary relief or restraining order. Upon the filing of any such petition the court shall cause notice thereof to be served upon such person, and thereupon shall have jurisdiction to grant to the Board such temporary relief or restraining order as it deems just and proper.

(k) Whenever it is charged that any person has engaged in an unfair labor practice within the meaning of paragraph (4)(D) of section 8(b), the Board is empowered and directed to hear and determine the dispute out of which such unfair labor practice shall have arisen, unless, within ten days after notice that such charge has been filed, the parties to such dispute submit to the Board satisfactory evidence that they have adjusted, or agreed upon methods for the voluntary adjustment of, the dispute. Upon compliance by the parties to the dispute with the decision of the Board or upon such voluntary adjustment of the dispute, such charge shall be dismissed.

(*l*) Whenever it is charged that any person has engaged in an unfair labor practice within the meaning of paragraph (4)(A), (B), or (C) of section 8(b), *or section 8(e) or section 8(b)(7)* **the preliminary investigation of such charge shall be made forthwith and given priority over all other cases except cases of like character in the office where it is filed or to which it is referred. If, after such investigation, the officer or regional attorney to whom the matter may be referred has reasonable cause to believe such charge is true and that a complaint should issue, he shall, on behalf of the Board, petition any United States district court within any district where the unfair labor practice in question has occurred, is alleged to have occurred, or wherein such person resides or transacts business, for appropriate injunctive relief pending the final adjudication of the Board with respect to such matter. Upon the filing of any such petition the district**

---

*   The Norris-LaGuardia Act of 1932.

court shall have jurisdiction to grant such injunctive relief or temporary restraining order as it deems just and proper, notwithstanding any other provision of law: *Provided further*, That no temporary restraining order shall be issued without notice unless a petition alleges that substantial and irreparable injury to the charging party will be unavoidable and such temporary restraining order shall be effective for no longer than five days and will become void at the expiration of such period[.]: *Provided further, That such officer or regional attorney shall not apply for any restraining order under section 8(b)(7) if a charge against the employer under section 8(a)(2) has been filed and after the preliminary investigation, he has reasonable cause to believe that such charge is true and that a complaint should issue.* Upon filing of any such petition the courts shall cause notice thereof to be served upon any person involved in the charge and such person, including the charging party, shall be given an opportunity to appear by counsel and present any relevant testimony: *Provided further*, That for the purposes of this subsection district courts shall be deemed to have jurisdiction of a labor organization (1) in the district in which such organization maintains its principal office, or (2) in any district in which its duly authorized officers or agents are engaged in promoting or protecting the interests of employee members. The service of legal process upon such officer or agent shall constitute service upon the labor organization and make such organization a party to the suit. In situations where such relief is appropriate the procedure specified herein shall apply to charges with respect to sections 8(b)(4)(D).

(m) *Whenever it is charged that any person has engaged in an unfair labor practice within the meaning of subsection (a)(3) or (b)(2) of section 8, such charge shall be given priority over all other cases except cases of like character in the office where it is filed or to which it is referred and cases given priority under subsection (l)* of this section.

INVESTIGATORY POWERS

Sec. 11. For the purpose of all hearings and investigations, which, in the opinion of the Board, are necessary and proper for the exercise of the powers vested in it by section 9 and section 10—

(1) The Board, or its duly authorized agents or agencies, shall at all reasonable times have access to, for the purpose of examination, and the right to copy any evidence of any person being investigated or proceeded against that relates to any matter under investigation or in question. The Board, or any member thereof, shall upon application of any party to such proceedings, forthwith issue to such party subpoenas requiring the attendance and testimony of witnesses or the production of any evidence in such proceeding or investigation requested in such application. Within five days after the service of a subpoena on any person

requiring the production of any evidence in his possession or under his control, such person may petition the Board to revoke, and the Board shall revoke, such subpena if in its opinion the evidence whose production is required does not relate to any matter under investigation, or any matter in question in such proceedings, or if in its opinion such subpena does not describe with sufficient particularity the evidence whose production is required. Any member of the Board, or any agent or agency designated by the Board for such purposes, may administer oaths and affirmations, examine witnesses, and receive evidence. Such attendance of witnesses and the production of such evidence may be required from any place in the United States or any Territory or possession thereof, at any designated place of hearing.

(2)   In case of contumacy or refusal to obey a subpena issued to any person, any district court of the United States or the United States courts of any Territory or possession, or the District Court of the United States for the District of Columbia, within the jurisdiction of which the inquiry is carried on or within the jurisdiction of which said person guilty of contumacy or refusal to obey is found or resides or transacts business, upon application by the Board shall have jurisdiction to issue to such person an order requiring such person to appear before the Board, its member, agent, or agency, there to produce evidence if so ordered, or there to give testimony touching the matter under investigation or in question; and any failure to obey such order of the court may be punished by said court as a contempt thereof.

[(3) No person shall be excused from attending and testifying or from producing books, records, correspondence, documents, or other evidence in obedience to the subpena of the Board, on the ground that the testimony or evidence required of him may tend to incriminate him or subject him to a penalty or forfeiture; but no individual shall be prosecuted or subjected to any penalty or forfeiture for or on account of any transaction, matter, or thing concerning which he is compelled, after having claimed his privilege against self-incrimination, to testify or produce evidence, except that such individual so testifying shall not be exempt from prosecution and punishment for perjury committed in so testifying.]*

(4)   Complaints, orders, and other process and papers of the Board, its member, agent, or agency, may be served either personally or by registered mail or by telegraph or by leaving a copy thereof at the principal office or place of business of the person required to be served. The verified return by the individual so serving the same setting forth the manner of such service shall be proof of the same, and the return post office receipt or telegraph receipt therefor when registered and mailed or telegraphed as aforesaid shall be proof of service of the same. Witnesses

---

*   Section 11(3) was repealed in 1970, by 84 Stat. 930. Similar immunity provisions were substituted; see 18 U.S.C. §§ 6001, 6002, 6004 (1970).

summoned before the Board, its member, agent, or agency, shall be paid the same fees and mileage that are paid witnesses in the courts of the United States, and witnesses whose depositions are taken and the persons taking the same shall severally be entitled to the same fees as are paid for like services in the courts of the United States.

(5)   All process of any court to which application may be made under this Act may be served in the judicial district wherein the defendant or other person required to be served resides or may be found.

(6)   The several departments and agencies of the Government, when directed by the President, shall furnish the Board, upon its request, all records, papers, and information in their possession relating to any matter before the Board.

Sec. 12. Any person who shall willfully resist, prevent, impede, or interfere with any member of the Board or any of its agents or agencies in the performance of duties pursuant to this Act shall be punished by a fine of not more than $5,000 or by imprisonment for not more than one year, or both.

LIMITATIONS

Sec. 13. Nothing in this Act, **except as specifically provided for herein,** shall be construed so as either to interfere with or impede or diminish in any way the right to strike, **or to affect the limitations or qualifications on that right.**

Sec. 14. (a) Nothing herein shall prohibit any individual employed as a supervisor from becoming or remaining a member of a labor organization, but no employer subject to this Act shall be compelled to deem individuals defined herein as supervisors as employees for the purpose of any law, either national or local, relating to collective bargaining.

(b) Nothing in this Act shall be construed as authorizing the execution or application of agreements requiring membership in a labor organization as a condition of employment in any State or Territory in which such execution or application is prohibited by State or Territorial law.

(c)(1) The Board, in its discretion, may, by rule of decision or by published rules adopted pursuant to the Administrative Procedure Act, decline to assert jurisdiction over any labor dispute involving any class or category of employers, where, in the opinion of the Board, the effect of such labor dispute on commerce is not sufficiently substantial to warrant the exercise of its jurisdiction: Provided, That the Board shall not decline to assert jurisdiction over any labor dispute over which it would assert jurisdiction under the standards prevailing upon August 1, 1959.

(2)   Nothing in this Act shall be deemed to prevent or bar any agency or the courts of any State or Territory (including the Commonwealth of Puerto Rico, Guam, and the Virgin Islands), from assuming and asserting

jurisdiction over labor disputes over which the Board declines, pursuant to paragraph (1) of this subsection, to assert jurisdiction.

Sec. 15. [Reference to repealed provisions of the Bankruptcy Act.]

Sec. 16. If any provision of this Act, or the application of such provision to any person or circumstances, shall be held invalid, the remainder of this Act, or the application of such provision to persons or circumstances other than those as to which it is held invalid, shall not be affected thereby.

Sec. 17. This Act may be cited as the "National Labor Relations Act."

Sec. 18. [This section, which refers to the now-repealed Sections 9(f), (g), (h), is omitted.]

INDIVIDUALS WITH RELIGIOUS CONVICTIONS

Sec. 19. Any employee who is a member of and adheres to established and traditional tenets or teachings of a bona fide religion, body, or sect which has historically held conscientious objections to joining or financially supporting labor organizations shall not be required to join or financially support any labor organization as a condition of employment; except that such employee may be required in a contract between such employee's employer and a labor organization in lieu of periodic dues and initiation fees, to pay sums equal to such dues and initiation fees to a nonreligious, nonlabor organization charitable fund exempt from taxation under section 501(c)(3) of title 26 of the Internal Revenue Code [section 501(c)(3) of title 26], chosen by such employee from a list of at least three such funds, designated in such contract or if the contract fails to designate such funds, then to any such fund chosen by the employee. If such employee who holds conscientious objections pursuant to this section requests the labor organization to use the grievance-arbitration procedure on the employee's behalf, the labor organization is authorized to charge the employee for the reasonable cost of using such procedure.*

---

* This section was added by Pub.L. 93–360, July 26, 1974, 88 Stat. 397, and amended, Pub.L. 96–593, Dec. 24, 1980, 94 Stat. 3452.

LABOR MANAGEMENT RELATIONS ACT

61 Stat. 136 (1947), as amended; 29 U.S.C. §§ 141–97 (1988).

SHORT TITLE AND DECLARATION OF POLICY

Sec. 1. (a) This Act may be cited as the "Labor Management Relations Act, 1947."

(b) Industrial strife which interferes with the normal flow of commerce and with the full production of articles and commodities for commerce, can be avoided or substantially minimized if employers, employees, and labor organizations each recognize under law one another's legitimate rights in their relations with each other, and above all recognize under law that neither party has any right in its relations with any other to engage in acts or practices which jeopardize the public health, safety, or interest.

It is the purpose and policy of this Act, in order to promote the full flow of commerce, to prescribe the legitimate rights of both employees and employers in their relations affecting commerce, to provide orderly and peaceful procedures for preventing the interference by either with the legitimate rights of the other, to protect the rights of individual employees in their relations with labor organizations whose activities affect commerce, to define and proscribe practices on the part of labor and management which affect commerce and are inimical to the general welfare, and to protect the rights of the public in connection with labor disputes affecting commerce.

TITLE I

AMENDMENT OF NATIONAL LABOR RELATIONS ACT

Sec. 101. The National Labor Relations Act is hereby amended to read as follows: [The text of the National Labor Relations Act as amended is set forth supra.]

TITLE II

CONCILIATION OF LABOR DISPUTES IN INDUSTRIES AFFECTING COMMERCE; NATIONAL EMERGENCIES

Sec. 201. That it is the policy of the United States that—

(a) sound and stable industrial peace and the advancement of the general welfare, health, and safety of the Nation and of the best interests of employers and employees can most satisfactorily be secured by the settlement of issues between employers and employees through the processes of conference and collective bargaining between employers and the representatives of their employees;

(b) the settlement of issues between employers and employees through collective bargaining may be advanced by making available full and adequate governmental facilities for conciliation, mediation, and voluntary arbitration to aid and encourage employers and the representatives of their employees to reach and maintain agreements concerning rates of pay, hours, and working conditions, and to make all reasonable efforts to settle their differences by mutual agreement reached through conferences and collective bargaining or by such methods as may be provided for in any applicable agreement for the settlement of disputes; and

(c) certain controversies which arise between parties to collective-bargaining agreements may be avoided or minimized by making available full and adequate governmental facilities for furnishing assistance to employers and the representatives of their employees in formulating for inclusion within such agreements provision for adequate notice of any proposed changes in the terms of such agreements, for the final adjustment of grievances or questions regarding the application or interpretation of such agreements, and other provisions designed to prevent the subsequent arising of such controversies.

Sec. 202. (a) There is hereby created an independent agency to be known as the Federal Mediation and Conciliation Service (herein referred to as the "Service," except that for sixty days after the date of the enactment of this Act such term shall refer to the Conciliation Service of the Department of Labor). The Service shall be under the direction of a Federal Mediation and Conciliation Director (hereinafter referred to as the "Director"), who shall be appointed by the President by and with the advice and consent of the Senate. The Director shall not engage in any other business, vocation, or employment.

(b) The Director is authorized, subject to the civil-service laws, to appoint such clerical and other personnel as may be necessary for the execution of the functions of the Service, and shall fix their compensation in accordance with chapter 51 and subchapter III of chapter 53 of title 5, and may, without regard to the provisions of the civil-service laws, appoint such conciliators and mediators as may be necessary to carry out the functions of the Service. The Director is authorized to make such expenditures for supplies, facilities, and services as he deems necessary. Such expenditures shall be allowed and paid upon presentation of itemized vouchers therefor approved by the Director or by any employee designated by him for that purpose.

(c) The principal office of the Service shall be in the District of Columbia, but the Director may establish regional offices convenient to localities in which labor controversies are likely to arise. The Director may by order, subject to revocation at any time, delegate any authority and discretion conferred upon him by this Act to any regional director, or other officer or employee of the Service. The Director may establish suitable procedures for cooperation with State and local mediation agencies. The Director shall make an annual report in writing to Congress at the end of the fiscal year.

(d) All mediation and conciliation functions of the Secretary of Labor or the United States Conciliation Service under section 8 of the Act entitled "An Act to create a Department of Labor," approved March 4, 1913 (U.S.C., title 29, sec. 51), and all functions of the United States Conciliation Service under any other law are transferred to the Federal Mediation and Conciliation Service, together with the personnel and records of the United States Conciliation Service. Such transfer shall take effect upon the sixtieth day after June 23, 1947. Such transfer shall not affect any proceedings pending before the United States Conciliation Service or any certification, order, rule, or regulation theretofore made by it or by the Secretary of Labor. The Director and the Service shall not be subject in any way to the jurisdiction or authority of the Secretary of Labor or any official or division of the Department of Labor.

FUNCTIONS OF THE SERVICE

Sec. 203. (a) It shall be the duty of the Service, in order to prevent or minimize interruptions of the free flow of commerce growing out of labor disputes, to assist parties to labor disputes in industries affecting commerce to settle such disputes through conciliation and mediation.

(b) The Service may proffer its services in any labor dispute in any industry affecting commerce, either upon its own motion or upon the request of one or more of the parties to the dispute, whenever in its judgment such dispute threatens to cause a substantial interruption of commerce. The Director and the Service are directed to avoid attempting to mediate disputes which would have only a minor effect on interstate commerce if State or other conciliation services are available to the parties. Whenever the Service does proffer its services in any dispute, it shall be the duty of the Service promptly to put itself in communication with the parties and to use its best efforts, by mediation and conciliation, to bring them to agreement.

(c) If the Director is not able to bring the parties to agreement by conciliation within a reasonable time, he shall seek to induce the parties voluntarily to seek other means of settling the dispute without resort to strike, lock-out, or other coercion, including submission to the employees in the bargaining unit of the employer's last offer of settlement for approval or rejection in a secret ballot. The failure or refusal of either party to agree to any procedure suggested by the Director shall not be deemed a violation of any duty or obligation imposed by this Act.

(d) Final adjustment by a method agreed upon by the parties is hereby declared to be the desirable method for settlement of grievance disputes arising over the application or interpretation of an existing collective-bargaining agreement. The Service is directed to make its conciliation and mediation services available in the settlement of such grievance disputes only as a last resort and in exceptional cases.

(e)* The Service is authorized and directed to encourage and support the establishment and operation of joint labor management activities conducted by plant, area, and industrywide committees designed to improve labor management relationships, job security and organizational effectiveness, in accordance with the provisions of section 205A.

Sec. 204.   (a) In order to prevent or minimize interruptions of the free flow of commerce growing out of labor disputes, employers and employees and their representatives, in any industry affecting commerce, shall—

(1) exert every reasonable effort to make and maintain agreements concerning rates of pay, hours, and working conditions, including provision for adequate notice of any proposed change in the terms of such agreements;

(2) whenever a dispute arises over the terms or application of a collective-bargaining agreement and a conference is requested by a party or prospective party thereto, arrange promptly for such a conference to be held and endeavor in such conference to settle such dispute expeditiously; and

(3) in case such dispute is not settled by conference, participate fully and promptly in such meetings as may be undertaken by the Service under this Act for the purpose of aiding in a settlement of the dispute.

Sec. 205.   (a) There is created a National Labor-Management Panel which shall be composed of twelve members appointed by the President, six of whom shall be selected from among persons outstanding in the field of management and six of whom shall be selected from among persons outstanding in the field of labor. Each member shall hold office for a term of three years, except that any member appointed to fill a vacancy occurring prior to the expiration of the term for which his predecessor was appointed shall be appointed for the remainder of such term, and the terms of office of the members first taking office shall expire, as designated by the President at the time of appointment, four at the end of the first year, four at the end of the second year, and four at the end of the third year after the date of appointment. Members of the panel, when serving on business of the panel, shall be paid compensation at the rate of $25 per day, and shall also be entitled to receive an allowance for actual and necessary travel and subsistence expenses while so serving away from their places of residence.

(b) It shall be the duty of the panel, at the request of the Director, to advise in the avoidance of industrial controversies and the manner in

---

* Subsection (e) was added in 1978, by Pub.L. 95–524, § 6(c)(1), 92 Stat. 2020.

which mediation and voluntary adjustment shall be administered, particularly with reference to controversies affecting the general welfare of the country.

Sec. 205A.* **(a)**(1) The Service is authorized and directed to provide assistance in the establishment and operation of plant, area and industrywide labor management committees which—

(A) have been organized jointly by employers and labor organizations representing employees in that plant, area, or industry; and

(B) are established for the purpose of improving labor management relationships, job security, organizational effectiveness, enhancing economic development or involving workers in decisions affecting their jobs including improving communication with respect to subjects of mutual interest and concern.

(2) The Service is authorized and directed to enter into contracts and to make grants, where necessary or appropriate, to fulfill its responsibilities under this section.

(b)(1) No grant may be made, no contract may be entered into and no other assistance may be provided under the provisions of this section to a plant labor management committee unless the employees in that plant are represented by a labor organization and there is in effect at that plant a collective bargaining agreement.

(2) No grant may be made, no contract may be entered into and no other assistance may be provided under the provisions of this section to an area or industrywide labor management committee unless its participants include any labor organizations certified or recognized as the representative of the employees of an employer participating in such committee. Nothing in this clause shall prohibit participation in an area or industrywide committee by an employer whose employees are not represented by a labor organization.

(3) No grant may be made under the provisions of this section to any labor management committee which the Service finds to have as one of its purposes the discouragement of the exercise of rights contained in section 7 of the National Labor Relations Act (29 U.S.C. § 157) [section 157 of this title], or the interference with collective bargaining in any plant, or industry.

(c) The Service shall carry out the provisions of this section through an office established for that purpose.

(d) There are authorized to be appropriated to carry out the provisions of this section $10,000,000 for the fiscal year 1979, and such sums as may be necessary thereafter.

---

*   This section was added in 1978, by Pub.L. 95–524, § 6(c)(2), 92 Stat. 2020.

NATIONAL EMERGENCIES

Sec. 206.   Whenever in the opinion of the President of the United States, a threatened or actual strike or lock-out affecting an entire industry or a substantial part thereof engaged in trade, commerce, transportation, transmission, or communication among the several States or with foreign nations, or engaged in the production of goods for commerce, will, if permitted to occur or to continue, imperil the national health or safety, he may appoint a board of inquiry to inquire into the issues involved in the dispute and to make a written report to him within such time as he shall prescribe. Such report shall include a statement of the facts with respect to the dispute, including each party's statement of its position but shall not contain any recommendations. The President shall file a copy of such report with the Service and shall make its contents available to the public.

Sec. 207.   (a) A board of inquiry shall be composed of a chairman and such other members as the President shall determine, and shall have power to sit and act in any place within the United States and to conduct such hearings either in public or in private, as it may deem necessary or proper, to ascertain the facts with respect to the causes and circumstances of the dispute.

(b) Members of a board of inquiry shall receive compensation at the rate of $50 for each day actually spent by them in the work of the board, together with necessary travel and subsistence expenses.

(c) For the purpose of any hearing or inquiry conducted by any board appointed under this title, the provisions of sections 9 and 10 (relating to the attendance of witnesses and the production of books, papers, and documents) of the Federal Trade Commission Act of September 16, 1914, as amended (U.S.C. 19, title 15, secs. 49 and 50, as amended), are made applicable to the powers and duties of such board.

Sec. 208.   (a) Upon receiving a report from a board of inquiry the President may direct the Attorney General to petition any district court of the United States having jurisdiction of the parties to enjoin such strike or lock-out or the continuing thereof, and if the court finds that such threatened or actual strike or lock-out—

(i) affects an entire industry or a substantial part thereof engaged in trade, commerce, transportation, transmission, or communication among the several States or with foreign nations, or engaged in the production of goods for commerce; and

(ii) if permitted to occur or to continue, will imperil the national health or safety, it shall have jurisdiction to enjoin any such strike or lock-out, or the continuing thereof, and to make such other orders as may be appropriate.

(b) In any case, the provisions of the Act of March 23, 1932, entitled "An Act to amend the Judicial Code and to define and limit the jurisdiction of courts sitting in equity, and for other purposes," shall not be applicable.

(c) The order or orders of the court shall be subject to review by the appropriate United States court of appeals and by the Supreme Court upon writ of certiorari or certification as provided in sections 239 and 240 of the Judicial Code, as amended (U.S.C., title 29, secs. 346 and 347).

Sec. 209. (a) Whenever a district court has issued an order under section 208 enjoining acts or practices which imperil or threaten to imperil the national health or safety, it shall be the duty of the parties to the labor dispute giving rise to such order to make every effort to adjust and settle their differences, with the assistance of the Service created by this Act. Neither party shall be under any duty to accept, in whole or in part, any proposal of settlement made by the Service.

(b) Upon the issuance of such order, the President shall reconvene the board of inquiry which has previously reported with respect to the dispute. At the end of a sixty-day period (unless the dispute has been settled by that time), the board of inquiry shall report to the President the current position of the parties and the efforts which have been made for settlement, and shall include a statement by each party of its position and a statement of the employer's last offer of settlement. The President shall make such report available to the public. The National Labor Relations Board, within the succeeding fifteen days, shall take a secret ballot of the employees of each employer involved in the dispute on the question of whether they wish to accept the final offer of settlement made by their employer as stated by him and shall certify the results thereof to the Attorney General within five days thereafter.

Sec. 210. Upon the certification of the results of such ballot or upon a settlement being reached, whichever happens sooner, the Attorney General shall move the court to discharge the injunction, which motion shall then be granted and the injunction discharged. When such motion is granted, the President shall submit to the Congress a full and comprehensive report of the proceedings, including the findings of the board of inquiry and the ballot taken by the National Labor Relations Board, together with such recommendations as he may see fit to make for consideration and appropriate action.

COMPILATION OF COLLECTIVE BARGAINING AGREEMENTS, ETC.

Sec. 211. (a) For the guidance and information of interested representatives of employers, employees, and the general public, the Bureau of Labor Statistics of the Department of Labor shall maintain a file of copies of all available collective-bargaining agreements and other available agreements and actions thereunder settling or adjusting labor disputes. Such file shall be open to inspection under appropriate conditions prescribed by the Secretary of Labor, except that no specific information submitted in confidence shall be disclosed.

(b) The Bureau of Labor Statistics in the Department of Labor is authorized to furnish upon request of the Service, or employers, employees, or their representatives, all available data and factual information which may aid in the settlement of any labor dispute, except that no specific information submitted in confidence shall be disclosed.

EXEMPTION OF RAILWAY LABOR ACT

Sec. 212.   The provisions of this title shall not be applicable with respect to any matter which is subject to the provisions of the Railway Labor Act, as amended from time to time.

CONCILIATION OF LABOR DISPUTES IN THE HEALTH CARE INDUSTRY

Sec. 213.   (a) If, in the opinion of the Director of the Federal Mediation and Conciliation Service a threatened or actual strike or lockout affecting a health care institution will, if permitted to occur or to continue, substantially interrupt the delivery of health care in the locality concerned, the Director may further assist in the resolution of the impasse by establishing within 30 days after the notice to the Federal Mediation and Conciliation Service under clause (A) of the last sentence of section 8(d) (which is required by clause (3) of such section 8(d)), or within 10 days after the notice under clause (B), an impartial Board of Inquiry to investigate the issues involved in the dispute and to make a written report thereon to the parties within fifteen (15) days after the establishment of such a Board. The written report shall contain the findings of fact together with the Board's recommendations for settling the dispute, with the objective of achieving a prompt, peaceful and just settlement of the dispute. Each such Board shall be composed of such number of individuals as the Director may deem desirable. No member appointed under this section shall have any interest or involvement in the health care institutions or the employee organizations involved in the dispute.

(b)(1)   Members of any board established under this section who are otherwise employed by the Federal Government shall serve without compensation but shall be reimbursed for travel, subsistence, and other necessary expenses incurred by them in carrying out its duties under this section.

(2) Members of any board established under this section who are not subject to paragraph (1) shall receive compensation at a rate prescribed by the Director but not to exceed the daily rate prescribed for GS-18 of the General Schedule under section 5332 of title 5, United States Code, including travel for each day they are engaged in the performance of their duties under this section and shall be entitled to reimbursement for travel, subsistence, and other necessary expenses incurred by them in carrying out their duties under this section.

(c) After the establishment of a board under subsection (a) of this section and for 15 days after any such board has issued its report, no change in the status quo in effect prior to the expiration of the contract in the case of negotiations for a contract renewal, or in effect prior to the time of the impasse in the case of an initial bargaining negotiation, except by agreement, shall be made by the parties to the controversy.

(d) There are authorized to be appropriated such sums as may be necessary to carry out the provisions of this section.

TITLE III
SUITS BY AND AGAINST LABOR ORGANIZATIONS

Sec. 301. (a) Suits for violation of contracts between an employer and a labor organization representing employees in an industry affecting commerce as defined in this Act, or between any such labor organizations, may be brought in any district court of the United States having jurisdiction of the parties, without respect to the amount in controversy or without regard to the citizenship of the parties.

(b) Any labor organization which represents employees in an industry affecting commerce as defined in this Act and any employer whose activities affect commerce as defined in this Act shall be bound by the acts of its agents. Any such labor organization may sue or be sued as an entity and in behalf of the employees whom it represents in the courts of the United States. Any money judgment against a labor organization in a district court of the United States shall be enforceable only against the organization as an entity and against its assets, and shall not be enforceable against any individual member or his assets.

(c) For the purposes of actions and proceedings by or against labor organizations in the district courts of the United States, district courts shall be deemed to have jurisdiction of a labor organization (1) in the district in which such organization maintains its principal office, or (2) in any district in which its duly authorized officers or agents are engaged in representing or acting for employee members.

(d) The service of summons, subpena, or other legal process of any court of the United States upon an officer or agent of a labor organization, in his capacity as such, shall constitute service upon the labor organization.

(e) For the purposes of this section, in determining whether any person is acting as an "agent" of another person so as to make such other person responsible for his acts, the question of whether the specific acts performed were actually authorized or subsequently ratified shall not be controlling.

RESTRICTIONS ON PAYMENTS TO
EMPLOYEE REPRESENTATIVES

Sec. 302. (a) It shall be unlawful for any employer or association of employers or any person who acts as a labor relations expert, adviser, or consultant to an employer or who acts in the interest of an employer to pay, lend, or deliver, or agree to pay, lend, or deliver, any money or other thing of value—

(1) to any representative of any of his employees who are employed in an industry affecting commerce; or

(2) to any labor organization, or any officer or employee thereof, which represents, seeks to represent, or would admit to membership, any of the employees of such employer who are employed in an industry affecting commerce; or

(3) to any employee or group or committee of employees of such employer employed in an industry affecting commerce in excess of their normal compensation for the purpose of causing such employee or group or committee directly or indirectly to influence any other employees in the exercise of the right to organize and bargain collectively through representatives of their own choosing; or

(4) to any officer or employee of a labor organization engaged in an industry affecting commerce with intent to influence him in respect to any of his actions, decisions, or duties as a representative of employees or as such officer or employee of such labor organization.

(b)(1) It shall be unlawful for any person to request, demand, receive, or accept, or agree to receive or accept, any payment, loan or delivery of any money or other thing of value prohibited by subsection (a).

(2) It shall be unlawful for any labor organization, or for any person acting as an officer, agent, representative, or employee of such labor organization, to demand or accept from the operator of any motor vehicle (as defined in part II of the Interstate Commerce Act) employed in the transportation of property in commerce, or the employer of any such operator, any money or other thing of value payable to such organization or to an officer, agent, representative or employee thereof as a fee or charge for the unloading, or in connection with the unloading, of the cargo of such vehicle: *Provided*, That nothing in this paragraph shall be construed to make unlawful any payment by an employer to any of his employees as compensation for their services as employees.

(c) The provisions of this section shall not be applicable (1) in respect to any money or other thing of value payable by an employer to any of his employees whose established duties include acting openly for such employer in matters of labor relations or personnel administration or to any representative of his employees, or to any officer or employee of a labor organization, who is also an employee or former employee of such employer, as compensation for, or by reason of, his service as an employee of such employer; (2) with respect to the payment or delivery of any money or other thing of value in satisfaction of a judgment of any court or a decision or award of an arbitrator or impartial chairman or in compromise, adjustment, settlement, or release of any claim, complaint, grievance, or dispute in the absence of fraud or duress; (3) with respect to the sale or purchase of an article or commodity at the prevailing market price in the regular course of business; (4) with respect to money deducted from the wages of employees in payment of membership dues in a labor organization: *Provided*, That the employer has received from each employee, on whose account such deductions are made, a written assignment which shall not be irrevocable for a period of more than one year, or beyond the termination date of the applicable collective agreement, whichever occurs sooner; (5) with respect to money or other thing of value paid to a trust fund established by such representative, for the sole and exclusive benefit of the employees of such employer, and their families and dependents (or of such employees, families, and dependents jointly with the employees of other employers making similar payments, and their families and dependents): *Provided*, That (A) such payments are held in trust for the purpose of paying, either from principal or income or both, for the benefit of employees, their families and dependents, for medical or hospital care, pensions on retirement or death of employees, compensation for injuries or illness resulting from occupational activity or insurance to provide any of the foregoing, or unemployment benefits or life insurance, disability and sickness insurance, or accident insurance; (B) the detailed basis on which such payments are to be made is specified in a written agreement with the employer, and employees and employers are equally represented in the administration of such fund, together with such neutral persons as the representatives of the employers and the representatives of employees may agree upon and in the event the employer and employee groups deadlock on the administration of such fund and there are no neutral persons empowered to break such deadlock, such agreement provides that the two groups shall agree on an impartial umpire to decide such dispute, or in event of their failure to agree within a reasonable length of time, an impartial umpire to decide such dispute shall, on petition of either group, be appointed by the district court of the United States for the district where the trust fund has its principal office, and shall also contain provisions for an annual audit of the trust fund, a statement of the results of which shall be available for inspection by interested persons at the principal office of the trust fund and at such other places as may be designated in such written agreement; and (C) such payments as are intended to be used for the purpose of providing pensions or annuities for employees are made to a separate trust which provides that the funds held therein cannot be used for any purpose other than paying such pensions or annuities; (6) with respect to money or other thing of value paid by any employer to a trust fund established by such representative for the purpose of pooled vacation, holiday, severance or similar benefits, or defraying costs of apprenticeship or other training programs: *Provided*, That the requirements of clause (B) of the proviso to clause (5) of this subsection, shall apply to such trust funds; (7) with respect to money or other thing of value paid by any employer to a pooled or individual trust fund established by such representative for the purpose of (A) scholarships for the benefit of employees, their families, and dependents for study at educational institutions, (B) child care centers for pre-school and school age dependents of employees, or (C) financial assistance for employee housing: *Provided*, That no labor organization or employer shall be required to bargain on the establishment of any such trust fund, and refusal to do so shall not constitute an unfair labor practice: *Provided further*, That the requirements of clause (B) of the proviso to clause (5) of this subsection shall apply to such trust funds; (8) with respect to money or any other thing of value paid by any employer to a trust fund established by such representative for the purpose of defraying the costs of legal services for employees, their families, and dependents for counsel or plan of their choice: *Provided*, That the requirements of clause (B) of the proviso to clause (5) of this subsection shall apply to such trust funds: *Provided further*, That no such legal services shall be furnished: (A) to initiate any proceeding directed (i) against any such employer or its officers or agents except in workman's compensation cases, or (ii) against such labor organization, or its parent or subordinate bodies, or their officers or agents, or (iii) against any other employer or labor organization, or their officers or agents, in any matter arising under the National Labor Relations Act, as amended, or this Act; and (B) in any proceeding where a labor organization would be prohibited from defraying the costs of legal services by the provisions of the Labor-Management Reporting and Disclosure Act of 1959; or (9) with respect to money or other things of value paid by an employer to a plant, area or industry-wide labor management committee established for one or more of the purposes set forth in section 5(b) of the Labor Management Cooperation Act of 1978.*

(d)(1) Any person who participates in a transaction involving a payment, loan, or delivery of money or other thing of value to a labor organization in payment of membership dues or to a joint labor-management trust fund as defined by clause (B) of the proviso to clause (5) of subsection (c) of this section or to a plant, area, or industry-wide labor-management committee that is received and used by such labor organization, trust fund, or committee, which transaction does not satisfy all the applicable requirements of subsections (c)(4) through (c)(9) of this section, and willfully and with intent to benefit himself or to benefit other persons he knows are not permitted to receive a payment, loan, money, or other thing of value under subsections (c)(4) through (c)(9) violates this subsection, shall, upon conviction thereof, be guilty of a felony and be subject to a fine of not more than $15,000, or imprisoned for not more than five years, or both; but if the value of the amount of money or thing of value involved in any violation of the provisions of this section does not exceed $1,000, such person shall be guilty of a misdemeanor and be

---

* Sec. 302(c)(7) was added by Pub.L. 91–86, Oct. 14, 1969, 83 Stat. 133; Sec. 302(c)(8) by Pub.L. 93–95, Aug. 15, 1973, 87 Stat. 314; and Sec. 302(c)(9) by Pub.L. 95–524, Oct. 27, 1978, 92 Stat. 2021.

subject to a fine of not more than $10,000, or imprisoned for not more than one year, or both.

(2) Except for violations involving transactions covered by subsection (d)(1) of this section, any person who willfully violates this section shall, upon conviction thereof, be guilty of a felony and be subject to a fine of not more than $15,000 or imprisoned for not more than five years, or both; but if the value of the amount of money or thing of value involved in any violation of the provisions of this section does not exceed $1,000, such person shall be guilty of a misdemeanor and be subject to a fine of not more than $10,000, or imprisoned for not more than one year, or both.*

(e) The district courts of the United States and the United States courts of the Territories and possessions shall have jurisdiction, for cause shown, and subject to the provisions of section 17 (relating to notice to opposite party) of the Act entitled "An Act to supplement existing laws against unlawful restraints and monopolies, and for other purposes," approved October 15, 1914, as amended (U.S.C., title 28, section 381), to restrain violations of this section, without regard to the provisions of sections 6 and 20 of such Act of October 15, 1914, as amended (U.S.C., title 15, section 17, and title 29, section 52), and the provisions of the Act entitled "An Act to amend the Judicial Code and to define and limit the jurisdiction of courts sitting in equity, and for other purposes," approved March 23, 1932 (U.S.C., title 29, sections 101–115).

(f) This section shall not apply to any contract in force on the date of enactment of this Act, until the expiration of such contract, or until July 1, 1948, whichever first occurs.

(g) Compliance with the restrictions contained in subsection (c)(5)(B) upon contributions to trust funds, otherwise lawful, shall not be applicable to contributions to such trust funds established by collective agreement prior to January 1, 1946, nor shall subsection (c)(5)(A) be construed as prohibiting contributions to such trust funds if prior to January 1, 1947, such funds contained provisions for pooled vacation benefits.

BOYCOTTS AND OTHER UNLAWFUL COMBINATIONS

Sec. 303.   (a) It shall be unlawful, for the purpose of this section only, in an industry or activity affecting commerce, for any labor organization to engage in any activity or conduct defined as an unfair labor practice in section 8(b)(4) of the National Labor Relations Act, as amended.

(b) Whoever shall be injured in his business or property by reason of any violation of subsection (a) may sue therefor in any district court of the United States subject to the limitations and provisions of section 301 hereof without respect to the amount in controversy, or in any other court

---

* Section 302(d) was amended by Pub.L. 98–473, Oct. 12, 1984, 98 Stat. 2131.

having jurisdiction of the parties, and shall recover the damages by him sustained and the cost of the suit.

Sec. 304.   [Repealed.]

Sec. 305.   [Repealed.]

TITLE IV

CREATION OF JOINT COMMITTEE TO STUDY AND REPORT ON BASIC PROBLEMS AFFECTING FRIENDLY LABOR RELATIONS AND PRODUCTIVITY

* * *

TITLE V

DEFINITIONS

Sec. 501.   When used in this Act—

(1) The term "industry affecting commerce" means any industry or activity in commerce or in which a labor dispute would burden or obstruct commerce or tend to burden or obstruct commerce or the free flow of commerce.

(2) The term "strike" includes any strike or other concerted stoppage of work by employees (including a stoppage by reason of the expiration of a collective-bargaining agreement) and any concerted slow-down or other concerted interruption of operations by employees.

(3) The terms "commerce", "labor disputes", "employer", "employee", "labor organization", "representative", "person", and "supervisor" shall have the same meaning as when used in the National Labor Relations Act as amended by this Act.

SAVING PROVISION

Sec. 502.   Nothing in this Act shall be construed to require an individual employee to render labor or service without his consent, nor shall anything in this Act be construed to make the quitting of his labor by an individual employee an illegal act; nor shall any court issue any process to compel the performance by an individual employee of such labor or service, without his consent; nor shall the quitting of labor by an employee or employees in good faith because of abnormally dangerous conditions for work at the place of employment of such employee or employees be deemed a strike under this Act.

SEPARABILITY

Sec. 503.   If any provision of this Act, or the application of such provision to any person or circumstance, shall be held invalid, the remainder of this Act, or the application of such provision to persons or circumstances other than those as to which it is held invalid, shall not be affected thereby.

LABOR-MANAGEMENT REPORTING AND DISCLOSURE ACT OF 1959

73 Stat. 519 (1959), as amended; 29 U.S.C. §§ 401–531 (1988).

SHORT TITLE

Sec. 1. This Act may be cited as the "Labor-Management Reporting and Disclosure Act of 1959".

DECLARATION OF FINDINGS, PURPOSES, AND POLICY

Sec. 2. (a) The Congress finds that, in the public interest, it continues to be the responsibility of the Federal Government to protect employees' rights to organize, choose their own representatives, bargain collectively, and otherwise engage in concerted activities for their mutual aid or protection; that the relations between employers and labor organizations and the millions of workers they represent have a substantial impact on the commerce of the Nation; and that in order to accomplish the objective of a free flow of commerce it is essential that labor organizations, employers, and their officials adhere to the highest standards of responsibility and ethical conduct in administering the affairs of their organizations, particularly as they affect labor-management relations.

(b) The Congress further finds, from recent investigations in the labor and management fields, that there have been a number of instances of breach of trust, corruption, disregard of the rights of individual employees, and other failures to observe high standards of responsibility and ethical conduct which require further and supplementary legislation that will afford necessary protection of the rights and interests of employees and the public generally as they relate to the activities of labor organizations, employers, labor relations consultants, and their officers and representatives.

(c) The Congress, therefore, further finds and declares that the enactment of this Act is necessary to eliminate or prevent improper practices on the part of labor organizations, employers, labor relations consultants, and their officers and representatives which distort and defeat the policies of the Labor Management Relations Act, 1947, as amended, and the Railway Labor Act, as amended, and have the tendency or necessary effect of burdening or obstructing commerce by (1) impairing the efficiency, safety, or operation of the instrumentalities of commerce; (2) occurring in the current of commerce; (3) materially affecting, restraining, or controlling the flow of raw materials or manufactured or processed goods into or from the channels of commerce, or the prices of such materials or goods in commerce; or (4) causing diminution of employment and wages in such volume as substantially to impair or disrupt the market for goods flowing into or from the channels of commerce.

DEFINITIONS

Sec. 3. For the purposes of titles I, II, III, IV, V (except section 505), and VI of this Act—

(a) "Commerce" means trade, traffic, commerce, transportation, transmission, or communication among the several States or between any State and any place outside thereof.

(b) "State" includes any State of the United States, the District of Columbia, Puerto Rico, the Virgin Islands, American Samoa, Guam, Wake Island, the Canal Zone, and Outer Continental Shelf lands defined in the Outer Continental Shelf Lands Act (43 U.S.C. §§ 1331–1343).

(c) "Industry affecting commerce" means any activity, business, or industry in commerce or in which a labor dispute would hinder or obstruct commerce or the free flow of commerce and includes any activity or industry "affecting commerce" within the meaning of the Labor Management Relations Act, 1947, as amended, or the Railway Labor Act, as amended.

(d) "Person" includes one or more individuals, labor organizations, partnerships, associations, corporations, legal representatives, mutual companies, joint-stock companies, trusts, unincorporated organizations, trustees, trustees in bankruptcy, or receivers.

(e) "Employer" means any employer or any group or association of employers engaged in an industry affecting commerce (1) which is, with respect to employees engaged in an industry affecting commerce, an employer within the meaning of any law of the United States relating to the employment of any employees or (2) which may deal with any labor organization concerning grievances, labor disputes, wages, rates of pay, hours of employment, or conditions of work, and includes any person acting directly or indirectly as an employer or as an agent of an employer in relation to an employee but does not include the United States or any corporation wholly owned by the Government of the United States or any State or political subdivision thereof.

(f) "Employee" means any individual employed by an employer, and includes any individual whose work has ceased as a consequence of, or in connection with, any current labor dispute or because of any unfair labor practice or because of exclusion or expulsion from a labor organization in any manner or for any reason inconsistent with the requirements of this Act.

(g) "Labor dispute" includes any controversy concerning terms, tenure, or conditions of employment, or concerning the association or representation of persons in negotiating, fixing, maintaining, changing or seeking to arrange terms or conditions of employment, regardless of whether the disputants stand in the proximate relation of employer and employee.

(h) "Trusteeship" means any receivership, trusteeship, or other method of supervision or control whereby a labor organization suspends the autonomy otherwise available to a subordinate body under its constitution or bylaws.

(i) "Labor organization" means a labor organization engaged in an industry affecting commerce and includes any organization of any kind, any agency, or employee representation committee, group, association, or plan so engaged in which employees participate and which exists for the purpose, in whole or in part, of dealing with employers concerning grievances, labor disputes, wages, rates of pay, hours, or other terms or conditions of employment, and any conference, general committee, joint or system board, or joint council so engaged which is subordinate to a national or international labor organization, other than a State or local central body.

(j) A labor organization shall be deemed to be engaged in an industry affecting commerce if it—

(1) is the certified representative of employees under the provisions of the National Labor Relations Act, as amended, or the Railway Labor Act, as amended; or

(2) although not certified, is a national or international labor organization or a local labor organization recognized or acting as the representative of employees of an employer or employers engaged in an industry affecting commerce; or

(3) has chartered a local labor organization or subsidiary body which is representing or actively seeking to represent employees of employers within the meaning of paragraph (1) or (2); or

(4) has been chartered by a labor organization representing or actively seeking to represent employees within the meaning of paragraph (1) or (2) as the local or subordinate body through which such employees may enjoy membership or become affiliated with such labor organization; or

(5) is a conference, general committee, joint or system board, or joint council, subordinate to a national or international labor organization, which includes a labor organization engaged in an industry affecting commerce within the meaning of any of the preceding paragraphs of this subsection, other than a State or local central body.

(k) "Secret ballot" means the expression by ballot, voting machine, or otherwise, but in no event by proxy, of a choice with respect to any election or vote taken upon any matter, which is cast in such a manner that the person expressing such choice cannot be identified with the choice expressed.

(*l*) "Trust in which a labor organization is interested" means a trust or other fund or organization (1) which was created or established by a labor organization, or one or more of the trustees or one or more members of the governing body of which is selected or appointed by a labor organization, and (2) a primary purpose of which is to provide benefits for the members of such labor organization or their beneficiaries.

(m) "Labor relations consultant" means any person who, for compensation, advises or represents an employer, employer organization, or labor organization concerning employee organizing, concerted activities, or collective bargaining activities.

(n) "Officer" means any constitutional officer, any person authorized to perform the functions of president, vice president, secretary, treasurer, or other executive functions of a labor organization, and any member of its executive board or similar governing body.

(o) "Member" or "member in good standing", when used in reference to a labor organization, includes any person who has fulfilled the requirements for membership in such organization, and who neither has voluntarily withdrawn from membership nor has been expelled or suspended from membership after appropriate proceedings consistent with lawful provisions of the constitution and bylaws of such organization.

(p) "Secretary" means the Secretary of Labor.

(q) "Officer, agent, shop steward, or other representative", when used with respect to a labor organization, includes elected officials and key administrative personnel, whether elected or appointed (such as business agents, heads of departments or major units, and organizers who exercise substantial independent authority), but does not include salaried nonsupervisory professional staff, stenographic, and service personnel.

(r) "District court of the United States" means a United States district court and a United States court of any place subject to the jurisdiction of the United States.

TITLE I—BILL OF RIGHTS OF MEMBERS OF LABOR ORGANIZATIONS

BILL OF RIGHTS

Sec. 101.   (a)(1) EQUAL RIGHTS.—Every member of a labor organization shall have equal rights and privileges within such organization to nominate candidates, to vote in elections or referendums of the labor organization, to attend membership meetings, and to participate in the deliberations and voting upon the business of such meetings, subject to reasonable rules and regulations in such organization's constitution and bylaws.

(2) FREEDOM OF SPEECH AND ASSEMBLY.—Every member of any labor organization shall have the right to meet and assemble freely with other members; and to express any views, arguments, or opinions; and to express at meetings of the labor organization his views, upon

candidates in an election of the labor organization or upon any business properly before the meeting, subject to the organization's established and reasonable rules pertaining to the conduct of meetings: *Provided,* That nothing herein shall be construed to impair the right of a labor organization to adopt and enforce reasonable rules as to the responsibility of every member toward the organization as an institution and to his refraining from conduct that would interfere with its performance of its legal or contractual obligations.

(3) DUES, INITIATION FEES, AND ASSESSMENTS.—Except in the case of a federation of national or international labor organizations, the rates of dues and initiation fees payable by members of any labor organization in effect on the date of enactment of this Act shall not be increased, and no general or special assessment shall be levied upon such members, except—

(A) in a case of a local labor organization, (i) by majority vote by secret ballot of the members in good standing voting at a general or special membership meeting, after reasonable notice of the intention to vote upon such question, or (ii) by majority vote of the members in good standing voting in a membership referendum conducted by secret ballot; or

(B) in the case of a labor organization, other than a local labor organization or a federation of national or international labor organizations, (i) by majority vote of the delegates voting at a regular convention, or at a special convention of such labor organization held upon not less than thirty days' written notice to the principal office of each local or constituent labor organization entitled to such notice, or (ii) by majority vote of the members in good standing of such labor organization voting in a membership referendum conducted by secret ballot, or (iii) by majority vote of the members of the executive board or similar governing body of such labor organization, pursuant to express authority contained in the constitution and bylaws of such labor organization: *Provided,* That such action on the part of the executive board or similar governing body shall be effective only until the next regular convention of such labor organization.

(4) PROTECTION OF THE RIGHT TO SUE.—No labor organization shall limit the right of any member thereof to institute an action in any court, or in a proceeding before any administrative agency, irrespective of whether or not the labor organization or its officers are named as defendants or respondents in such action or proceeding, or the right of any member of a labor organization to appear as a witness in any judicial, administrative, or legislative proceeding, or to petition any legislature or to communicate with any legislator: *Provided,* That any such member may be required to exhaust reasonable hearing procedures (but not to exceed a four-month lapse of time) within such organization, before instituting legal or administrative proceedings against such organizations or any officer thereof: *And provided further,* That no

interested employer or employer association shall directly or indirectly finance, encourage, or participate in, except as a party, any such action, proceeding, appearance, or petition.

(5) SAFEGUARDS AGAINST IMPROPER DISCIPLINARY ACTION.—No member of any labor organization may be fined, suspended, expelled, or otherwise disciplined except for nonpayment of dues by such organization or by any officer thereof unless such member has been (A) served with written specific charges; (B) given a reasonable time to prepare his defense; (C) afforded a full and fair hearing.

(b) Any provision of the constitution and bylaws of any labor organization which is inconsistent with the provisions of this section shall be of no force or effect.

CIVIL ENFORCEMENT

Sec. 102.   Any person whose rights secured by the provisions of this title have been infringed by any violation of this title may bring a civil action in a district court of the United States for such relief (including injunctions) as may be appropriate. Any such action against a labor organization shall be brought in the district court of the United States for the district where the alleged violation occurred, or where the principal office of such labor organization is located.

RETENTION OF EXISTING RIGHTS

Sec. 103.   Nothing contained in this title shall limit the rights and remedies of any member of a labor organization under any State or Federal law or before any court or other tribunal, or under the constitution and bylaws of any labor organization.

RIGHT TO COPIES OF COLLECTIVE BARGAINING AGREEMENTS

Sec. 104.   It shall be the duty of the secretary or corresponding principal officer of each labor organization, in the case of a local labor organization, to forward a copy of each collective bargaining agreement made by such labor organization with any employer to any employee who requests such a copy and whose rights as such employee are directly affected by such agreement, and in the case of a labor organization other than a local labor organization, to forward a copy of any such agreement to each constituent unit which has members directly affected by such agreement; and such officer shall maintain at the principal office of the labor organization of which he is an officer copies of any such agreement made or received by such labor organization, which copies shall be available for inspection by any member or by any employee whose rights are affected by such agreement. The provisions of section 210 shall be applicable in the enforcement of this section.

INFORMATION AS TO ACT

Sec. 105.   Every labor organization shall inform its members concerning the provisions of this Act.

TITLE II—REPORTING BY LABOR ORGANIZATIONS, OFFICERS AND EMPLOYEES OF LABOR ORGANIZATIONS, AND EMPLOYERS

REPORT OF LABOR ORGANIZATIONS

Sec. 201. (a) Every labor organization shall adopt a constitution and bylaws and shall file a copy thereof with the Secretary, together with a report, signed by its president and secretary or corresponding principal officers, containing the following information—

(1) the name of the labor organization, its mailing address, and any other address at which it maintains its principal office or at which it keeps the records referred to in this title;

(2) the name and title of each of its officers;

(3) the initiation fee or fees required from a new or transferred member and fees for work permits required by the reporting labor organization;

(4) the regular dues or fees or other periodic payments required to remain a member of the reporting labor organization; and

(5) detailed statements, or references to specific provisions of documents filed under this subsection which contain such statements, showing the provision made and procedures followed with respect to each of the following: (A) qualifications for or restrictions on membership, (B) levying of assessments, (C) participation in insurance or other benefit plans, (D) authorization for disbursement of funds of the labor organization, (E) audit of financial transactions of the labor organization, (F) the calling of regular and special meetings, (G) the selection of officers and stewards and of any representatives to other bodies composed of labor organizations' representatives, with a specific statement of the manner in which each officer was elected, appointed, or otherwise selected, (H) discipline or removal of officers or agents for breaches of their trust, (I) imposition of fines, suspensions and expulsions of members, including the grounds for such action and any provision made for notice, hearing, judgment on the evidence, and appeal procedures, (J) authorization for bargaining demands, (K) ratification of contract terms, (L) authorization for strikes, and (M) issuance of work permits. Any change in the information required by this subsection shall be reported to the Secretary at the time the reporting labor organization files with the Secretary the annual financial report required by subsection (b).

(b) Every labor organization shall file annually with the Secretary a financial report signed by its president and treasurer or corresponding principal officers containing the following information in such detail as may be necessary accurately to disclose its financial condition and operations for its preceding fiscal year—

(1)   assets and liabilities at the beginning and end of the fiscal year;

(2)   receipts of any kind and the sources thereof;

(3)   salary, allowances, and other direct or indirect disbursements (including reimbursed expenses) to each officer and also to each employee who, during such fiscal year, received more than $10,000 in the aggregate from such labor organization and any other labor organization affiliated with it or with which it is affiliated, or which is affiliated with the same national or international labor organization;

(4)   direct and indirect loans made to any officer, employee, or member, which aggregated more than $250 during the fiscal year, together with a statement of the purpose, security, if any, and arrangements for repayment;

(5)   direct and indirect loans to any business enterprise, together with a statement of the purpose, security, if any, and arrangements for repayment; and

(6)   other disbursements made by it including the purposes thereof;

all in such categories as the Secretary may prescribe.

(c)   Every labor organization required to submit a report under this title shall make available the information required to be contained in such report to all of its members, and every such labor organization and its officers shall be under a duty enforceable at the suit of any member of such organization in any State court of competent jurisdiction or in the district court of the United States for the district in which such labor organization maintains its principal office, to permit such member for just cause to examine any books, records, and accounts necessary to verify such report. The court in such action may, in its discretion, in addition to any judgment awarded to the plaintiff or plaintiffs, allow a reasonable attorney's fee to be paid by the defendant, and costs of the action.

REPORT OF OFFICERS AND EMPLOYEES OF LABOR ORGANIZATIONS

Sec. 202.   (a) Every officer of a labor organization and every employee of a labor organization (other than an employee performing exclusively clerical or custodial services) shall file with the Secretary a signed report listing and describing for his preceding fiscal year—

(1)   any stock, bond, security, or other interest, legal or equitable, which he or his spouse or minor child directly or indirectly held in, and any income or any other benefit with monetary value (including reimbursed expenses) which he or his spouse or minor child derived directly or indirectly from, an employer whose employees such labor organization represents or is actively seeking

to represent, except payments and other benefits received as a bona fide employee of such employer;

(2) any transaction in which he or his spouse or minor child engaged, directly or indirectly, involving any stock, bond, security, or loan to or from, or other legal or equitable interest in the business of an employer whose employees such labor organization represents or is actively seeking to represent;

(3) any stock, bond, security, or other interest, legal or equitable, which he or his spouse or minor child directly or indirectly held in, and any income or any other benefit with monetary value (including reimbursed expenses) which he or his spouse or minor child directly or indirectly derived from, any business a substantial part of which consists of buying from, selling or leasing to, or otherwise dealing with, the business of an employer whose employees such labor organization represents or is actively seeking to represent;

(4) any stock, bond, security, or other interest, legal or equitable, which he or his spouse or minor child directly or indirectly held in, and any income or any other benefit with monetary value (including reimbursed expenses) which he or his spouse or minor child directly or indirectly derived from, a business any part of which consists of buying from, or selling or leasing directly or indirectly to, or otherwise dealing with such labor organization;

(5) any direct or indirect business transaction or arrangement between him or his spouse or minor child and any employer whose employees his organization represents or is actively seeking to represent, except work performed and payments and benefits received as a bona fide employee of such employer and except purchases and sales of goods or services in the regular course of business at prices generally available to any employee of such employer; and

(6) any payment of money or other thing of value (including reimbursed expenses) which he or his spouse or minor child received directly or indirectly from any employer or any person who acts as a labor relations consultant to an employer, except payments of the kinds referred to in section 302(c) of the Labor Management Relations Act, 1947, as amended.

(b) The provisions of paragraphs (1), (2), (3), (4), and (5) of subsection (a) shall not be construed to require any such officer or employee to report his bona fide investments in securities traded on a securities exchange registered as a national securities exchange under the Securities Exchange Act of 1934, in shares in an investment company registered under the Investment Company Act of 1940, or in securities of a public utility holding company registered under the Public Utility Holding Company Act of 1935, or to report any income derived therefrom.

(c) Nothing contained in this section shall be construed to require any officer or employee of a labor organization to file a report under subsection (a) unless he or his spouse or minor child holds or has held an interest, has received income or any other benefit with monetary value or a loan, or has engaged in a transaction described therein.

REPORT OF EMPLOYERS

Sec. 203.   (a) Every employer who in any fiscal year made—

(1) any payment or loan, direct or indirect, of money or other thing of value (including reimbursed expenses), or any promise or agreement therefor, to any labor organization or officer, agent, shop steward, or other representative of a labor organization, or employee of any labor organization, except (A) payments or loans made by any national or State bank, credit union, insurance company, savings and loan association or other credit institution and (B) payments of the kind referred to in section 302(c) of the Labor Management Relations Act, 1947, as amended;

(2) any payment (including reimbursed expenses) to any of his employees, or any group or committee of such employees, for the purpose of causing such employee or group or committee of employees to persuade other employees to exercise or not to exercise, or as the manner of exercising, the right to organize and bargain collectively through representatives of their own choosing unless such payments were contemporaneously or previously disclosed to such other employees;

(3) any expenditure, during the fiscal year, where an object thereof, directly or indirectly, is to interfere with, restrain, or coerce employees in the exercise of the right to organize and bargain collectively through representatives of their own choosing, or is to obtain information concerning the activities of employees or a labor organization in connection with a labor dispute involving such employer, except for use solely in conjunction with an administrative or arbitral proceeding or a criminal or civil judicial proceeding;

(4) any agreement or arrangement with a labor relations consultant or other independent contractor or organization pursuant to which such person undertakes activities where an object thereof, directly or indirectly, is to persuade employees to exercise or not to exercise, or persuade employees as to the manner of exercising, the right to organize and bargain collectively through representatives of their own choosing, or undertakes to supply such employer with information concerning the activities of employees or a labor organization in connection with a labor dispute involving such employer, except information for use solely in conjunction with an administrative or arbitral proceeding or a criminal or civil judicial proceeding; or

(5) any payment (including reimbursed expenses) pursuant to an agreement or arrangement described in subdivision (4);

shall file with the Secretary a report, in a form prescribed by him, signed by its president and treasurer or corresponding principal officers showing in detail the date and amount of each such payment, loan, promise, agreement, or arrangement and the name, address, and position, if any, in any firm or labor organization of the person to whom it was made and a full explanation of the circumstances of all such payments, including the terms of any agreement or understanding pursuant to which they were made.

(b) Every person who pursuant to any agreement or arrangement with an employer undertakes activities where an object thereof is, directly or indirectly—

(1) to persuade employees to exercise or not to exercise, or persuade employees as to the manner of exercising, the right to organize and bargain collectively through representatives of their own choosing; or

(2) to supply an employer with information concerning the activities of employees or a labor organization in connection with a labor dispute involving such employer, except information for use solely in conjunction with an administrative or arbitral proceeding or a criminal or civil judicial proceeding;

shall file within thirty days after entering into such agreement or arrangement a report with the Secretary, signed by its president and treasurer or corresponding principal officers, containing the name under which such person is engaged in doing business and the address of its principal office, and a detailed statement of the terms and conditions of such agreement or arrangement. Every such person shall file annually, with respect to each fiscal year during which payments were made as a result of such an agreement or arrangement, a report with the Secretary, signed by its president and treasurer or corresponding principal officers, containing a statement (A) of its receipts of any kind from employers on account of labor relations advice or services, designating the sources thereof, and (B) of its disbursements of any kind, in connection with such services and the purposes thereof. In each such case such information shall be set forth in such categories as the Secretary may prescribe.

(c) Nothing in this section shall be construed to require any employer or other person to file a report covering the services of such person by reason of his giving or agreeing to give advice to such employer or representing or agreeing to represent such employer before any court, administrative agency, or tribunal of arbitration or engaging or agreeing to engage in collective bargaining on behalf of such employer with respect to wages, hours, or other terms or conditions of employment or the negotiation of an agreement or any question arising thereunder.

(d) Nothing contained in this section shall be construed to require an employer to file a report under subsection (a) unless he has made an expenditure, payment, loan, agreement, or arrangement of the kind described therein. Nothing contained in this section shall be construed to require any other person to file a report under subsection (b) unless he was a party to an agreement or arrangement of the kind described therein.

(e) Nothing contained in this section shall be construed to require any regular officer, supervisor, or employee of an employer to file a report in connection with services rendered to such employer nor shall any employer be required to file a report covering expenditures made to any regular officer, supervisor, or employee of an employer as compensation for service as a regular officer, supervisor, or employee of such employer.

(f) Nothing contained in this section shall be construed as an amendment to, or modification of the rights protected by, section 8(c) of the National Labor Relations Act, as amended.

(g) The term "interfere with, restrain, or coerce" as used in this section means interference, restraint, and coercion which, if done with respect to the exercise of rights guaranteed in section 7 of the National Labor Relations Act, as amended, would, under section 8(a) of such Act, constitute an unfair labor practice.

ATTORNEY-CLIENT COMMUNICATIONS EXEMPTED

Sec. 204.   Nothing contained in this Act shall be construed to require an attorney who is a member in good standing of the bar of any State, to include in any report required to be filed pursuant to the provisions of this Act any information which was lawfully communicated to such attorney by any of his clients in the course of a legitimate attorney-client relationship.

REPORTS MADE PUBLIC INFORMATION

Sec. 205.   (a) The contents of the reports and documents filed with the Secretary pursuant to sections 201, 202, 203, and 211 shall be public information, and the Secretary may publish any information and data which he obtains pursuant to the provisions of this title. The Secretary may use the information and data for statistical and research purposes, and compile and publish such studies, analyses, reports, and surveys based thereon as he may deem appropriate.

(b) The Secretary shall by regulation make reasonable provision for the inspection and examination, on the request of any person, of the information and data contained in any report or other document filed with him pursuant to section 201, 202, 203, or 211.

(c) The Secretary shall by regulation provide for the furnishing by the Department of Labor of copies of reports or other documents filed with the Secretary pursuant to this title, upon payment of a charge based upon the cost of the service. The Secretary shall make available without payment of a charge, or require any person to furnish, to such State agency as is designated by law or by the Governor of the State in which such person has his principal place of business or headquarters, upon request of the Governor of such State, copies of any reports and documents filed by such person with the Secretary pursuant to section 201, 202, 203, or 211, or of information and data contained therein. No person shall be required by reason of any law of any State to furnish to any officer or agency of such State any information included in a report filed by such person with the Secretary pursuant to the provisions of this title, if a copy of such report, or of the portion thereof containing such information, is furnished to such officer or agency. All moneys received in payment of such charges fixed by the Secretary pursuant to this subsection shall be deposited in the general fund of the Treasury.

RETENTION OF RECORDS

Sec. 206.   Every person required to file any report under this title shall maintain records on the matters required to be reported which will provide in sufficient detail the necessary basic information and data from which the documents filed with the Secretary may be verified, explained or clarified, and checked for accuracy and completeness, and shall include vouchers, worksheets, receipts, and applicable resolutions, and shall keep such records available for examination for a period of not less than five years after the filing of the documents based on the information which they contain.

EFFECTIVE DATE

Sec. 207.   (a)   Each labor organization shall file the initial report required under section 201(a) within ninety days after the date on which it first becomes subject to this Act.

(b)   Each person required to file a report under section 201(b), 202, 203(a), or the second sentence of 203(b), or section 211 shall file such report within ninety days after the end of each of its fiscal years; except that where such person is subject to section 201(b), 202, 203(a), the second sentence of 203(b), or section 211, as the case may be, for only a portion of such a fiscal year (because the date of enactment of this Act occurs during such person's fiscal year or such person becomes subject to this Act during its fiscal year) such person may consider that portion as the entire fiscal year in making such report.

RULES AND REGULATIONS

Sec. 208.   The Secretary shall have authority to issue, amend, and rescind rules and regulations prescribing the form and publication of reports required to be filed under this title and such other reasonable rules and regulations (including rules prescribing reports concerning trusts in which a labor organization is interested) as he may find necessary to prevent the circumvention or evasion of such reporting requirements. In exercising his power under this section the Secretary shall prescribe by general rule simplified reports for labor organizations or employers for whom he finds that by virtue of their size a detailed report would be unduly burdensome, but the Secretary may revoke such provision for simplified forms of any labor organization or employer if he determines, after such investigation as he deems proper and due notice and opportunity for a hearing, that the purposes of this section would be served thereby.

CRIMINAL PROVISIONS

Sec. 209.   (a) Any person who willfully violates this title shall be fined not more than $10,000 or imprisoned for not more than one year, or both.

(b) Any person who makes a false statement or representation of a material fact, knowing it to be false, or who knowingly fails to disclose a material fact, in any document, report, or other information required under the provisions of this title shall be fined not more than $10,000 or imprisoned for not more than one year, or both.

(c) Any person who willfully makes a false entry in or willfully conceals, withholds, or destroys any books, records, reports, or statements required to be kept by any provision of this title shall be fined not more than $10,000 or imprisoned for not more than one year, or both.

(d) Each individual required to sign reports under sections 201 and 203 shall be personally responsible for the filing of such reports and for any statement contained therein which he knows to be false.

CIVIL ENFORCEMENT

Sec. 210.   Whenever it shall appear that any person has violated or is about to violate any of the provisions of this title, the Secretary may bring a civil action for such relief (including injunctions) as may be appropriate. Any such action may be brought in the district court of the United States where the violation occurred or, at the option of the parties, in the United States District Court for the District of Columbia.

SURETY COMPANY REPORTS

Sec. 211.   Each surety company which issues any bond required by this Act or the Employee Retirement Income Security Act of 1974 shall file annually with the Secretary, with respect to each fiscal year during which any such bond was in force, a report, in such form and detail as he may prescribe by regulation, filed by the president and treasurer or corresponding principal officers of the surety company, describing its bond experience under each such Act, including information as to the premiums received, total claims paid, amounts recovered by way of subrogation, administrative and legal expenses and such related data and information as the Secretary shall determine to be necessary in the public interest and to carry out the policy of the Act. Notwithstanding the foregoing, if the Secretary finds that any such specific information cannot be practicably ascertained or would be uninformative, the Secretary may modify or waive the requirement for such information.

TITLE III—TRUSTEESHIPS
REPORTS

Sec. 301. (a) Every labor organization which has or assumes trusteeship over any subordinate labor organization shall file with the Secretary within thirty days after the date of the enactment of this Act or the imposition of any such trusteeship, and semiannually thereafter, a report, signed by its president and treasurer or corresponding principal officers, as well as by the trustees of such subordinate labor organization, containing the following information: (1) the name and address of the subordinate organization; (2) the date of establishing the trusteeship; (3) a detailed statement of the reason or reasons for establishing or continuing the trusteeship; and (4) the nature and extent of participation by the membership of the subordinate organization in the selection of delegates to represent such organization in regular or special conventions or other policy-determining bodies and in the election of officers of the labor organization which has assumed trusteeship over such subordinate organization. The initial report shall also include a full and complete account of the financial condition of such subordinate organization as of the time trusteeship was assumed over it. During the continuance of a trusteeship the labor organization which has assumed trusteeship over a subordinate labor organization shall file on behalf of the subordinate labor organization the annual financial report required by section 201(b) signed by the president and treasurer or corresponding principal officers of the labor organization which has assumed such trusteeship and the trustees of the subordinate labor organization.

(b) The provisions of sections 201(c), 205, 206, 208, and 210 shall be applicable to reports filed under this title.

(c) Any person who willfully violates this section shall be fined not more than $10,000 or imprisoned for not more than one year, or both.

(d) Any person who makes a false statement or representation of a material fact, knowing it to be false, or who knowingly fails to disclose a material fact, in any report required under the provisions of this section or willfully makes any false entry in or willfully withholds, conceals, or destroys any documents, books, records, reports, or statements upon which such report is based, shall be fined not more than $10,000 or imprisoned for not more than one year, or both.

(e) Each individual required to sign a report under this section shall be personally responsible for the filing of such report and for any statement contained therein which he knows to be false.

PURPOSES FOR WHICH A TRUSTEESHIP
MAY BE ESTABLISHED

Sec. 302. Trusteeships shall be established and administered by a labor organization over a subordinate body only in accordance with the constitution and bylaws of the organization which has assumed trusteeship over the subordinate body and for the purpose of correcting corruption or financial malpractice, assuring the performance of collective bargaining agreements or other duties of a bargaining representative, restoring democratic procedures, or otherwise carrying out the legitimate objects of such labor organization.

UNLAWFUL ACTS RELATING TO LABOR ORGANIZATION UNDER TRUSTEESHIP

Sec. 303.   (a) During any period when a subordinate body of a labor organization is in trusteeship, it shall be unlawful (1) to count the vote of delegates from such body in any convention or election of officers of the labor organization unless the delegates have been chosen by secret ballot in an election in which all the members in good standing of such subordinate body were eligible to participate, or (2) to transfer to such organization any current receipts or other funds of the subordinate body except the normal per capita tax and assessments payable by subordinate bodies not in trusteeship: *Provided*, That nothing herein contained shall prevent the distribution of the assets of a labor organization in accordance with its constitution and bylaws upon the bona fide dissolution thereof.

(b) Any person who willfully violates this section shall be fined not more than $10,000 or imprisoned for not more than one year, or both.

ENFORCEMENT

Sec. 304.   (a) Upon the written complaint of any member or subordinate body of a labor organization alleging that such organization has violated the provisions of this title (except section 301) the Secretary shall investigate the complaint and if the Secretary finds probable cause to believe that such violation has occurred and has not been remedied he shall, without disclosing the identity of the complainant, bring a civil action in any district court of the United States having jurisdiction of the labor organization for such relief (including injunctions) as may be appropriate. Any member or subordinate body of a labor organization affected by any violation of this title (except section 301) may bring a civil action in any district court of the United States having jurisdiction of the labor organization for such relief (including injunctions) as may be appropriate.

(b) For the purpose of actions under this section, district courts of the United States shall be deemed to have jurisdiction of a labor organization (1) in the district in which the principal office of such labor organization is located, or (2) in any district in which its duly authorized officers or agents are engaged in conducting the affairs of the trusteeship.

(c) In any proceeding pursuant to this section a trusteeship established by a labor organization in conformity with the procedural requirements of its constitution and bylaws and authorized or ratified after a fair hearing either before the executive board or before such other body as may be provided in accordance with its constitution or bylaws shall be presumed valid for a period of eighteen months from the date of its establishment and shall not be subject to attack during such period except upon clear and convincing proof that the trusteeship was not established or maintained in good faith for a purpose allowable under section 302. After the expiration of eighteen months the trusteeship shall be presumed invalid in any such proceeding and its discontinuance shall be decreed unless the labor organization shall show by clear and convincing proof that the continuation of the trusteeship is necessary for a purpose allowable under section 302. In the latter event the court may dismiss the complaint or retain jurisdiction of the cause on such conditions and for such period as it deems appropriate.

REPORT TO CONGRESS

Sec. 305.   The Secretary shall submit to the Congress at the expiration of three years from the date of enactment of this Act a report upon the operation of this title.

COMPLAINT BY SECRETARY

Sec. 306.   The rights and remedies provided by this title shall be in addition to any and all other rights and remedies at law or in equity: *Provided*, That upon the filing of a complaint by the Secretary the jurisdiction of the district court over such trusteeship shall be exclusive and the final judgment shall be res judicata.

TITLE IV—ELECTIONS

TERMS OF OFFICE; ELECTION PROCEDURES

Sec. 401.   (a) Every national or international labor organization, except a federation of national or international labor organizations, shall elect its officers not less often than once every five years either by secret ballot among the members in good standing or at a convention of delegates chosen by secret ballot.

(b) Every local labor organization shall elect its officers not less often than once every three years by secret ballot among the members in good standing.

(c) Every national or international labor organization, except a federation of national or international labor organizations, and every local labor organization, and its officers, shall be under a duty, enforceable at the suit of any bona fide candidate for office in such labor organization in the district court of the United States in which such labor organization maintains its principal office, to comply with all reasonable requests of any candidate to distribute by mail or otherwise at the candidate's expense campaign literature in aid of such person's candidacy to all members in good standing of such labor organization and to refrain from discrimination in favor of or against any candidate with respect to the use of lists of members, and whenever such labor organizations or its officers authorize the distribution by mail or otherwise to members of campaign literature on behalf of any candidate or of the labor organization itself with reference to such election, similar distribution at the request of any other bona fide candidate shall be made by such labor organization and its officers, with equal treatment as to the expense of such distribution. Every bona fide candidate shall have the right, once within 30 days prior to an election of a labor organization in which he is a candidate, to inspect a list containing the names and last known addresses of all members of the labor organization who are subject to a collective bargaining agreement requiring membership therein as a condition of employment, which list shall be maintained and kept at the principal office of such labor organization by a designated official thereof. Adequate safeguards to insure a fair election shall be provided, including the right of any candidate to have an observer at the polls and at the counting of the ballots.

(d) Officers of intermediate bodies, such as general committees, system boards, joint boards, or joint councils, shall be elected not less often than once every four years by secret ballot among the members in good standing or by labor organization officers representative of such members who have been elected by secret ballot.

(e) In any election required by this section which is to be held by secret ballot a reasonable opportunity shall be given for the nomination of candidates and every member in good standing shall be eligible to be a candidate and to hold office (subject to section 504 and to reasonable qualifications uniformly imposed) and shall have the right to vote for or otherwise support the candidate or candidates of his choice, without being subject to penalty, discipline, or improper interference or reprisal of any kind by such organization or any member thereof. Not less than fifteen days prior to the election notice thereof shall be mailed to each member at his last known home address. Each member in good standing shall be entitled to one vote. No member whose dues have been withheld by his employer for payment to such organization pursuant to his voluntary authorization provided for in a collective bargaining agreement, shall be declared ineligible to vote or be a candidate for office in such organization by reason of alleged delay or default in the payment of dues. The votes cast by members of each local labor organization shall be counted, and the results published, separately. The election officials designated in the constitution and bylaws or the secretary, if no other official is designated, shall preserve for one year the ballots and all other records pertaining to the election. The election shall be conducted in accordance with the constitution and bylaws of such organization insofar as they are not inconsistent with the provisions of this title.

(f) When officers are chosen by a convention of delegates elected by secret ballot, the convention shall be conducted in accordance with the constitution and bylaws of the labor organization insofar as they are not inconsistent with the provisions of this title. The officials designated in the constitution and bylaws or the secretary, if no other is designated, shall preserve for one year the credentials of the delegates and all minutes and other records of the convention pertaining to the election of officers.

(g)   No moneys received by any labor organization by way of dues, assessment, or similar levy, and no moneys of an employer shall be contributed or applied to promote the candidacy of any person in an election subject to the provisions of this title. Such moneys of a labor organization may be utilized for notices, factual statements of issues not involving candidates, and other expenses necessary for the holding of an election.

(h)   If the Secretary, upon application of any member of a local labor organization, finds after hearing in accordance with the Administrative Procedure Act that the constitution and bylaws of such labor organization do not provide an adequate procedure for the removal of an elected officer guilty of serious misconduct, such officer may be removed, for cause shown and after notice and hearing, by the members in good standing voting in a secret ballot conducted by the officers of such labor organization in accordance with its constitution and bylaws insofar as they are not inconsistent with the provisions of this title.

(i)   The Secretary shall promulgate rules and regulations prescribing minimum standards and procedures for determining the adequacy of the removal procedures to which reference is made in subsection (h).

ENFORCEMENT

Sec. 402.   (a)   A member of a labor organization—

(1)   who has exhausted the remedies available under the constitution and bylaws of such organization and of any parent body or

(2)   who has invoked such available remedies without obtaining a final decision within three calendar months after their invocation,

may file a complaint with the Secretary within one calendar month thereafter alleging the violation of any provision of section 401 (including violation of the constitution and bylaws of the labor organization pertaining to the election and removal of officers). The challenged election shall be presumed valid pending a final decision thereon (as hereinafter provided) and in the interim the affairs of the organization shall be conducted by the officers elected or in such other manner as its constitution and bylaws may provide.

(b)   The Secretary shall investigate such complaint and, if he finds probable cause to believe that a violation of this title has occurred and has not been remedied, he shall, within sixty days after the filing of such complaint, bring a civil action against the labor organization as an entity in the district court of the United States in which such labor organization maintains its principal office to set aside the invalid election, if any, and to direct the conduct of an election or hearing and vote upon the removal of officers under the supervision of the Secretary and in accordance with the provisions of this title and such rules and regulations as the Secretary may prescribe. The court shall have power to take such action as it deems proper to preserve the assets of the labor organization.

(c) If, upon a preponderance of the evidence after a trial upon the merits, the court finds—

(1) that an election has not been held within the time prescribed by section 401, or

(2) that the violation of section 401 may have affected the outcome of an election

the court shall declare the election, if any, to be void and direct the conduct of a new election under supervision of the Secretary and, so far as lawful and practicable, in conformity with the constitution and bylaws of the labor organization. The Secretary shall promptly certify to the court the names of the persons elected, and the court shall thereupon enter a decree declaring such persons to be the officers of the labor organization. If the proceeding is for the removal of officers pursuant to subsection (h) of section 401, the Secretary shall certify the results of the vote and the court shall enter a decree declaring whether such persons have been removed as officers of the labor organization.

(d) An order directing an election, dismissing a complaint, or designating elected officers of a labor organization shall be appealable in the same manner as the final judgment in a civil action, but an order directing an election shall not be stayed pending appeal.

APPLICATION OF OTHER LAWS

Sec. 403. No labor organization shall be required by law to conduct elections of officers with greater frequency or in a different form or manner than is required by its own constitution or bylaws, except as otherwise provided by this title. Existing rights and remedies to enforce the constitution and bylaws of a labor organization with respect to elections prior to the conduct thereof shall not be affected by the provisions of this title. The remedy provided by this title for challenging an election already conducted shall be exclusive.

EFFECTIVE DATE

Sec. 404. The provisions of this title shall become applicable—

(1) ninety days after the date of enactment of this Act in the case of a labor organization whose constitution and bylaws can lawfully be modified or amended by action of its constitutional officers or governing body, or

(2) where such modification can only be made by a constitutional convention of the labor organization, not later than the next constitutional convention of such labor organization after the date of enactment of this Act, or one year after such date, whichever is sooner. If no such convention is held within such one-

year period, the executive board or similar governing body empowered to act for such labor organization between conventions is empowered to make such interim constitutional changes as are necessary to carry out the provisions of this title.

TITLE V—SAFEGUARDS FOR LABOR ORGANIZATIONS

FIDUCIARY RESPONSIBILITY OF OFFICERS OF LABOR ORGANIZATIONS

Sec. 501. (a) The officers, agents, shop stewards, and other representatives of a labor organization occupy positions of trust in relation to such organization and its members as a group. It is, therefore, the duty of each such person, taking into account the special problems and functions of a labor organization, to hold its money and property solely for the benefit of the organization and its members and to manage, invest, and expend the same in accordance with its constitution and bylaws and any resolutions of the governing bodies adopted thereunder, to refrain from dealing with such organization as an adverse party or in behalf of an adverse party in any matter connected with his duties and from holding or acquiring any pecuniary or personal interest which conflicts with the interests of such organization, and to account to the organization for any profit received by him in whatever capacity in connection with transactions conducted by him or under his direction on behalf of the organization. A general exculpatory provision in the constitution and bylaws of such a labor organization or a general exculpatory resolution of a governing body purporting to relieve any such person of liability for breach of the duties declared by this section shall be void as against public policy.

(b) When any officer, agent, shop steward, or representative of any labor organization is alleged to have violated the duties declared in subsection (a) and the labor organization or its governing board or officers refuse or fail to sue or recover damages or secure an accounting or other appropriate relief within a reasonable time after being requested to do so by any member of the labor organization, such member may sue such officer, agent, shop steward, or representative in any district court of the United States or in any State court of competent jurisdiction to recover damages or secure an accounting or other appropriate relief for the benefit of the labor organization. No such proceeding shall be brought except upon leave of the court obtained upon verified application and for good cause shown which application may be made ex parte. The trial judge may allot a reasonable part of the recovery in any action under this subsection to pay the fees of counsel prosecuting the suit at the instance of the member of the labor organization and to compensate such member for any expenses necessarily paid or incurred by him in connection with the litigation.

(c) Any person who embezzles, steals, or unlawfully and willfully abstracts or converts to his own use, or the use of another, any of the moneys, funds, securities, property, or other assets of a labor organization of which he is an officer, or by which he is employed, directly or indirectly, shall be fined not more than $10,000 or imprisoned for not more than five years, or both.

BONDING

Sec. 502.   (a) Every officer, agent, shop steward, or other representative or employee of any labor organization (other than a labor organization whose property and annual financial receipts do not exceed $5,000 in value), or of a trust in which a labor organization is interested, who handles funds or other property thereof shall be bonded to provide protection against loss by reason of acts of fraud or dishonesty on his part directly or through connivance with others. The bond of each such person shall be fixed at the beginning of the organization's fiscal year and shall be in an amount not less than 10 per centum of the funds handled by him and his predecessor or predecessors, if any, during the preceding fiscal year, but in no case more than $500,000. If the labor organization or the trust in which a labor organization is interested does not have a preceding fiscal year, the amount of the bond shall be, in the case of a local labor organization, not less than $1,000, and in the case of any other labor organization or of a trust in which a labor organization is interested, not less than $10,000. Such bonds shall be individual or schedule in form, and shall have a corporate surety company as surety thereon. Any person who is not covered by such bonds shall not be permitted to receive, handle, disburse, or otherwise exercise custody or control of the funds or other property of a labor organization or of a trust in which a labor organization is interested. No such bond shall be placed through an agent or broker or with a surety company in which any labor organization or any officer, agent, shop steward, or other representative of a labor organization has any direct or indirect interest. Such surety company shall be a corporate surety which holds a grant of authority from the Secretary of the Treasury under the Act of July 30, 1947 (6 U.S.C. 6–13), as an acceptable surety on Federal bonds: *Provided*, That when in the opinion of the Secretary a labor organization has made other bonding arrangements which would provide the protection required by this section at comparable cost or less, he may exempt such labor organization from placing a bond through a surety company holding such grant of authority.

(b)   Any person who willfully violates this section shall be fined not more than $10,000 or imprisoned for not more than one year, or both.

MAKING OF LOANS; PAYMENT OF FINES

Sec. 503.   (a) No labor organization shall make directly or indirectly any loan or loans to any officer or employee of such organization which results in a total indebtedness on the part of such officer or employee to the labor organization in excess of $2,000.

(b) No labor organization or employer shall directly or indirectly pay the fine of any officer or employee convicted of any willful violation of this Act.

(c) Any person who willfully violates this section shall be fined not more than $5,000 or imprisoned for not more than one year, or both.

PROHIBITION AGAINST CERTAIN PERSONS HOLDING OFFICE

Sec. 504.*   (a) No person who is or has been a member of the Communist Party or who has been convicted of, or served any part of a prison term resulting from his conviction of, robbery, bribery, extortion, embezzlement, grand larceny, burglary, arson, violation of narcotics laws, murder, rape, assault with intent to kill, assault which inflicts grievous bodily injury, or a violation of subchapter III or IV of this chapter, any felony involving abuse or misuse of such person's position or employment in a labor organization or employee benefit plan to seek or obtain an illegal gain at the expense of the members of the labor organization or the beneficiaries of the employee benefit plan, or conspiracy to commit any such crimes or attempt to commit any such crimes, or a crime in which any of the foregoing crimes is an element, shall serve or be permitted to serve—

(1) as a consultant or adviser to any labor organization,

(2) as an officer, director, trustee, member of any executive board or similar governing body, business agent, manager, organizer, employee, or representative in any capacity of any labor organization,

(3) as a labor relations consultant or adviser to a person engaged in an industry or activity affecting commerce, or as an officer, director, agent, or employee of any group or association of employers dealing with any labor organization, or in a position having specific collective bargaining authority or direct responsibility in the area of labor-management relations in any corporation or association engaged in an industry or activity affecting commerce, or

(4) in a position which entitles its occupant to a share of the proceeds of, or as an officer or executive or administrative employee of, any entity whose activities are in whole or substantial part devoted to providing goods or services to any labor organization, or

(5) in any capacity, other than in his capacity as a member of such labor organization, that involves decisionmaking authority concerning, or decisionmaking authority over, or custody of, or control of the moneys, funds, assets, or property of any labor organization,

---

*   This section was amended by Pub.L. 98–473, Title II, § 803, Oct. 12, 1984, 98 Stat. 2133.

during or for the period of thirteen years after such conviction or after the end of such imprisonment, whichever is later, unless the sentencing court on the motion of the person convicted sets a lesser period of at least three years after such conviction or after the end of such imprisonment, whichever is later, or unless prior to the end of such period, in the case of a person so convicted or imprisoned, (A) his citizenship rights, having been revoked as a result of such conviction, have been fully restored, or (B) the United States Parole Commission determines that such person's service in any capacity referred to in clauses (1) through (5) would not be contrary to the purposes of this chapter. Prior to making any such determination the Commission shall hold an administrative hearing and shall give notice of such proceeding by certified mail to the Secretary of Labor and to State, county, and Federal prosecuting officials in the jurisdiction or jurisdictions in which such person was convicted. The Commission's determination in any such proceeding shall be final. No person shall knowingly hire, retain, employ, or otherwise place any other person to serve in any capacity in violation of this subsection.

(b) Any person who willfully violates this section shall be fined not more than $10,000 or imprisoned for not more than five years, or both.

(c) For the purpose of this section—

(1) A person shall be deemed to have been "convicted" and under the disability of "conviction" from the date of the judgment of the trial court, regardless of whether that judgment remains under appeal.

(2) A period of parole shall not be considered as part of a period of imprisonment.

(d) Whenever any person—

(1) by operation of this section, has been barred from office or other position in a labor organization as a result of a conviction, and

(2) has filed an appeal of that conviction,

any salary which would be otherwise due such person by virtue of such office or position, shall be placed in escrow by the individual employer or organization responsible for payment of such salary. Payment of such salary into escrow shall continue for the duration of the appeal or for the period of time during which such salary would be otherwise due, whichever period is shorter. Upon the final reversal of such person's conviction on appeal, the amounts in escrow shall be paid to such person. Upon the final sustaining of such person's conviction on appeal, the amounts in escrow shall be returned to the individual employer or organization responsible for payments of those amounts. Upon final reversal of such person's conviction, such person shall no longer be barred by this statute from assuming any position from which such person was previously barred.

TITLE VI—MISCELLANEOUS PROVISIONS
INVESTIGATIONS

Sec. 601.   (a) The Secretary shall have power when he believes it necessary in order to determine whether any person has violated or is about to violate any provision of this Act (except title I or amendments made by this Act to other statutes) to make an investigation and in connection therewith he may enter such places and inspect such records and accounts and question such persons as he may deem necessary to enable him to determine the facts relative thereto. The Secretary may report to interested persons or officials concerning the facts required to be shown in any report required by this Act and concerning the reasons for failure or refusal to file such a report or any other matter which he deems to be appropriate as a result of such an investigation.

(b) For the purpose of any investigation provided for in this Act, the provisions of sections 9 and 10 (relating to the attendance of witnesses and the production of books, papers, and documents) of the Federal Trade Commission Act of September 16, 1914, as amended (15 U.S.C. 49, 50), are hereby made applicable to the jurisdiction, powers, and duties of the Secretary or any officers designated by him.

EXTORTIONATE PICKETING

Sec. 602.   (a) It shall be unlawful to carry on picketing on or about the premises of any employer for the purpose of, or as part of any conspiracy or in furtherance of any plan or purpose for, the personal profit or enrichment of any individual (except a bona fide increase in wages or other employee benefits) by taking or obtaining any money or other thing of value from such employer against his will or with his consent.

(b) Any person who willfully violates this section shall be fined not more than $10,000 or imprisoned not more than twenty years, or both.

RETENTION OF RIGHTS UNDER OTHER
FEDERAL AND STATE LAWS

Sec. 603.   (a) Except as explicitly provided to the contrary, nothing in this Act shall reduce or limit the responsibilities of any labor organization or any officer, agent, shop steward, or other representative of a labor organization, or of any trust in which a labor organization is interested, under any other Federal law or under the laws of any State, and, except as explicitly provided to the contrary, nothing in this Act shall take away any right or bar any remedy to which members of a labor organization are entitled under such other Federal law or law of any State.

(b) Nothing contained in titles I, II, III, IV, V, or VI of this Act shall be construed to supersede or impair or otherwise affect the provisions of the Railway Labor Act, as amended, or any of the obligations, rights, benefits, privileges, or immunities of any carrier, employee, organization, representative, or person subject thereto; nor shall anything contained in said titles (except section 505) of this Act be construed to confer any rights, privileges, immunities, or defenses upon employers, or to impair or otherwise affect the rights of any person under the National Labor Relations Act, as amended.

EFFECT ON STATE LAWS

Sec. 604.   Nothing in this Act shall be construed to impair or diminish the authority of any State to enact and enforce general criminal laws with respect to robbery, bribery, extortion, embezzlement, grand larceny, burglary, arson, violation of narcotics laws, murder, rape, assault with intent to kill, or assault which inflicts grievous bodily injury, or conspiracy to commit any of such crimes.

STATE AUTHORITY TO ENACT AND ENFORCE LEGISLATION

Sec. 604a.   Notwithstanding this or any other Act regulating labor-management relations, each State shall have the authority to enact and enforce, as part of a comprehensive statutory system to eliminate the threat of pervasive racketeering activity in an industry that is, or over time has been, affected by such activity, a provision of law that applies equally to employers, employees, and collective bargaining representatives, which provision of law governs service in any position in a local labor organization which acts or seeks to act in that State as a collective bargaining representative pursuant to the National Labor Relations Act [29 U.S.C.A. § 151 et seq.], in the industry that is subject to that program.*

SERVICE OF PROCESS

Sec. 605.   For the purposes of this Act, service of summons, subpena, or other legal process of a court of the United States upon an officer or agent of a labor organization in his capacity as such shall constitute service upon the labor organization.

ADMINISTRATIVE PROCEDURE ACT

Sec. 606.   The provisions of the Administrative Procedure Act shall be applicable to the issuance, amendment, or rescission of any rules or regulations, or any adjudication, authorized or required pursuant to the provisions of this Act.

OTHER AGENCIES AND DEPARTMENTS

Sec. 607.   In order to avoid unnecessary expense and duplication of functions among Government agencies, the Secretary may make such arrangements or agreements for cooperation or mutual assistance in the performance of his functions under this Act and the functions of any such agency as he may find to be practicable and consistent with law. The Secretary may utilize the facilities or services of any department, agency,

---

*   Pub.L. 98–473, Title II, § 2201, Oct. 12, 1984, 98 Stat. 2192.

or establishment of the United States or of any State or political subdivision of a State, including the services of any of its employees, with the lawful consent of such department, agency, or establishment; and each department, agency, or establishment of the United States is authorized and directed to cooperate with the Secretary and, to the extent permitted by law, to provide such information and facilities as he may request for his assistance in the performance of his functions under this Act. The Attorney General or his representative shall receive from the Secretary for appropriate action such evidence developed in the performance of his functions under this Act as may be found to warrant consideration for criminal prosecution under the provisions of this Act or other Federal law.

CRIMINAL CONTEMPT

Sec. 608.   No person shall be punished for any criminal contempt allegedly committed outside the immediate presence of the court in connection with any civil action prosecuted by the Secretary or any other person in any court of the United States under the provisions of this Act unless the facts constituting such criminal contempt are established by the verdict of the jury in a proceeding in the district court of the United States, which jury shall be chosen and empaneled in the manner prescribed by the law governing trial juries in criminal prosecutions in the district courts of the United States.

PROHIBITION ON CERTAIN DISCIPLINE BY LABOR ORGANIZATION

Sec. 609.   It shall be unlawful for any labor organization, or any officer, agent, shop steward, or other representative of a labor organization, or any employee thereof to fine, suspend, expel, or otherwise discipline any of its members for exercising any right to which he is entitled under the provisions of this Act. The provisions of section 102 shall be applicable in the enforcement of this section.

DEPRIVATION OF RIGHTS UNDER ACT BY VIOLENCE

Sec. 610.   It shall be unlawful for any person through the use of force or violence, or threat of the use of force or violence, to restrain, coerce, or intimidate, or attempt to restrain, coerce, or intimidate any member of a labor organization for the purpose of interfering with or preventing the exercise of any right to which he is entitled under the provisions of this Act. Any person who willfully violates this section shall be fined not more than $1,000 or imprisoned for not more than one year, or both.

SEPARABILITY PROVISIONS

Sec. 611.   If any provision of this Act, or the application of such provision to any person or circumstances, shall be held invalid, the remainder of this Act or the application of such provision to persons or circumstances other than those as to which it is held invalid, shall not be affected thereby.

CIVIL RIGHTS ACT OF 1964

78 Stat. 253 (1964), as amended; 42 U.S.C. § 2000e et seq. (1988); as amended Pub.L. 102–166 (Nov. 21, 1991).

TITLE VII—EQUAL EMPLOYMENT OPPORTUNITY

DEFINITIONS

Sec. 701. (§ 2000e) For the purposes of this title—

(a) The term "person" includes one or more individuals, governments, governmental agencies, political subdivisions, labor unions, partnerships, associations, corporations, legal representatives, mutual companies, joint-stock companies, trusts, unincorporated organizations, trustees, trustees in bankruptcy, or receivers.

(b) The term "employer" means a person engaged in an industry affecting commerce who has fifteen or more employees for each working day in each of twenty or more calendar weeks in the current or preceding calendar year, and any agent of such a person, but such term does not include (1) the United States, a corporation wholly owned by the Government of the United States, an Indian tribe, or any department or agency of the District of Columbia subject by statute to procedures of the competitive service (as defined in section 2102 of Title 5), or (2) a bona fide private membership club (other than a labor organization) which is exempt from taxation under section 501(c) of Title 26, except that during the first year after March 24, 1972, persons having fewer than twenty-five employees (and their agents) shall not be considered employers.

(c) The term "employment agency" means any person regularly undertaking with or without compensation to procure employees for an employer or to procure for employees opportunities to work for an employer and includes an agent of such a person.

(d) The term "labor organization" means a labor organization engaged in an industry affecting commerce, and any agent of such an organization, and includes any organization of any kind, any agency, or employee representation committee, group, association, or plan so engaged in which employees participate and which exists for the purpose, in whole or in part, of dealing with employers concerning grievances, labor disputes, wages, rates of pay, hours, or other terms or conditions of employment, and any conference, general committee, joint or system board, or joint council so engaged which is subordinate to a national or international labor organization.

(e) A labor organization shall be deemed to be engaged in an industry affecting commerce if (1) it maintains or operates a hiring hall or hiring office which procures employees for an employer or procures for employees opportunities to work for an employer, or (2) the number of its members (or, where it is a labor organization composed of other labor organizations or their representatives, if the aggregate number of the members of such other labor organization) is (A) twenty-five or more during the first year after March 24, 1972, or (B) fifteen or more thereafter, and such labor organization—

(1) is the certified representative of employees under the provisions of the National Labor Relations Act, as amended, or the Railway Labor Act, as amended;

(2) although not certified, is a national or international labor organization or a local labor organization recognized or acting as the representative of employees of an employer or employers engaged in an industry affecting commerce; or

(3) has chartered a local labor organization or subsidiary body which is representing or actively seeking to represent employees of employers within the meaning of paragraph (1) or (2); or

(4) has been chartered by a labor organization representing or actively seeking to represent employees within the meaning of paragraph (1) or (2) as the local or subordinate body through which such employees may enjoy membership or become affiliated with such labor organization; or

(5) is a conference, general committee, joint or system board, or joint council subordinate to a national or international labor organization, which includes a labor organization engaged in an industry affecting commerce within the meaning of any of the preceding paragraphs of this subsection.

(f) The term "employee" means an individual employed by an employer, except that the term "employee" shall not include any person elected to public office in any State or political subdivision of any State by the qualified voters thereof, or any person chosen by such officer to be on such officer's personal staff, or an appointee on the policy making level or an immediate adviser with respect to the exercise of the constitutional or legal powers of the office. The exemption set forth in the preceding sentence shall not include employees subject to the civil service laws of a State government, governmental agency or political subdivision. With respect to employment in a foreign country, such term includes an individual who is a citizen of the United States.

(g) The term "commerce" means trade, traffic, commerce, transportation, transmission, or communication among the several States; or between a State and any place outside thereof; or within the District of Columbia, or a possession of the United States; or between points in the same State but through a point outside thereof.

(h) The term "industry affecting commerce" means any activity, business, or industry in commerce or in which a labor dispute would hinder or obstruct commerce or the free flow of commerce and includes any activity or industry "affecting commerce" within the meaning of the Labor-Management Reporting and Disclosure Act of 1959, and further includes any governmental industry, business, or activity.

(i)   The term "State" includes a State of the United States, the District of Columbia, Puerto Rico, the Virgin Islands, American Samoa, Guam, Wake Island, the Canal Zone, and Outer Continental Shelf lands defined in the Outer Continental Shelf Lands Act.

(j)   The term "religion" includes all aspects of religious observance and practice, as well as belief, unless an employer demonstrates that he is unable to reasonably accommodate to an employee's or prospective employee's religious observance or practice without undue hardship on the conduct of the employer's business.

(k)   The terms "because of sex" or "on the basis of sex" include, but are not limited to, because of or on the basis of pregnancy, childbirth, or related medical conditions; and women affected by pregnancy, childbirth, or related medical conditions shall be treated the same for all employment-related purposes, including receipt of benefits under fringe benefit programs, as other persons not so affected but similar in their ability or inability to work, and nothing in section 2(h) of this Act shall be interpreted to permit otherwise. This subsection shall not require an employer to pay for health insurance benefits for abortion, except where the life of the mother would be endangered if the fetus were carried to term, or except where medical complications have arisen from an abortion: *Provided*, That nothing herein shall preclude an employer from providing abortion benefits or otherwise affect bargaining agreements in regard to abortion.

(*l*)   The term "complaining party" means the Commission, the Attorney General, or a person who may bring an action or proceeding under this subchapter.

(m) The term "demonstrates" means meets the burdens of production and persuasion.

(n) The term "respondent" means an employer, employment agency, labor organization, joint labor-management committee controlling apprenticeship or other training or retraining program, including an on-the-job training program, or Federal entity subject to section 2000e–16 of this title.

FOREIGN AND RELIGIOUS EMPLOYMENT

Sec. 702.   (§ 2000e–1)(a) This Subchapter shall not apply to an employer with respect to the employment of aliens outside any State, or to a religious corporation, association, educational institution, or society with respect to the employment of individuals of a particular religion to perform work connected with the carrying on by such corporation, association, educational institution, or society of its activities.

(b)   It shall not be unlawful under section 2000e–2 or 2000e–3 of this title for an employer (or a corporation controlled by an employer), labor organization, employment agency, or joint labor-management committee controlling apprenticeship or other training or retraining (including on-the-job training programs) to take any action otherwise prohibited by such section, with respect to an employee in a workplace in a foreign country if compliance with such section would cause such employer (or such corporation), such organization, such agency, or such committee to violate the law of the foreign country in which such workplace is located.

(c)(1) If an employer controls a corporation whose place of incorporation is a foreign country, any practice prohibited by section 2000e–2 or 2000e–3 of this title engaged in by such corporation shall be presumed to be engaged in by such employer.

(2) Sections 2000e–2 and 2000e–3 of this title shall not apply with respect to the foreign operations of an employer that is a foreign person not controlled by an American employer.

(3) For purposes of this subsection, the determination of whether an employer controls a corporation shall be based on—

(A) the interrelation of operations;

(B) the common management;

(C) the centralized control of labor relations; and

(D) the common ownership or financial control,

of the employer and the corporation.

DISCRIMINATION BECAUSE OF RACE, COLOR, RELIGION, SEX, OR NATIONAL ORIGIN

Sec. 703.   (§ 2000e–2)(a) It shall be an unlawful employment practice for an employer—

(1) to fail or refuse to hire or to discharge any individual, or otherwise to discriminate against any individual with respect to his compensation, terms, conditions, or privileges of employment, because of such individual's race, color, religion, sex, or national origin; or

(2) to limit, segregate, or classify his employees or applicants for employment in any way which would deprive or tend to deprive any individual of employment opportunities or otherwise adversely affect his status as an employee, because of such individual's race, color, religion, sex, or national origin.

(b) It shall be an unlawful employment practice for an employment agency to fail or refuse to refer for employment, or otherwise to discriminate against, any individual because of his race, color, religion, sex, or national origin, or to classify or refer for employment any individual on the basis of his race, color, religion, sex, or national origin.

(c) It shall be an unlawful employment practice for a labor organization—

(1) to exclude or to expel from its membership, or otherwise to discriminate against, any individual because of his race, color, religion, sex, or national origin;

(2) to limit, segregate, or classify its membership or applicants for membership, or to classify or fail or refuse to refer for employment any individual, in any way which would deprive or tend to deprive any individual of employment opportunities, or would limit such employment opportunities or otherwise adversely affect his status as an employee or as an applicant for employment, because of such individual's race, color, religion, sex, or national origin; or

(3) to cause or attempt to cause an employer to discriminate against an individual in violation of this section.

(d) It shall be an unlawful employment practice for any employer, labor organization, or joint labor-management committee controlling apprenticeship or other training or retraining, including on-the-job training programs to discriminate against any individual because of his race, color, religion, sex, or national origin in admission to, or employment in, any program established to provide apprenticeship or other training.

(e) Notwithstanding any other provision of this Subchapter (1) it shall not be an unlawful employment practice for an employer to hire and employ employees, for an employment agency to classify, or refer for employment any individual, for a labor organization to classify its membership or to classify or refer for employment any individual, or for an employer, labor organization, or joint labor-management committee controlling apprenticeship or other training or retraining programs to admit or employ any individual in any such program, on the basis of his religion, sex, or national origin in those certain instances where religion, sex, or national origin is a bona fide occupational qualification reasonably necessary to the normal operation of that particular business or enterprise, and (2) it shall not be an unlawful employment practice for a school, college, university, or other educational institution or institution of learning to hire and employ employees of a particular religion if such school, college, university, or other educational institution or institution of learning is, in whole or in substantial part, owned, supported, controlled, or managed by a particular religion or by a particular religious corporation, association, or society, or if the curriculum of such school, college, university, or other educational institution or institution of learning is directed toward the propagation of a particular religion.

(f) As used in this Subchapter, the phrase "unlawful employment practice" shall not be deemed to include any action or measure taken by an employer, labor organization, joint labor-management committee, or employment agency with respect to an individual who is a member of the Communist Party of the United States or of any other organization required to register as a Communist-action or Communist-front organization by final order of the Subversive Activities Control Board pursuant to the Subversive Activities Control Act of 1950.

(g)   Notwithstanding any other provision of this Subchapter, it shall not be an unlawful employment practice for an employer to fail or refuse to hire and employ any individual for any position, for an employer to discharge any individual from any position, or for an employment agency to fail or refuse to refer any individual for employment in any position, or for a labor organization to fail or refuse to refer any individual for employment in any position, if—

(1)   the occupancy of such position, or access to the premises in or upon which any part of the duties of such position is performed or is to be performed, is subject to any requirement imposed in the interest of the national security of the United States under any security program in effect pursuant to or administered under any statute of the United States or any Executive order of the President; and

(2)   such individual has not fulfilled or has ceased to fulfill that requirement.

(h)   Notwithstanding any other provision of this Subchapter, it shall not be an unlawful employment practice for an employer to apply different standards of compensation, or different terms, conditions, or privileges of employment pursuant to a bona fide seniority or merit system, or a system which measures earnings by quantity or quality of production or to employees who work in different locations, provided that such differences are not the result of an intention to discriminate because of race, color, religion, sex, or national origin, nor shall it be an unlawful employment practice for an employer to give and to act upon the results of any professionally developed ability test provided that such test, its administration or action upon the results is not designed, intended or used to discriminate because of race, color, religion, sex or national origin. It shall not be an unlawful employment practice under this subchapter for any employer to differentiate upon the basis of sex in determining the amount of the wages or compensation paid or to be paid to employees of such employer if such differentiation is authorized by the provisions of section 206(d) of Title 29.

(i)   Nothing contained in this Subchapter shall apply to any business or enterprise on or near an Indian reservation with respect to any publicly announced employment practice of such business or enterprise under which a preferential treatment is given to any individual because he is an Indian living on or near a reservation.

(j)   Nothing contained in this Subchapter shall be interpreted to require any employer, employment agency, labor organization, or joint labor-management committee subject to this subchapter to grant preferential treatment to any individual or to any group because of the race, color, religion, sex, or national origin of such individual or group on account of an imbalance which may exist with respect to the total number of percentage of persons of any race, color, religion, sex, or national origin employed by any employer, referred or classified for employment by any employment agency or labor organization, admitted to membership or classified by any labor organization, or admitted to, or employed in, any apprenticeship or other training program, in comparison with the total number or percentage of persons of such race, color, religion, sex, or national origin in any community, State, section, or other area, or in the available work force in any community, State, section, or other area.

(k)(1)**(A)** An unlawful employment practice based on disparate impact is established under this subchapter only if—

> (i) a complaining party demonstrates that a respondent uses a particular employment practice that causes a disparate impact on the basis of race, color, religion, sex, or national origin and the respondent fails to demonstrate that the challenged practice is job related for the position in question and consistent with business necessity; or

> (ii) the complaining party makes the demonstration described in subparagraph (C) with respect to an alternative employment practice and the respondent refuses to adopt such alternative employment practice.

(B)(i) With respect to demonstrating that a particular employment practice causes a disparate impact as described in subparagraph (A)(i), the complaining party shall demonstrate that each particular challenged employment practice causes a disparate impact, except that if the complaining party can demonstrate to the court that the elements of a respondent's decisionmaking process are not capable of separation for analysis, the decisionmaking process may be analyzed as one employment practice.

> (ii) If the respondent demonstrates that a specific employment practice does not cause the disparate impact, the respondent shall not be required to demonstrate that such practice is required by business necessity.

(C) The demonstration referred to by subparagraph (A)(ii) shall be in accordance with the law as it existed on June 4, 1989, with respect to the concept of "alternative employment practice".

(2) A demonstration that an employment practice is required by business necessity may not be used as a defense against a claim of intentional discrimination under this subchapter.

(3) Notwithstanding any other provision of this subchapter, a rule barring the employment of an individual who currently and knowingly uses or possesses a controlled substance, as defined in schedules I and II of section 102(6) of the Controlled Substances Act (21 U.S.C. 802(6)), other than the use or possession of a drug taken under the supervision of a licensed health care professional, or any other use or possession authorized by the Controlled Substances Act or any other provision of Federal law, shall be considered an unlawful employment practice under this subchapter only if such

rule is adopted or applied with an intent to discriminate because of race, color, religion, sex, or national origin.

(*l*) It shall be an unlawful employment practice for a respondent, in connection with the selection or referral of applicants or candidates for employment or promotion, to adjust the scores of, use different cutoff scores for, or otherwise alter the results of, employment related tests on the basis of race, color, religion, sex, or national origin.

(m) Except as otherwise provided in this subchapter, an unlawful employment practice is established when the complaining party demonstrates that race, color, religion, sex, or national origin was a motivating factor for any employment practice, even though other factors also motivated the practice.

(n)(1)**(A)** Notwithstanding any other provision of law, and except as provided in paragraph (2), an employment practice that implements and is within the scope of a litigated or consent judgment or order that resolves a claim of employment discrimination under the Constitution or Federal civil rights laws may not be challenged under the circumstances described in subparagraph (B).

(B) A practice described in subparagraph (A) may not be challenged in a claim under the Constitution or Federal civil rights laws—

(i) by a person who, prior to the entry of the judgment or order described in subparagraph (A), had—

(I) actual notice of the proposed judgment or order sufficient to apprise such person that such judgment or order might adversely affect the interests and legal rights of such person and that an opportunity was available to present objections to such judgment or order by a future date certain; and

(II) a reasonable opportunity to present objections to such judgment or order; or

(ii) by a person whose interests were adequately represented by another person who had previously challenged the judgment or order on the same legal grounds and with a similar factual situation, unless there has been an intervening change in law or fact.

(2) Nothing in this subsection shall be construed to—

(A) alter the standards for intervention under rule 24 of the Federal Rules of Civil Procedure or apply to the rights of parties who have successfully intervened pursuant to such rule in the proceeding in which the parties intervened;

(B) apply to the rights of parties to the action in which a litigated or consent judgment or order was entered, or of members of a class represented or sought to be represented in such action, or of members of a group on whose behalf relief was sought in such action by the Federal Government;

(C) prevent challenges to a litigated or consent judgment or order on the ground that such judgment or order was obtained through collusion or fraud, or is transparently invalid or was entered by a court lacking subject matter jurisdiction; or

(D) authorize or permit the denial to any person of the due process of law required by the Constitution.

(3) Any action not precluded under this subsection that challenges an employment consent judgment or order described in paragraph (1) shall be brought in the court, and if possible before the judge, that entered such judgment or order. Nothing in this subsection shall preclude a transfer of such action pursuant to section 1404 of Title 28.

OTHER UNLAWFUL EMPLOYMENT PRACTICES

Sec. 704.   (§ 2000e–3)(a) It shall be an unlawful employment practice for an employer to discriminate against any of his employees or applicants for employment, for an employment agency, or joint labor-management committee controlling apprenticeship or other training or retraining, including on-the-job training programs, to discriminate against any individual, or for a labor organization to discriminate against any member thereof or applicant for membership, because he has opposed any practice made an unlawful employment practice by this subchapter, or because he has made a charge, testified, assisted, or participated in any manner in an investigation, proceeding, or hearing under this subchapter.

(b) It shall be an unlawful employment practice for an employer, labor organization, employment agency, or joint labor-management committee controlling apprenticeship or other training or retraining; including on-the-job training programs, to print or publish or cause to be printed or published any notice or advertisement relating to employment by such an employer or membership in or any classification or referral for employment by such a labor organization, or relating to any classification or referral for employment by such an employment agency, or relating to admission to, or employment in, any program established to provide apprenticeship or other training by such a joint labor management committee, indicating any preference, limitation, specification, or discrimination, based on race, color, religion, sex, or national origin, except that such a notice or advertisement may indicate a preference, limitation, specification, or discrimination based on religion, sex, or national origin when religion, sex, or national origin is a bona fide occupational qualification for employment.

* * *

WORKER ADJUSTMENT AND RETRAINING NOTIFICATION ACT

102 Stat. 890 (1988), 29 U.S.C. §§ 2101–2109 (1988).

§ 2101. Definitions; exclusions from definition of loss of employment

(a) **Definitions.**—As used in this chapter—

(1) the term "employer" means any business enterprise that employs—

    (A) 100 or more employees, excluding part-time employees; or

    (B) 100 or more employees who in the aggregate work at least 4,000 hours per week (exclusive of hours of overtime);

(2) the term "plant closing" means the permanent or temporary shutdown of a single site of employment, or one or more facilities or operating units within a single site of employment, if the shutdown results in an employment loss at the single site of employment during any 30-day period for 50 or more employees excluding any part-time employees;

(3) the term "mass layoff" means a reduction in force which—

    (A) is not the result of a plant closing; and

    (B) results in an employment loss at the single site of employment during any 30-day period for—

        (i)(I) at least 33 percent of the employees (excluding any part-time employees); and

            (II) at least 50 employees (excluding any part-time employees); or

        (ii) at least 500 employees (excluding any part-time employees);

(4) the term "representative" means an exclusive representative of employees within the meaning of section 158(f) or 159(a) of this title or section 152 of Title 45;

(5) the term "affected employees" means employees who may reasonably be expected to experience an employment loss as a consequence of a proposed plant closing or mass layoff by their employer;

(6) subject to subsection (b) of this section the term "employment loss" means (A) an employment termination, other than a discharge for cause, voluntary departure, or retirement, (B) a layoff exceeding 6 months, or (C) a reduction in hours of work of more than 50 percent during each month of any 6-month period;

(7) the term "unit of local government" means any general purpose political subdivision of a State which has the power to levy taxes and spend funds, as well as general corporate and police powers; and

(8) the term "part-time employee" means an employee who is employed for an average of fewer than 20 hours per week or who has been employed for fewer than 6 of the 12 months preceding the date on which notice is required.

(b) Exclusions from definition of employment loss.—**(1)** In the case of a sale of part or all of an employer's business, the seller shall be responsible for providing notice for any plant closing or mass layoff in accordance with section 2102 of this title, up to and including the effective date of the sale. After the effective date of the sale of part or all of an employer's business, the purchaser shall be responsible for providing notice for any plant closing or mass layoff in accordance with section 2102 of this title. Notwithstanding any other provision of this chapter, any person who is an employee of the seller (other than a part-time employee) as of the effective date of the sale shall be considered an employee of the purchaser immediately after the effective date of the sale.

(2) Notwithstanding subsection (a)(6) of this section, an employee may not be considered to have experienced an employment loss if the closing or layoff is the result of the relocation or consolidation of part or all of the employer's business and, prior to the closing or layoff—

(A) the employer offers to transfer the employee to a different site of employment within a reasonable commuting distance with no more than a 6-month break in employment; or

(B) the employer offers to transfer the employee to any other site of employment regardless of distance with no more than a 6-month break in employment, and the employee accepts within 30 days of the offer or of the closing or layoff, whichever is later.

§ 2102. Notice required before plant closings and mass layoffs

(a) Notice to employees, state dislocated worker units, and local governments.—An employer shall not order a plant closing or mass layoff until the end of a 60-day period after the employer serves written notice of such an order—

(1) to each representative of the affected employees as of the time of the notice or, if there is no such representative at that time, to each affected employee; and

(2) to the State dislocated worker unit (designated or created under title III of the Job Training Partnership Act [29 U.S.C.A.

§ 1651 et seq.]), and the chief elected official of the unit of local government within which such closing or layoff is to occur.

If there is more than one such unit, the unit of local government which the employer shall notify is the unit of local government to which the employer pays the highest taxes for the year preceding the year for which the determination is made.

(b) Reduction of notification period.—**(1)** An employer may order the shutdown of a single site of employment before the conclusion of the 60-day period if as of the time that notice would have been required the employer was actively seeking capital or business which, if obtained, would have enabled the employer to avoid or postpone the shutdown and the employer reasonably and in good faith believed that giving the notice required would have precluded the employer from obtaining the needed capital or business.

(2)(A) An employer may order a plant closing or mass layoff before the conclusion of the 60-day period if the closing or mass layoff is caused by business circumstances that were not reasonably foreseeable as of the time that notice would have been required.

(B) No notice under this chapter shall be required if the plant closing or mass layoff is due to any form of natural disaster, such as a flood, earthquake, or the drought currently ravaging the farmlands of the United States.

(3) An employer relying on this subsection shall give as much notice as is practicable and at that time shall give a brief statement of the basis for reducing the notification period.

(c) Extension of layoff period.—A layoff of more than 6 months which, at its outset, was announced to be a layoff of 6 months or less, shall be treated as an employment loss under this chapter unless—

(1) the extension beyond 6 months is caused by business circumstances (including unforeseeable changes in price or cost) not reasonably foreseeable at the time of the initial layoff; and

(2) notice is given at the time it becomes reasonably foreseeable, that the extension beyond 6 months will be required.

(d) Determinations with respect to employment loss.—For purposes of this section, in determining whether a plant closing or mass layoff has occurred or will occur, employment losses for 2 or more groups at a single site of employment, each of which is less than the minimum number of employees specified in section 2101(a)(2) or (3) of this title but which in the aggregate exceed that minimum number, and which occur within any 90-day period shall be considered to be a plant closing or mass layoff unless the employer demonstrates that the employment losses are the result of separate and distinct actions and causes and are not an attempt by the employer to evade the requirements of this chapter.

§ 2103. Exemptions

This chapter shall not apply to a plant closing or mass layoff if—

(1) the closing is of a temporary facility or the closing or layoff is the result of the completion of a particular project or undertaking, and the affected employees were hired with the understanding that their employment was limited to the duration of the facility or the project or undertaking; or

(2) the closing or layoff constitutes a strike or constitutes a lockout not intended to evade the requirements of this chapter. Nothing in this chapter shall require an employer to serve written notice pursuant to section 2102(a) of this title when permanently replacing a person who is deemed to be an economic striker under the National Labor Relations Act [29 U.S.C.A. § 151 et seq.]: *Provided*, That nothing in this chapter shall be deemed to validate or invalidate any judicial or administrative ruling relating to the hiring of permanent replacements for economic strikers under the National Labor Relations Act.

§ 2104. Administration and enforcement of requirements

(a) Civil actions against employers.—**(1)** Any employer who orders a plant closing or mass layoff in violation of section 2102 of this title shall be liable to each aggrieved employee who suffers an employment loss as a result of such closing or layoff for—

(A) back pay for each day of violation at a rate of compensation not less than the higher of—

(i) the average regular rate received by such employee during the last 3 years of the employee's employment; or

(ii) the final regular rate received by such employee; and

(B) benefits under an employee benefit plan described in section 1002(3) of this title, including the cost of medical expenses incurred during the employment loss which would have been covered under an employee benefit plan if the employment loss had not occurred.

Such liability shall be calculated for the period of the violation, up to a maximum of 60 days, but in no event for more than one-half the number of days the employee was employed by the employer.

(2) The amount for which an employer is liable under paragraph (1) shall be reduced by—

(A) any wages paid by the employer to the employee for the period of the violation;

(B) any voluntary and unconditional payment by the employer to the employee that is not required by any legal obligation; and

(C) any payment by the employer to a third party or trustee (such as premiums for health benefits or payments to a defined contribution pension plan) on behalf of and attributable to the employee for the period of the violation.

In addition, any liability incurred under paragraph (1) with respect to a defined benefit pension plan may be reduced by crediting the employee with service for all purposes under such a plan for the period of the violation.

(3) Any employer who violates the provisions of section 2102 of this title with respect to a unit of local government shall be subject to a civil penalty of not more than $500 for each day of such violation, except that such penalty shall not apply if the employer pays to each aggrieved employee the amount for which the employer is liable to that employee within 3 weeks from the date the employer orders the shutdown or layoff.

(4) If an employer which has violated this chapter proves to the satisfaction of the court that the act or omission that violated this chapter was in good faith and that the employer had reasonable grounds for believing that the act or omission was not a violation of this chapter the court may, in its discretion, reduce the amount of the liability or penalty provided for in this section.

(5) A person seeking to enforce such liability, including a representative of employees or a unit of local government aggrieved under paragraph (1) or (3), may sue either for such person or for other persons similarly situated, or both, in any district court of the United States for any district in which the violation is alleged to have occurred, or in which the employer transacts business.

(6) In any such suit, the court, in its discretion, may allow the prevailing party a reasonable attorney's fee as part of the costs.

(7) For purposes of this subsection, the term, "aggrieved employee" means an employee who has worked for the employer ordering the plant closing or mass layoff and who, as a result of the failure by the employer to comply with section 2102 of this title, did not receive timely notice either directly or through his or her representative as required by section 2102 of this title.

(b) Exclusivity of remedies.—The remedies provided for in this section shall be the exclusive remedies for any violation of this chapter. Under this chapter, a Federal court shall not have authority to enjoin a plant closing or mass layoff.

§ 2105. Procedures in addition to other rights of employees

The rights and remedies provided to employees by this chapter are in addition to, and not in lieu of, any other contractual or statutory rights and remedies of the employees, and are not intended to alter or affect such rights and remedies, except that the period of notification required by this chapter shall run concurrently with any period of notification required by contract or by any other statute.

§ 2106. Procedures encouraged where not required

It is the sense of Congress that an employer who is not required to comply with the notice requirements of section 2102 of this title should, to the extent possible, provide notice to its employees about a proposal to close a plant or permanently reduce its workforce.

§ 2107. Authority to prescribe regulations

(a) The Secretary of Labor shall prescribe such regulations as may be necessary to carry out this chapter. Such regulations shall, at a minimum, include interpretative regulations describing the methods by which employers may provide for appropriate service of notice as required by this chapter.

(b) The mailing of notice to an employee's last known address or inclusion of notice in the employee's paycheck will be considered acceptable methods for fulfillment of the employer's obligation to give notice to each affected employee under this chapter.

§ 2108. Effect on other laws

The giving of notice pursuant to this chapter, if done in good faith compliance with this chapter, shall not constitute a violation of the National Labor Relations Act [29 U.S.C.A. § 151 et seq.] or the Railway Labor Act [45 U.S.C.A. 151 et seq.].

§ 2109. Report on employment and international competitiveness

Two years after Aug. 4, 1988, the Comptroller General shall submit to the Committee on Small Business of both the House and Senate, the Committee on Labor and Human Resources, and the Committee on Education and Labor a report containing a detailed and objective analysis of the effect of this chapter on employers (especially small- and medium-sized businesses), the economy (international competitiveness), and employees (in terms of levels and conditions of employment). The Comptroller General shall assess both costs and benefits, including the effect on productivity, competitiveness, unemployment rates and compensation, and worker retraining and readjustment.

COLLECTIVE BARGAINING AGREEMENT

PREAMBLE

This Agreement is made and entered into by and between the MAJOR CONTAINER COMPANY ("Company"), their successors or assigns, and the UNITED PAPERWORKERS INTERNATIONAL UNION, AFL-CIO ("Union").

I. PURPOSE

Section 1.   WITNESSETH, whereas the parties hereto have reached agreement as a result of collective bargaining for the purpose of facilitating the peaceful adjustment of differences which may arise from time to time between this Company and the Union, and to promote harmony and efficiency and to the end that the employees and the Company and the general public may mutually benefit, the parties hereto contract and agree with each other as follows:

II. RECOGNITION AND UNION SECURITY

Section 1.   The Company recognizes the Union as the sole agency for collective bargaining on behalf of all employees, with the exception of timekeepers, clerks, office employees, watchmen and non-working foremen and non-working supervisors, in charge of any classes of labor.

Section 2.   This recognition is interpreted by the parties to apply to any transfer or relocation of the Company's present facility to another location within or outside of the metropolitan area, which are an accretion to the existing bargaining unit, where the jobs performed are substantially the same as are covered by the present Agreement.

Section 3.   All employees with the exceptions noted in Section 1 who are members of the Union in good standing on the effective date of this Agreement, shall as a condition of continued employment, maintain their membership in good standing in the Union. All employees, who on the effective date of this Agreement, are not as yet members in good standing of the Union, shall become members of the Union in good standing by no later than thirty (30) days following the effective date of this Agreement and shall maintain membership in good standing in the Union in order to continue in employment. All new employees, shall as a condition of continued employment, become members and maintain membership in good standing in the Union by no later than thirty (30) days following the date of their employment or the effective date of this Agreement, whichever is the later.

Section 4.   The Company agrees to discharge any employee who does not join or maintain his membership in good standing in the Union within seven (7) calendar days after receipt of written notice from the Union that such employee is delinquent in initiation fee or dues. The Union will indemnify and save harmless the Company against any and all claims, demands, or suits that may arise out of the discharge of any employee under this section.

Section 5.   During the term of this Agreement, and at the written request of the Union, the Company will deduct from their wages and remit promptly to the Union the regular monthly membership dues and/or initiation fees established by the Union in accordance with the Constitution and By-Laws of the Union for all employees who have executed and caused to be delivered to the Company a written authorization for such deductions, on a form in conformity with the applicable statutes, which shall not be irrevocable for a period of more than one (1) year, or the termination date of this Agreement, whichever occurs sooner.

III. MANAGEMENT RIGHTS

Section 1.   It is understood and agreed that the management of the Plant and the direction of the work force, including but not limited to the right to hire, suspend, transfer or discharge for proper cause and the right to relieve employees from duty because of lack of work, the right to establish, determine, and maintain reasonable standards of production, to introduce new and improved methods, materials, equipment or facilities and change or eliminate methods, materials, equipment or facilities are vested exclusively in the Company, subject to the provisions of this Agreement.

IV. DISCRIMINATION

Section 1.   No employee shall be discriminated against by the Company for activity in or on behalf of the Union, but shall not be exempted from discipline that is not discriminatory.

Section 2.   The Company and the Union agree that there shall be no discrimination in regard to hiring, tenure of employment or any condition of employment, or in regard to membership in the Union, because of race, color, religion, sex, age, disability, national origin, marital status, sexual orientation, veteran status, or any other classification protected by law.

Section 3.   The parties recognize that in complying with this Article they are subject to the specific provisions and exemptions of Title VII of the Civil Rights Act of 1964, the Age Discrimination in Employment Act of 1967, the Americans with Disabilities Act, as well as the specific statutes of the various states and pertinent Executive Orders issued by the President of the United States.

V. WAGES

Section 1.   The schedule of rates attached hereto as "Exhibit A" shall become a part of this Agreement and they shall be the minimum rates of pay to be paid by the Company to its employees for the duration of this Agreement.

Section 2.   All employees shall receive their pay weekly.

VI. HOURS OF WORK; OVERTIME

Section 1.   Eight (8) consecutive hours, shall constitute a normal day's work; five (5) days, shall constitute a normal work week. Employees assigned to work days will be granted an unpaid lunch period of thirty (30) minutes. Shift employees will be granted a paid twenty (20) minutes lunch period during the shift, when operating requirements permit. Any employee who works over eight (8) hours in any twenty-four (24) hour period, or forty (40) hours (for which overtime has not previously been paid) in any one work week, shall be paid at the rate of time and a half. This provision shall not be construed to guarantee any specific hours or days of work.

Any employee who works over sixty (60) hours (for which double-time has not previously been paid) in any one work week shall be paid at the rate of double-time.

Section 2.   Overtime shall be distributed as equitably as possible among the employees who can perform the work. The Company shall maintain open overtime records for the purpose of distributing over time equitably.

Section 3.   All work performed on Sundays and holidays shall be paid for at the rate of double time.

Section 4.   All work performed on Saturdays shall be paid for at the rate of time and one-half.

Section 5.   Employees working on second shift shall receive a shift premium of fifteen (15) cents per hour.

Section 6.   Employees working on third shift shall receive a shift premium of twenty-five (25) cents per hour.

VII. HOLIDAYS

Section 1.   The following holidays or days celebrated in place thereof shall be observed and shall be paid for even though not worked at eight hours of the regular hourly rate of pay for all employees who have worked sixty (60) days or more in the Company. Holidays falling on Sunday shall be observed on the following Monday.

New Year's Day

Decoration Day

Fourth of July

Good Friday

Labor Day

Employee's Birthday

Thanksgiving Day

Day after Thanksgiving

Christmas Day

Christmas Eve Day

New Year's Eve Day

Section 2.   Any employee entitled to a holiday with pay shall not be required to work on said holiday.

Section 3.   It is agreed that to qualify for such holiday pay an employee shall have worked the regular scheduled work day immediately preceding and succeeding said holiday, provided work is available unless excused from such work by the plant management.

VIII. VACATIONS

Section 1.   Vacation pay shall be computed on the basis of regular hourly rates of pay.

Section 2.   The following schedule shall be the method of application of vacation periods and vacation pay.

Length of Service	Vacation Periods	Vacation Pay at Regular Hourly Rates of Pay
1 Year	1	42 Hours Pay
3 Years	2	84 Hours Pay
8 Years	3	126 Hours Pay
15 Years	4	168 Hours Pay
20 Years	5	210 Hours Pay
25 Years	6	252 Hours Pay

Section 3.   The Company may shut down the plant completely or partially to grant vacations to all or part of the employees at one time provided it shall notify the employees of such a plan at least sixty (60) days before a vacation commences. Otherwise, vacations will be scheduled according to employees' desires, subject to the exclusive right of the Company to change vacation periods to assure orderly and efficient operation of the Plant. In the event of a dispute between two or more employees as to the time of their vacations, the employee with the greatest seniority with the Company shall receive the preference.

Section 4.   Any employee eligible for a vacation, who is severed from the payroll of the Company in any calendar year before having taken his or her vacation, except one who is discharged for cause or who quits without two weeks' notice, shall receive vacation pay.

IX. SENIORITY

Section 1.   Seniority is defined as the length of an employee's service with the Company within the bargaining unit; it shall apply plant-wide.

Section 2.   The Company agrees to draw up a plant-wide Seniority list as of June 1st of each year, which shall be posted in a location available to all employees.

Section 3.   The Union may select from the employees covered by this Agreement a Steward who has been employed by the Company for a period of at least one (1) year, whose duty it is to see that this contract is not broken by either the employees or the Employer. The Union shall notify the Company, in writing, of the name of the Shop Steward.

Section 4.   In the event of layoff, all Union officers, shop stewards, and shop committee members shall have seniority during their terms of office only, over other employees of the Company provided they have at least one (1) year service with the Company.

Section 5.   Production foremen, or other non-bargaining unit employees, shall not do any work, the performance of which, would cause any employee to suffer lay-off or loss of overtime.

Section 6.   An employee shall be terminated and shall lose all accumulated seniority when he or she:

a)   quits

b)   is discharged

c)   is laid off for lack of work for a continuous period of 15 calendar months or a period of time equal to the employee's plant seniority, whichever comes first.

d)   fails to return to work within four (4) days of notice to return to work, unless such failure to return is for reason satisfactory to the Company

e)   engages in gainful employment during a leave of absence except in cases where such leave of absence is expressly granted for this purpose

f)   fails to return to work within three (3) working days from the date of expiration of his leave of absence

g)   is absent due to non-industrial accident or illness for a period of two (2) years

h)   is retired under the Company's Pension Plan.

X.   PERMANENT VACANCIES

Section 1.   Each permanent job vacancy and each permanent new job which falls within the scope of the Union's certification shall be filled as follows:

(a)   Notice of such job shall be posted in the plant for two (2) days. Such job postings shall include the job classification, department, and the shift on which the new job or vacancy exists. Any employee who wishes to bid for such jobs shall sign the posting. Job postings shall be placed in three locations throughout the plant for official signing in the presence of a member of management, who will initial the posting. Two postings will be provided in the supervisory offices assigned in the plant; a third posting will be placed in the Human Resources office for signing. At all posting locations, job descriptions for all jobs will be available for review. At the end of the two (2) days, the Company shall remove the posting.

(b) Where skill and ability are relatively equal, seniority shall prevail, providing the employee is physically able to perform the work without endangering his or her health or safety. The most senior qualified employee will be awarded the job and be notified by the Human Resources office within five (5) days after removal of the posting. The Company will transfer the employee awarded the vacancy hereunder to the new job within fifteen (15) calendar days, provided the release of the employee does not interfere with the efficient operations of the department. Multiple postings will be awarded from the highest pay grade posting to the lowest pay grade posting.

(c) An employee awarded the vacancy hereunder shall be given up to sixteen (16) working days in which to demonstrate his or her ability to perform the work involved. In some circumstances, extensions may be required, not to exceed sixteen (16) additional workdays. During the qualifying period, employees are unable to bid. During this period, the Company may remove the employee from the job if the Company considers the employee's work to be unsatisfactory. The employee may then bid on any other vacancy. An employee disqualified from a job will be unable to bid that job for a period of three (3) months.

Section 2. The Union and the Company may, by mutual agreement, provide rules whereby disabled employees may be assigned to jobs which they are able to satisfactorily perform without regard to this Article. When the Union and the Company agree to placement of an employee hereunder, the conditions pertaining to that placement shall be reduced to writing and signed by the parties.

XI. LAYOFF AND RECALL

Section 1. If the Company decides to reduce the number of employees in a job classification in a department, and the reduction is expected to continue for more than four (4) days, the reduction shall be made as follows:

(a) The least senior employee or employees shall be removed from the classification provided the skill and ability of the employees in the classification are relatively equal.

(b) An employee removed from his or her classification and/or shift pursuant to (a) shall be afforded the opportunity to move into a job classification in an equal or lower labor grade on any shift provided he or she has the proven skill and ability to perform such work which is held by an employee with less seniority. An employee displaced from his job classification by the exercise of the seniority rights granted in this paragraph shall also be afforded the opportunity to displace other employees in accordance with this paragraph and the exercise of seniority hereunder.

(c)   In the operation of (a) and (b) above, a senior employee has the prerogative of accepting layoff instead of displacing a junior employee, if he or she so desires.

(d)   The Company will post a notice of layoff expected to last more than four (4) days at least ten (10) days in advance of such layoff, unless the conditions leading to such layoff resulted from an Act of God, labor dispute, or other condition beyond the control of the Company.

Section 2.   (a) Employees affected by a reduction of forces shall be recalled to their regular job classification and department in the inverse order of the force reduction. If the employee refuses such recall, he will be terminated as a voluntary quit. Employees recalled to their regular job classification and department, but not to their regular shift, shall be returned to their regular shift in order of seniority as openings occur.

(b)   When a vacancy exists after exhausting paragraph (a), the job will be posted for bid according to the bidding procedure. If no employee is awarded such job vacancy, the most senior employee on layoff shall be afforded the vacancy providing he or she has the skill and ability to perform the work.

Section 3.   Nothing in this Agreement shall prohibit the Company's laying off the employees for the purpose of taking inventory and offering the work available during such period to the senior qualified employees in the department.

XII.   EMPLOYEE SAFETY

Section 1.   The Company agrees to provide a place of employment which shall be safe for the employees therein, shall furnish and use safety devices and safeguards, and shall adopt and use methods and processes adequate to render such places of employment safe. The term "safe" or "safety" as applied to employment or place of employment shall include conditions and methods of sanitation and hygiene necessary for the protection of life, health and safety of the employees.

Section 2.   The Company agrees that all machinery, equipment and facilities the Company furnishes shall meet with all required legal standards of safety and sanitation. Accident records shall be kept and maintained by the Company and shall be made available on request to the Safety Committee

Section 3.   The Company agrees to maintain a Joint Labor-Management Safety Committee. The Safety Committee shall be composed of at least two (2) representatives of Management and at least two (2) representatives of the Union. The Union representatives shall be selected by the local Union. The Safety Committee shall be able to sit in on any safety investigation when any employee is questioned and shall:

Meet at least once every month on definitely established dates;

Make inspections of the plant at least once every month;

Make recommendations for the correction of unsafe or harmful work practices;

Review and analyze all reports of industrial injury and illness, investigate causes of same and recommend rules and procedures for the prevention of accidents and disease and for the promotion of health and safety of employees;

Promote health and safety education.

Section 4.   All disputes and disagreements brought to the attention of the Safety Committee, arising under the Safety clause of this contract, if not disposed of by the Safety Committee, shall be subject to the Grievance Procedure.

Section 5.   In the event of special circumstances, the Safety Committee may seek advice, opinion and suggestions of experts and authorities on safety matters. Such experts shall have access to the plant for the purpose of applying this article at any time upon providing reasonable notice. The Personnel Manager or his/her designee and a Union designee shall accompany the Safety representative.

Section 6.   Employees injured in the plant shall be furnished medical aid or treatment on Company time, and shall receive full pay for the shift on which they were working when injured.

Section 7.   The Union agrees to participate on the Safety Committee and will endeavor to have its members observe all safety rules and use all equipment and safeguards provided. The Union representative on the Safety Committee, upon request, shall be allowed to leave his or her work during working hours for the purpose of performing his or duties as outlined in this Article without loss of time or pay.

XIII. DISCIPLINE

Section 1.   The Employer may not discipline or discharge except for just cause and only after due regard for principles of progressive discipline, except as specified otherwise herein.

Section 2.   The following shall be causes for immediate discharge:

(a) Bringing intoxicants, narcotics or other dangerous drugs into or consuming intoxicants or such narcotics or drugs in the plant or on the plant premises.

(b) Reporting for duty under the influence of liquor, narcotics or drugs.

(c) Smoking while on duty or in prohibited areas.

(d) Deliberate destruction or removal of Company's or another employee's property.

(e) Refusal to comply with Company rules, provided that such rules shall be posted in a conspicuous place where they may be read by all employees; and further provided that no changes in present rules or no additional rules shall be made that are inconsistent with this Agreement.

(f)   Disorderly conduct.

(g)   Sleeping on duty.

(h)   Giving or taking a bribe of any nature, as an inducement to obtaining work or retaining a position.

(i)   Failure to report for duty without bona fide reasons.

(j)   Reading of books, magazines or newspapers while on duty except where required in line of duty.

(k)   Unsanitary practice endangering the health of others.

(*l*)   Gambling during working hours.

Section 3.   Except for the infractions noted in Section 2, above, the Employer shall not discharge or suspend an employee without first having discussed such action with the employee and Shop Steward or, in absence of both, having given notice to the Union. Such notice may be by telephone, telegram, or letter, and such notice must include the reason or reasons for an employee's discharge or suspension.

Section 4.   No employee in the bargaining unit shall be required to take any polygraph test, but an employee may, of his own volition, take such a test.

XIV.   GRIEVANCE PROCEDURE

Section 1.   Should grievances arise, a diligent effort shall be made to settle all grievances as soon as possible after they have been presented either by the Union or an employee.

Any employee having a grievance shall submit same in writing as promptly as possible after its occurrence but no grievance shall be valid if not presented within fifteen (15) days from the time the cause for complaint became known to the employee.

If at any time a grievance remains at any step below Step 4 for more than seven (7) working days, the Local Union may, by written notice to local management, request that such grievance be heard at the next step.

Section 2.   When grievances arise, the following steps shall be followed, each to be exhausted before resorting to the next:

Step 1. Between the immediate supervisor and the aggrieved employee; the appropriate Union representative shall be given an opportunity to be present.

Step 2. Between the Production Superintendent and the Union Committee.

Step 3. Between the Operations Manager and the Union Committee.

Step 4.   Between the Divisional Vice President of the Company, or his representative, and the President of the International Union, or his representative.

XV.   ARBITRATION

Section 1.   In the event that a grievance based upon the interpretation, application or compliance with the terms of this Agreement shall not have been satisfactorily settled, the Union within thirty (30) days after the Company's answer to the last step in the grievance procedure may submit the matter to the American Arbitration Association under their rules then in effect. Expenses of the arbitrator shall be shared equally by the Company and the Union. The decision of the arbitrator shall be binding upon both parties to this Agreement. Such decision shall be within the scope and terms of this Agreement, but shall not change any of its terms or conditions.

XVI.   STRIKES AND LOCKOUTS

Section 1.   The Union and the Company agree that there shall be no strikes, sympathy strikes, boycotts, lockouts or general slowing down of production by employees, during the life of this Agreement, and that in the event differences should arise between the Company and the Union or its members employed by the Company, as to the meaning and application of this Agreement, or should any local trouble of any kind arise in the plant, there shall be no suspension of work by the employees on account of such differences.

XVII.   EMPLOYEE BENEFITS

The benefits as shown in this section shall continue in effect during the life of this Agreement.

Medical Insurance: Blue Cross Preferred Comprehensive; Blue Shield, 100; and Major Medical Insurance shall continue to be provided at Company expense for employees until age 70. The Major Medical Insurance referred to herein shall be provided on the basis of $10,000 maximum; $100 deductible per person, and 80/20 participation.

A Blue Shield Eye Examination and Refraction Program shall be provided for employees and certain of their dependents at Company expense as promptly as arrangements can be made.

Dental Insurance: A dental insurance plan to be agreed upon by the parties shall be effective April 1, 2017. This plan shall provide dental benefits for employees and their covered dependents. Company shall contribute $20.00 per month per covered employee toward the cost of this coverage and any excess cost shall be made up by employee contributions.

Death in Family: Should death occur to the Mother, Father, Stepmother, Stepfather, Wife, Children, Stepchildren, Sister or Brother of any employee, he or she shall be entitled to a three-day leave of absence and should death occur to the Grandparent of any employee he or she shall be entitled to a one-day leave of absence. For all such leaves of absence the employee will be paid at his or her straight-time rate provided the leave is taken during the normal week, i.e., Monday through Friday.

Jury Duty: The Company agrees to pay to any employee who shall serve on a bona fide jury panel an amount equal to the difference between the employee's earnings from such service and his or her regular eight (8) hours straight time pay for the days, not in excess of fifteen days for any single period of jury service, during which the employee shall be absent and on jury service.

Sick Benefits: Provision is made for the payment of Sick Benefits to hourly paid employees who have been on the payroll for not less than one year immediately prior to the event of sickness.

On presentation of a licensed physician's, dentist's, chiropodist's, or chiropractor's certificate, an employee who has been ill seven (7) or more consecutive days is entitled to an amount equal to fifty (50) percent of his or her forty-hour weekly wages or the amount to which the employee would be entitled under the State Temporary Disability Law, whichever is greater, from the day he became ill, for a period not in excess of twenty-six weeks in any twelve-month period.

Sick benefits have no connection with illness due to injury in the plant. Disabilities due to injuries in the plant are compensated for under Employers' Liability Insurance in accordance with State regulations.

Retirement: All employees covered by this Agreement are also covered by the Pension Plan which went into operation July 1, 1990, as amended: This is a funded pension plan.

A copy of the Summary Plan Description will be regularly furnished to each new employee. Additional copies may be obtained upon request at the Personnel Office.

Life Insurance: A group life insurance policy will be purchased by the Company so that each employee with one or more years of continuous service with the Company shall have life insurance protection in the amount of $10,000 in the event such employee shall die while employed by the Company and before such employee's retirement. Beneficiary designations shall be made by each such employee in accordance with the provisions of such group policy.

XVIII.   NEW EMPLOYEES

Section 1.   New employees shall be considered probationary employees and shall not rank for seniority until they shall have been in the employ of the Company for sixty (60) calendar days, unless otherwise extended by mutual agreement. After the expiration of the sixty (60) day period, they shall cease to be probationary employees and rates of pay and all other provisions of this Agreement shall be applicable to them. They shall then rank for seniority from the date of original hiring in the plant. During the probationary period the Company may pay the employee the regular job wage rate.

XIX.   SCOPE OF WORK; NEW TECHNOLOGIES

Section 1.   It is the intent of the parties to permit the Company to remain technologically competitive and to meet its customer's needs so long as work opportunities now and in the future are preserved for the employees within the bargaining unit identified in Article II. As new technologies develop, the parties pledge their best efforts to fully train and include bargaining unit employees in the implementation of such technologies.

Section 2.   In furtherance of the parties' intent, a technology committee consisting of two (2) Union and two (2) Company representatives shall be established and shall meet at the request of either the Union or the Company. The committee shall be empowered to investigate and discuss all issues involving the impact of new technology on bargaining unit work. The committee shall reach agreement on issues investigated and discussed.

Section 3.   The Company shall provide training, if required, on any new technology used to perform bargaining unit work. The Company will not permit its proprietary or licensed software, data, hardware, equipment or facilities to be used by others to perform work or functions that replace work or functions being performed by bargaining unit employees.

XX.   COMPLETE AGREEMENT

Section 1.   The parties hereto acknowledge that, during the negotiations which resulted in this Agreement, each had the unlimited right and opportunity to make demands and proposals with respect to any subject or matter not removed by law from the area of collective bargaining, and that the understandings and Agreements arrived at by the parties after the exercise of the right and opportunity are set forth in this Agreement. Therefore, the parties hereto, for the life of this Agreement, each voluntarily and unqualifiedly waives the right, and each expressly agrees that the other shall not be obligated, to bargain collectively with respect to any subject or matter referred to, or covered or not specifically referred to or covered in the Agreement, even though such subject or matter may not have been within the knowledge or contemplation of either or both of the parties at the time that they negotiated or signed this Agreement.

Section 2.   The parties hereto expressly agree that this contract is the sole and complete Agreement between them and that any other previous understandings or Agreements, oral or written (inconsistent with the provisions of this Agreement), are superseded and are of no effect during the term of this Agreement (except as elsewhere provided in the Agreement).

XXI. TERM OF AGREEMENT

Section 1.   This Agreement shall be effective April 1, 2016, and shall continue in full force and effect to and including March 31, 2019, and from year to year after the latter date, unless and until either of the parties hereto shall give to the other three (3) months' written notice prior to the end of the original term, or three (3) months' written notice prior to the end of any subsequent year, of an intention to modify or terminate at the end of the original term or of the then current year.

XXII. SUCCESSORS AND ASSIGNS

Section 1.   This Agreement shall be binding upon the successors, purchasers, transferees and assignees of the Company.

Section 2.   The Company shall give notice of the existence of this Agreement to any successor, purchaser, transferee or assignee. Such notice shall be in writing, with a copy to the Union, at least sixty (60) days in advance of the effective date of transfer. After such notice is given, upon the request of either party, the parties shall bargain in good faith about any matter not covered by this Agreement.

Exhibit A

All incumbent employees shall receive the following wages:

Effective June 1, 2016

Work Level A	Start	$10.71	–$14.06
Work Level B	Start	$11.64	–$15.02
Work Level C	Start	$12.53	–$16.48
Work Level D	Start	$13.01	–$16.96
Work Level E	Start	$15.15	–$19.10

Effective June 1, 2017

Work Level A	Start	$10.88	–$14.34
Work Level B	Start	$11.83	–$15.32
Work Level C	Start	$12.74	–$16.81
Work Level D	Start	$13.23	–$17.30
Work Level E	Start	$15.41	–$19.48

Effective June 1, 2018

Work Level A	Start	$11.20	–$14.84
Work Level B	Start	$12.18	–$15.86
Work Level C	Start	$13.12	–$17.40
Work Level D	Start	$13.62	–$17.91
Work Level E	Start	$15.88	–$20.16

MEMORANDUM OF UNDERSTANDING #1
ABSENTEE CONTROL PROGRAM
Executed by Company and Union on June 1, 2003

The Company shall have the sole option of placing an employee on the absentee watch list by issuing a written notice to the employee, with a copy to the Union. The Company's decision to place an employee on the absentee watch list shall not be subject to the grievance or arbitration provisions of the contract.

Once an employee is placed on the absentee watch list, termination will take place in the event there are two (2) unexcused absences or four (4) tardinesses, or any combination thereof in any rolling 90-calendar day period. An unexcused absence is defined as *any* absence that is not approved by the Company in writing and signed by the Company President or a designee. In the event a termination based upon absenteeism or tardiness is processed to arbitration, the arbitrator shall be limited to determining whether or not an individual had two (2) or more unexcused absences or four (4) or more tardinesses, or any combination thereof, in the rolling 90-day period. It is further understood that an individual placed on the absentee watch list shall remain on that list for 300 calendar days provided there is no intervening unexcused absence or tardiness and otherwise for 365 calendar days from the date of written notice provided for above.

MEMORANDUM OF UNDERSTANDING #2
CHEMICAL SUBSTANCE ABUSE POLICY
Executed by Company and Union on October 15, 2015

1.   An employee who is found or reasonable believed to be under the influence of alcohol, drugs or an intoxicant in the employee's system during the course of business on Company premises or when conducting Company business *at any time* will be subject to discipline including discharge, or may be referred to the Employee Assistance Program. Being "under the influence" of alcohol is defined as a blood alcohol content of .04 or higher; and being "under the influence" of an unauthorized controlled substance, illegal drug, prescription, or non-prescription drug is defined as testing positive at specified ng/ml levels.

2.   It is the responsibility of each employee to report promptly to the Medical Department the use or possession of any prescribed medication which may affect judgment, performance, or behavior. No prescription drug will be brought on the Company premises or business in any manner, combination, or quantity other than that prescribed by a licensed physician. Failure to comply may result in discipline, including discharge, or the employee may be referred to the Employee Assistance Program.

3.   All new hires will be tested for the use of drugs, alcohol, and intoxicating substances. Refusal to submit to testing, or testing positive, will result in rejection of employment by the Company. Applicants who

are denied employment because of a positive test result may reapply for employment and be re-tested after one year from the time of initial rejection.

4.   If Management has reasonable suspicion (as herein defined) that an employee is under the influence or, impaired by, or unfit for work due to a chemical substance, including but not limited to a drug, alcohol, or intoxicating substance, or in the event of an accident when the cause may be human error, the subject employee shall be required to submit to medical chemical screening, which may include breath, saliva, urine, and/or blood specimen testing. Positive test results may result in the employee being disciplined, up to and including discharge, or the employee may be referred to the Employee Assistance Program.

5.   "Reasonable suspicion" means objective belief based upon reasonable, individualized suspicion that can be described with particularity that a specific employee may be under the influence of alcohol, drugs, or other intoxicating substances based on direct observation by a supervisor or management representative.

NATIONAL LABOR RELATIONS BOARD FORMS

(1) Petition for Election.

(2) Stipulated Election Agreement, and

(3) Unfair Labor Practice Charge Against Employer.

(4) Unfair Labor Practice Charge Against Union.

(5) Remedial Notice.

INTERNET FORM NLRB-502 (2-08)	UNITED STATES GOVERNMENT NATIONAL LABOR RELATIONS BOARD **PETITION**	FORM EXEMPT UNDER 44 U.S.C. **DO NOT WRITE IN THIS SPACE**	
		Case No.	Date Filed

INSTRUCTIONS: Submit an original of this Petition to the NLRB Regional Office in the Region in which the employer concerned is located.

The Petitioner alleges that the following circumstances exist and requests that the NLRB proceed under its proper authority pursuant to Section 9 of the NLRA.

1. PURPOSE OF THIS PETITION (if box RC, RM, or RD is checked and a charge under Section 8(b)(7) of the Act has been filed involving the Employer named herein, the statement following the description of the type of petition shall not be deemed made.) (Check One)

☐ **RC-CERTIFICATION OF REPRESENTATIVE** - A substantial number of employees wish to be represented for purposes of collective bargaining by Petitioner and Petitioner desires to be certified as representative of the employees.

☐ **RM-REPRESENTATION (EMPLOYER PETITION)** - One or more individuals or labor organizations have presented a claim to Petitioner to be recognized as the representative of employees of Petitioner.

☐ **RD-DECERTIFICATION (REMOVAL OF REPRESENTATIVE)** - A substantial number of employees assert that the certified or currently recognized bargaining representative is no longer their representative.

☐ **UD-WITHDRAWAL OF UNION SHOP AUTHORITY (REMOVAL OF OBLIGATION TO PAY DUES)** - Thirty percent (30%) or more of employees in a bargaining unit covered by an agreement between their employer and a labor organization desire that such authority be rescinded.

☐ **UC-UNIT CLARIFICATION** - A labor organization is currently recognized by Employer, but Petitioner seeks clarification of placement of certain employees: (Check one) ☐ In unit not previously certified. ☐ In unit previously certified in Case No. _____

☐ **AC-AMENDMENT OF CERTIFICATION** - Petitioner seeks amendment of certification issued in Case No. _____ Attach statement describing the specific amendment sought.

2. Name of Employer	Employer Representative to contact	Tel. No.
3. Address(es) of Establishment(s) involved (Street and number, city, State, ZIP code)		Fax No.

4a. Type of Establishment (Factory, mine, wholesaler, etc.)	4b. Identify principal product or service	Cell No.
		e-Mail

5. Unit Involved (In UC petition, describe present bargaining unit and attach description of proposed clarification.)	6a. Number of Employees in Unit:
Included	Present
Excluded	Proposed (By UC/AC)
	6b. Is this petition supported by 30% or more of the employees in the unit? ☐ Yes ☐ No *Not applicable in RM, UC, and AC

(If you have checked box RC in 1 above, check and complete EITHER item 7a or 7b, whichever is applicable)

7a. ☐ Request for recognition as Bargaining Representative was made on (Date) _____ and Employer declined recognition on or about (Date) _____ (If no reply received, so state).
7b. ☐ Petitioner is currently recognized as Bargaining Representative and desires certification under the Act.

8. Name of Recognized or Certified Bargaining Agent (If none, so state.)	Affiliation	
Address	Tel. No.	Date of Recognition or Certification
	Cell No.	Fax No.	e-Mail

9. Expiration Date of Current Contract. If any (Month, Day, Year)	10. If you have checked box UD in 1 above, show here the date of execution of agreement granting union shop (Month, Day and Year)

11a. Is there now a strike or picketing at the Employer's establishment(s) Involved? Yes ☐ No ☐	11b. If so, approximately how many employees are participating?

11c. The Employer has been picketed by or on behalf of (Insert Name) _____ , a labor organization, of (Insert Address) _____ Since (Month, Day, Year) _____

12. Organizations or individuals other than Petitioner (and other than those named in items 8 and 11c), which have claimed recognition as representatives and other organizations and individuals known to have a representative interest in any employees in unit described in item 5 above. (If none, so state)

Name	Address	Tel. No.	Fax No.
		Cell No.	e-Mail

13. Full name of party filing petition (If labor organization, give full name, including local name and number)

14a. Address (street and number, city, state, and ZIP code)	14b. Tel. No. EXT	14c. Fax No.
	14d. Cell No.	14e. e-Mail

15. Full name of national or international labor organization of which Petitioner is an affiliate or constituent (to be filled in when petition is filed by a labor organization)

I declare that I have read the above petition and that the statements are true to the best of my knowledge and belief.

Name (Print)	Signature	Title (if any)
Address (street and number, city, state, and ZIP code)	Tel. No.	Fax No.
	Cell No.	eMail

WILLFUL FALSE STATEMENTS ON THIS PETITION CAN BE PUNISHED BY FINE AND IMPRISONMENT (U.S. CODE, TITLE 18, SECTION 1001)

PRIVACY ACT STATEMENT

Solicitation of the information on this form is authorized by the National Labor Relations Act (NLRA), 29 U.S.C. § 151 et seq. The principal use of the information is to assist the National Labor Relations Board (NLRB) in processing unfair labor practice and related proceedings or litigation. The routine uses for the information are fully set forth in the Federal Register, 71 Fed. Reg. 74942-43 (Dec. 13, 2006). The NLRB will further explain these uses upon request. Disclosure of this information to the NLRB is voluntary; however, failure to supply the information will cause the NLRB to decline to invoke its processes.

FORM NLRB-652
(4-85)

UNITED STATES OF AMERICA
NATIONAL LABOR RELATIONS BOARD
STIPULATED ELECTION AGREEMENT

The parties agree that a hearing is waived, that approval of this Agreement constitutes withdrawal of any notice of hearing previously issued in this matter, that the petition is amended to conform to this Agreement, and further **AGREE AS FOLLOWS:**

1. **SECRET BALLOT.** A secret-ballot election shall be held under the supervision of the Regional Director in the unit defined below at the agreed time and place, under the Board's Rules and Regulations.

2. **ELIGIBLE VOTERS.** The eligible voters shall be unit employees employed during the payroll period for eligibility, including employees who did not work during that period because they were ill, on vacation, or temporarily laid off, employees engaged in an economic strike which commenced less than 12 months before the election date and who retained their status as such during the eligibility period and their replacements, and employees in the military services of the United States who appear in person at the polls. Ineligible to vote are employees who have quit or been discharged for cause since the payroll period for eligibility, employees engaged in a strike who have been discharged for cause since the commencement thereof and who have not been rehired or reinstated before the election date, and employees engaged in an economic strike which commenced more than 12 months before the election date and who have been permanently replaced. The Employer shall provide to the Regional Director, within 7 days after the Regional Director has approved this Agreement, an election eligibility list containing the full names and addresses of all eligible voters. *Excelsior Underwear, Inc.*, 156 NLRB 1236 (1966). *North Macon Health Care Facility*, 315 NLRB 359 (1994).

3. **NOTICE OF ELECTION.** Copies of the Notice of Election shall be posted by the Employer in conspicuous places and usual posting places easily accessible to the voters at least three (3) full working days prior to 12:01 a.m. of the day of the election. As soon as the election arrangements are finalized, the Employer will be informed when the Notices must be posted in order to comply with the posting requirement. Failure to post the Election Notices as required shall be grounds for setting aside the election whenever proper and timely objections are filed.

4. **ACCOMMODATIONS REQUIRED.** All parties should notify the Regional Director as soon as possible of any voters, potential voters, or other participants in this election who have handicaps falling within the provisions of Section 504 of the Rehabilitation Act of 1973, as amended, and 29 C.F.R. 100.603, and who in order to participate in this election need appropriate auxiliary aids, as defined in 29 C.F.R. 100.603, and request the necessary assistance.

5. **OBSERVERS.** Each party may station an equal number of authorized, nonsupervisory-employee observers at the polling places to assist in the election, to challenge the eligibility of voters, and to verify the tally.

6. **TALLY OF BALLOTS.** Upon conclusion of the election, the ballots will be counted and a tally of ballots prepared and immediately made available to the parties.

7. **POSTELECTION AND RUNOFF PROCEDURES.** All procedures after the ballots are counted shall conform with the Board's Rules and Regulations.

8. **RECORD.** The record in this case shall include this Agreement and be governed by the Board's Rules and Regulations.

(Over)

9. **COMMERCE.** The Employer is engaged in commerce within the meaning of Section 2(6) and (7) of the National Labor Relations Act and a question affecting commerce has arisen concerning the representation of employees within the meaning of Section 9(c). (Insert commerce facts.)

10. **WORDING ON THE BALLOT.** When only one labor organization is on the ballot, the choice shall be "Yes" or "No." If more than one labor organization is on the ballot, the choices shall appear as follows, reading left to right or top to bottom. (If more than one labor organization is on the ballot, any labor organization may have its name removed by the approval of the Regional Director of a timely written request.)

First.

Second.

Third.

11. **PAYROLL PERIOD FOR ELIGIBILITY - THE PERIOD ENDING** _____

12. **DATE, HOURS, AND PLACE OF ELECTION.**

13. **THE APPROPRIATE COLLECTIVE-BARGAINING UNIT.**

_____
            (Employer)

By _____
          (Name)   (Date)

            (Title)
Recommended:

_____
     (Board Agent)   (Date)

Date approved _____

Regional Director
National Labor Relations Board

Case _____

_____
          (Labor Organization)

By _____
          (Name)   (Date)

            (Title)

_____
          (Labor Organization)

By _____
          (Name)   (Date)

            (Title)

FORM EXEMPT UNDER 44 U.S.C. 3512

INTERNET FORM NLRB-501 (2-08)	UNITED STATES OF AMERICA NATIONAL LABOR RELATIONS BOARD **CHARGE AGAINST EMPLOYER**	**DO NOT WRITE IN THIS SPACE**	
		Case	Date Filed

INSTRUCTIONS:
File an original with NLRB Regional Director for the region in which the alleged unfair labor practice occurred or is occurring.

1. EMPLOYER AGAINST WHOM CHARGE IS BROUGHT

a. Name of Employer	b. Tel. No.
	c. Cell No.
d. Address *(Street, city, state, and ZIP code)* e. Employer Representative	f. Fax No.
	g. e-Mail
	h. Number of workers employed

i. Type of Establishment *(factory, mine, wholesaler, etc.)*	j. Identify principal product or service

k. The above-named employer has engaged in and is engaging in unfair labor practices within the meaning of section 8(a), subsections (1) and *(list subsections)* _____ of the National Labor Relations Act, and these unfair labor practices are practices affecting commerce within the meaning of the Act, or these unfair labor practices are unfair practices affecting commerce within the meaning of the Act and the Postal Reorganization Act.

2. Basis of the Charge *(set forth a clear and concise statement of the facts constituting the alleged unfair labor practices)*

3. Full name of party filing charge *(if labor organization, give full name, including local name and number)*

4a. Address *(Street and number, city, state, and ZIP code)*	4b. Tel. No.
	4c. Cell No.
	4d. Fax No.
	4e. e-Mail

5. Full name of national or international labor organization of which it is an affiliate or constituent unit *(to be filled in when charge is filed by a labor organization)*

6. DECLARATION I declare that I have read the above charge and that the statements are true to the best of my knowledge and belief.	Tel. No.
	Office, if any, Cell No.
By _____ _____ *(signature of representative or person making charge)* *(Print/type name and title or office, if any)*	Fax No.
	e-Mail
Address _____ *(date)*	

WILLFUL FALSE STATEMENTS ON THIS CHARGE CAN BE PUNISHED BY FINE AND IMPRISONMENT (U.S. CODE, TITLE 18, SECTION 1001)

PRIVACY ACT STATEMENT

Solicitation of the information on this form is authorized by the National Labor Relations Act (NLRA), 29 U.S.C. § 151 *et seq.* The principal use of the information is to assist the National Labor Relations Board (NLRB) in processing unfair labor practice and related proceedings or litigation. The routine uses for the information are fully set forth in the Federal Register, 71 Fed. Reg. 74942-43 (Dec. 13, 2006). The NLRB will further explain these uses upon request. Disclosure of this information to the NLRB is voluntary; however, failure to supply the information will cause the NLRB to decline to invoke its processes.

INTERNET
FORM NLRB-508
(2-08)

FORM EXEMPT UNDER 44 U.S.C 3512

UNITED STATES OF AMERICA
NATIONAL LABOR RELATIONS BOARD
**CHARGE AGAINST LABOR ORGANIZATION
OR ITS AGENTS**

DO NOT WRITE IN THIS SPACE	
Case	Date Filed

INSTRUCTIONS: File an original with NLRB Regional Director for the region in which the alleged unfair labor practice occurred or is occurring.

1. LABOR ORGANIZATION OR ITS AGENTS AGAINST WHICH CHARGE IS BROUGHT

a. Name	b. Union Representative to contact	
c. Address (Street, city, state, and ZIP code)	d. Tel. No.	e. Cell No.
	f. Fax No.	g. e-Mail

h. The above-named organization(s) or its agents has (have) engaged in and is (are) engaging in unfair labor practices within the meaning of section 8(b), subsection(s) (list subsections) _____ of the National Labor Relations Act, and these unfair labor practices are unfair practices affecting commerce within the meaning of the Act, or these unfair labor practices are unfair practices affecting commerce within the meaning of the Act and the Postal Reorganization Act.

2. Basis of the Charge (set forth a clear and concise statement of the facts constituting the alleged unfair labor practices)

3. Name of Employer	4a. Tel. No.	b. Cell No.
	c. Fax No.	d. e-Mail

5. Location of plant involved (street, city, state and ZIP code)	6. Employer representative to contact

7. Type of establishment (factory, mine, wholesaler, etc.)	8. Identify principal product or service	9. Number of workers employed

10. Full name of party filing charge	11a. Tel. No.	b. Cell No.
	c. Fax No.	d. e-Mail

11. Address of party filing charge (street, city, state and ZIP code)	

12. DECLARATION
I declare that I have read the above charge and that the statements therein are true to the best of my knowledge and belief.

By _____   _____
(signature of representative or person making charge)   (Print/type name and title or office, if any)

Tel. No.
Cell No.
Fax No.
e-Mail

Address _____ (date) _____

WILLFUL FALSE STATEMENTS ON THIS CHARGE CAN BE PUNISHED BY FINE AND IMPRISONMENT (U.S. CODE, TITLE 18, SECTION 1001)

PRIVACY ACT STATEMENT

Solicitation of the information on this form is authorized by the National Labor Relations Act (NLRA). 29 U.S.C. § 151 et seq. The principal use of the information is to assist the National Labor Relations Board (NLRB) in processing unfair labor practice and related proceedings or litigation. The routine uses for the information are fully set forth in the Federal Register, 71 Fed. Reg. 74942-43 (Dec. 13, 2006). The NLRB will further explain these uses upon request. Disclosure of this information to the NLRB is voluntary; however, failure to supply the information will cause the NLRB to decline to invoke its processes.

NATIONAL LABOR RELATIONS BOARD

AN AGENCY OF THE UNITED STATES GOVERNMENT

The National Labor Relations Act gives employees these rights:

To engage in self-organization;

To form, join, or help unions;

To bargain collectively through a representative of their own choosing

To act together for collective bargaining or other mutual aid or protection;

To refrain from all of these things.

WE WILL NOT promulgate, maintain or enforce a rule which prohibits employees from posting pro-Union literature on Company bulletin boards without permission.

WE WILL NOT threaten employees with discipline for violating such a rule.

WE WILL NOT promulgate, maintain or enforce a rule which prohibits the distribution of materials related to union or other activity by Section 7 of the National Labor Relations Act in nonwork areas without prior approval.

WE WILL NOT interrogate job applicants about their union affiliation, their feelings about working for a non-union employer or whether their past employers were unionized.

WE WILL NOT request employees to report to management if they are harassed by employees who support [Union], or any other labor organization.

WE WILL NOT refer to employees interested in or engaged in union activity as "trouble" and WE WILL NOT threaten to discharge such employees because of their union activities.

WE WILL NOT in any other manner interfere with, restrain or coerce employees in the exercise of the rights guaranteed by Section 7 of the Act.

WE WILL notify our employees, in writing, by memorandum or letter separate from this document, that the rules referred to above are no longer in effect.

WE WILL allow our employees to wear union and/or other buttons, insignia, stickers, writings or other markings on their clothing. We will not allow our employees to put union or other buttons, insignia, stickers, writings or other markings on their hard hats, except for safety and security items specifically required by the Company.

WE WILL amend our rule with respect to hard hats to specify that the only items permitted to be put on the hard hats are safety and security items specifically required by the Company. WE WILL NOT promulgate, maintain or enforce a rule which allows any other items.

<u>XYZ COMPANY, INC.</u>
(Employer)

Dated: _____   By _____
                                           (Representative)   (Title)

THIS IS AN OFFICIAL NOTICE AND MUST NOT BE DEFACED BY ANYONE

This notice must remain posted for 60 consecutive days from the date of posting and must not be altered, defaced, or covered by any other material. Any questions concerning this notice or compliance with its provisions may be directed to the Board's Office.

615 Chestnut Street, One Independence Mall, 7th Floor,
Philadelphia, Pennsylvania 19106 (215) 597-7601

Notice may be posted in a language other than English when commonly spoken by the workforce. In Durham School Services, 360 N.L.R.B. No. 85 (2014), a unanimous five-member Board ordered that in all future cases the notice will include a hyperlink to a copy of the decision on the Board's website. Even if employees cannot use the hyperlink, it will give them an electronic address where they can obtain a copy of the decision for those employees who do not have access to or do not wish to use a computer to obtain an electronic copy of the decision, the notice also will provide an address to which they may write, and a telephone number which they may call, to obtain a printed copy of the decision from the Board's Executive Secretary.

PART ONE

THE EVOLUTION OF LABOR RELATIONS LAWS

II. JURISDICTION, ORGANIZATION AND PROCEDURE OF THE NLRB

A. NLRB JURISDICTION

2. EXCLUDED EMPLOYERS

Page 59. Add the following at the end of section 2:

CHARTER SCHOOLS: A STRAW IN THE WIND?

In *Excalibur Charter School, Inc.*, 366 NLRB No. 49 (2018), the Board affirmed that it had jurisdiction over the charter school before it under the standards defining what is a "political subdivision" discussed in the casebook. However, Chairman Kaplan appended the following footnote:

> Chairman Kaplan notes that even if statutory jurisdiction exists under Sec. 2(2), the Board may nonetheless decline to exercise jurisdiction over charter schools as a class or category of employer, consistent with Sec. 14(c)(1) of the Act. However, the Respondent does not argue that the Board should decline jurisdiction on this basis and, in any event, the Board has expressly rejected declining jurisdiction over charter schools as a class . . . (references omitted). Chairman Kaplan believes this precedent might warrant review by a full five-member Board in a future case.

In Voices for International Business and Education, Inc. v. NLRB, 905 F.3d 770 (5th Cir. 2018), the Fifth Circuit upheld the Board's finding that employing charter school is not a political subdivision of the State of Louisiana and therefore subject to the Act. In so holding, the court emphasized that the charter school and its leadership lack political accountability by design—indeed, one of the central virtues of charter schools is that the lack of political oversight gives them the freedom to innovate. Moreover, the court found the public lacked control over the selection of the school's key policy makers, since its board of directors are selected through a private process not subject to public override.

QUESTION FOR DISCUSSION

On what basis could the determination rest that charter schools' effect "on commerce is not sufficiently substantial to warrant" the Board's exercise of jurisdiction, such being the text of § 14(c)(1)? That they are educational and not commercial in nature? That was the Board's position for many years regarding private colleges and universities. Trustees of Columbia University, 97 NLRB 424 (1951). But it abandoned that rationale forty years ago. Cornell University, 183 NLRB 329 (1970). If the Board were to return to the non-commercial nature of the work being done, what rights would the employees of charter schools have? Would this rationale extend to other private entities that run or replace other public services such as private prisons, or contracted in public parks or hospitals?

3.   EXCLUDED EMPLOYEES

Page 65. Add at the end of the discussion of *FedEx Home Delivery*:

On March 3, 2017, the D.C. Circuit reiterated its prior holding. FedEx Home Delivery v. NLRB, 849 F.3d 1123 (D.C. Cir. 2017). Two years later, in a three-to-one decision in *SuperShuttle DFW, Inc.*, 367 NLRB No. 75 (2019), the Board overruled its 2014 *FedEx* decision and expressed agreement with the D.C. Circuit's approach to the role of entrepreneurial opportunity in the independent contractor analysis. The *SuperShuttle* majority found that the Board's 2014 decision had impermissibly diminished the significance of entrepreneurial opportunity and had revived an "economic dependency" standard that Congress had rejected with the Taft-Hartley amendments of 1947. The majority reiterated that the Board has, over time, shifted the emphasis of its independent-contractor analysis from control to entrepreneurial opportunity as "a principle by which to evaluate the overall effect of the common-law factors on a putative contractor's independence to pursue economic gain." The majority stated that it is not required to apply mechanically the entrepreneurial opportunity principle to each common-law factor in every case, but it is likely to find independent-contractor status when, in light of the particular factual circumstances of the case, the common-law factors demonstrate that the workers are afforded significant entrepreneurial opportunity. Applying the common-law test to the specific facts of the case, the majority found that the SuperShuttle van drivers' ownership of the vehicles, the method of their compensation, and their significant control over their daily work schedules and working conditions provide the them with significant entrepreneurial opportunity. The majority further found that these factors, combined with the absence of supervision and the parties' understanding that the drivers are independent contractors outweigh other factors supporting employee status. In her dissent, Member McFerran disagreed with the majority's overruling of *FedEx*, its description and analysis of Board precedent, and its application of that precedent to the circumstances in this case.

The use of independent contractors instead of employees has economic advantages for business: workers so classified are not protected by a variety of labor protective laws such as the Fair Labor Standards

Act (wage & hour law) and anti-discrimination law, nor are taxes attendant to employment status paid. Consequently, the misclassification of employees as independent contractors has become a significant problem outside the Labor Act. An Administrative Law Judge of the NLRB held that misclassification of employees under the Labor Act is a per se violation of section 8(a)(1) of the Act. The Board has invited *amicus* briefs addressing this question: "Under what circumstances, if any, should the Board deem an employer's act of misclassifying statutory employees as independent contractors a violation of Section 8(a)(1) of the Act?" Volex Express Inc., Case 15–CA–184006, 2018 BL 51451 (Feb. 15, 2018).

Page 66. Add after the second paragraph of Question 4:

As for Uber drivers, the NLRB's General Counsel has now opined, in an advice memorandum addressing several pending cases, that UberX and Uber Black drivers are independent contractors. *See* NLRB Gen. Counsel Advice Memorandum, Uber Technologies Inc., 13–CA–163062 (April 16, 2019). Relying heavily on *SuperShuttle* (*supra*), the GC concluded that the significant amount of entrepreneurial control each driver exercises outweighs other factors that favor of employee status. With regard to UberX drivers, the GC summarized as follows:

> Considering all the common-law factors through "the prism of entrepreneurial opportunity" set forth in *SuperShuttle*, we conclude that UberX drivers were independent contractors. Drivers' virtually complete control of their cars, work schedules, and log-in locations, together with their freedom to work for competitors of Uber, provided them with significant entrepreneurial opportunity. On any given day, at any free moment, UberX drivers could decide how best to serve their economic objectives: by fulfilling ride requests through the App, working for a competing rideshare service, or pursuing a different venture altogether. The surge pricing and other financial incentives Uber utilized to meet rider demand not only reflect Uber's "hands off" approach, they also constituted a further entrepreneurial opportunity for drivers. Although Uber limited drivers' selection of trips, established fares, and exercised less significant forms of control, overall UberX drivers operated with a level of entrepreneurial freedom consistent with independent-contractor status. In addition, drivers' lack of supervision, significant capital investments in their work, and their understanding that they were independent contractors also weigh heavily in favor of that status. Although Uber retained portions of drivers' fares under a commission-based system that may usually support employee status, that factor is neutral here because Uber's business model avoids the control of drivers traditionally associated with such systems and affords drivers significant entrepreneurial opportunity. The other factors supporting employee status—the skill required and our assumption that

drivers operated as part of Uber's regular business, and not in a distinct business or occupation—are also of lesser importance in this factual context. Accordingly, we conclude that UberX drivers were independent contractors.

Id. at 14 (footnotes omitted). The GC went on to conclude that UberBlack drivers also are independent contractors because they operate almost exactly like UberX drivers, and the minor differences weigh in favor of independent contractor status.

Do you agree with the GC's conclusions? While it is true that the drivers are free to choose among trips based on time, location, customer rating, and financial incentives (surge pricing, etc.), Uber, not the drivers, establishes these choices. Perhaps most importantly, all financial aspects—pricing and commissions—except for customer tips are controlled and subject to change by Uber. Is this kind of arrangement really one that reflects genuine entrepreneurial freedom?

Page 72. Add at the end of *Medical residents and graduate assistants*:

In Columbia University, 364 N.L.R.B. No. 40 (2016), the Board decided by vote of three to one to overrule *Brown University* and held that student assistants who have a common-law employment relationship with their university are statutory employees within the meaning of the Labor Act. Although the broader effects of the decision remain to be seen, it has obvious implications for organizing campaigns at other private universities, which appear to be on the rise.

Page 72. Add at the end of *Students on Athletic Scholarships*:

In early 2017, the NLRB General Counsel issued a "Report on the Statutory Rights of University Faculty and Students in the Unfair Labor Practice Context," reviewing the law under these headings. NLRB Gen Counsel Memorandum 17–01 (Jan. 31, 2017). With respect to "scholarship football players at Northwestern and other Division 1 FBS private colleges and universities," the General Counsel opined that that office will consider them to be statutory employees regardless of whether the Board will certify a bargaining unit. Thus, they would have the section 7 right to "advocate for greater protections against concussive head trauma and unsafe practice methods, reform NCAA rules so that football players can share in the profit derived from their talents, or self-organize."

B. NLRB ORGANIZATION AND PROCEDURE

Page 81. Add to end of section on Unfair labor practice cases

It is worth noting that, while the number of ULP cases has declined fairly steadily over the last two decades, this decline has accelerated since President Trump took office. According to one news account, the 11% drop under the current administration is due at least in part to unions' reluctance to seek charges under the Republican-controlled board. They fear both adverse outcomes and the establishment of new precedents that will adversely affect worker rights in the future. *See* Andrew Wallender and Hassan A. Kanu, *Trump's Labor Board Has Unions Shelving Complaints*, BLOOMBERG LAW NEWS (May 10, 2019).

Page 87. Add at end of discussion of "New Election Rules":

The Fifth Circuit affirmed the trial court. It found the new election rules to be consistent with the Labor Act and the Administrative Procedure Act. Associated Builders and Contractors of Texas, Inc. v. NLRB, 826 F.3d 215 (5th Cir. 2016).

According to one study, the new election new rules have expedited elections—most of which were stipulated to—but have not significantly affected the outcome.

Union Election Timelines

	2014–2015 (before new rules)	2016–2017 (after new rules)
Median days to election	39	24
No. of petitions filed	2,677	2,302
No. of elections held	1,502	1,542
Elections held in 2 weeks or less	6	62
Labor win rate	66.6%	66.9%

Source: Reported in DLR No. 83 (May 2, 2017) at p. AA–3

On the other hand, it was reported that unions did have a higher win rate in elections held within two weeks or less, although the precise figure was not given.

On December 7, 2018, the NLRB issued its Strategic Plan for FY2019–FY2022, which is required under the Government Performance and Results Act of 2010. *See* NLRB Gen. Counsel Memorandum 19–02 (December 7, 2018). The Plan first provides an overview of the NLRB and data on FY2018, including that it received over 20,000 new cases that year: 18,870 involving unfair labor practice charges and 2,090 representation petitions. The Strategic Plan then identifies and discusses four mission-related goals: (1) achieving a collective 20% increase (5% over each of four years) in timeliness in case processing of unfair labor practice charges, (2) achieving resolution of a greater number of representation cases within 100 days of the filing of an election petition, (3) achieving organizational excellence and productivity, and (4) managing agency resources efficiently and in a manner that instills public trust. To meet these goals, the plan offers some specific objectives, but also acknowledges that some factors—budget, case filings, and case settlements—are not entirely within its control.

PART TWO

THE ESTABLISHMENT OF THE COLLECTIVE BARGAINING RELATIONSHIP

I. PROTECTION OF THE RIGHT OF SELF-ORGANIZATION

A. INTERFERENCE, RESTRAINT AND COERCION

1. RESTRICTIONS ON SOLICITATION AND DISTRIBUTION

Page 97. Add at end of Problem 6:

Compare Boch Imports, Inc. v. NLRB, 826 F.3d 558 (1st Cir. 2016).

Page 97. Add to Problem 7:

May a fast-food chain apply a "no pins" rule in its dress code to forbid workers from displaying a "Fight for $15" button? The button is about the size of a quarter. It shows a "$15" imposed on a raised fist. It is part of a national campaign for a higher minimum wage. The employer argues that its rule is necessary to protect its corporate image and assure food safety. In-N-Out Burger, Inc. v. NLRB, 894 F.3d 707 (5th Cir. 2018). If the Board holds that the employer must allow the button to be worn would this "compel[ ] the employer to endorse and/or subsidize a pro-union message"? Petition for Writ of Certiorari in In-N-Out Burger, Inc. v. NLRB, U.S. Sup. Ct. No. 18–340 (Sept. 11, 2018).

Page 105. Add before "A Note on Company Rules":

4. Suppose an employee refuses to sign a confidentiality agreement that is facially unlawful because it expressly prohibits protected concerted activity, such as barring the employee from discussing the terms of employment (including compensation) with other employees. Does the employer violate Section 8(a)(1) by terminating the employee for such a refusal even in the absence of proof that the employee engaged or attempted to engage in concerted activity? *See* NLRB v. Long Island Ass'n for Aids Care, Inc., 870 F.3d 82 (2d Cir. 2017).

The Boeing Company
365 NLRB No. 154 (2017).

■ By CHAIRMAN MISCIMARRA and MEMBERS PEARCE, McFERRAN, KAPLAN, and EMANUEL.

This case involves the legality of an employer policy, which is one of a multitude of work rules, policies and employee handbook provisions that have been reviewed by the Board using a test set forth in *Lutheran*

Heritage Village-Livonia[, 343 NLRB 646 (2004) (*Lutheran Heritage*).] In this case, the issue is whether Respondent's mere maintenance of a facially neutral rule is unlawful under the *Lutheran Heritage* "reasonably construe" standard, which is also sometimes called *Lutheran Heritage* "prong one" (because it is the first prong of a three-prong standard in *Lutheran Heritage*). Thus, in *Lutheran Heritage*, the Board stated:

> [O]ur inquiry into whether the maintenance of a challenged rule is unlawful begins with the issue of whether the rule explicitly restricts activities protected by Section 7. If it does, we will find the rule unlawful. If the rule does not explicitly restrict activity protected by Section 7, the violation is dependent upon a showing of one of the following: (1) *employees would reasonably construe the language to prohibit Section 7 activity*; (2) the rule was promulgated in response to union activity; or (3) the rule has been applied to restrict the exercise of Section 7 rights.

Most of the cases decided under *Lutheran Heritage* have involved the *Lutheran Heritage* "reasonably construe" standard, which the judge relied upon in the instant case. Specifically, the judge ruled that Respondent . . . maintained a no-camera rule that constituted unlawful interference with the exercise of protected rights in violation of Section 8(a)(1) of the National Labor Relations Act (NLRA or Act).

. . . . Boeing maintains a policy restricting the use of camera-enabled devices such as cell phones on its property. For convenience, we refer to this policy . . . as the "no-camera rule." Boeing's no-camera rule does not explicitly restrict activity protected by Section 7 of the Act, it was not adopted in response to NLRA-protected activity, and it has not been applied to restrict such activity. Nevertheless, applying prong one of the test set forth in *Lutheran Heritage*, the judge found that Boeing's maintenance of this rule violated Section 8(a)(1) of the Act. Based on *Lutheran Heritage*, the judge reasoned that maintenance of Boeing's no-camera rule was unlawful because employees "would reasonably construe" the rule to prohibit Section 7 activity. In finding the no-camera rule unlawful, the judge gave no weight to Boeing's security needs for the rule.

The judge's decision in this case exposes fundamental problems with the Board's application of *Lutheran Heritage* when evaluating the maintenance of work rules, policies and employee handbook provisions. For the reasons set forth below, we have decided to overrule the *Lutheran Heritage* "reasonably construe" standard. . . .

I.   BACKGROUND

For decades, Boeing has had rules in place restricting the use of cameras to capture images or videos on Boeing property. . . . The current version of Boeing's "camera rule" . . . provides in relevant part as follows:

> Possession of the following camera-enabled devices is permitted on all company property and locations, except as restricted by

government regulation, contract requirements or by increased local security requirements.

However, use of [*inter alia*, personal digital assistants, cell phones, iPod/MPS devices, laptop or personal computers with web cameras, and bar code scanners and readers] to capture images or video is prohibited without a valid business need and an approved Camera Permit that has been reviewed and approved by Security. . . .

Boeing's no-camera rule defines "business need" as "a determination made by the authorizing manager that images or video are needed for a contractual requirement, training, technical manuals, advertising, technical analysis, or other purpose that provides a positive benefit to the company." Id. Boeing's no-camera rule applies to "all Boeing." [According to Boeing's testimony, the rule's purposes are as follows:]

First, Boeing's no-camera rule is an integral component of Boeing's security protocols, which are necessary to maintain Boeing's accreditation as a federal contractor to perform classified work for the United States Government.

Second, Boeing's no-camera rule plays a key role in ensuring that Boeing complies with its federally mandated duty to prevent the disclosure of export-controlled information or the exposure of export-controlled materials to unauthorized persons.

Third, Boeing's no-camera rule helps prevent the disclosure of Boeing's proprietary information . . . such as "manufacturing methods and processes" and "material usage."

Fourth, Boeing's no-camera rule limits the risk that employees' personally identifiable information will be released. . . . In addition, if a photograph shows an employee's badge, that image could be used to create a counterfeit badge that an unauthorized person may use to gain entry to Boeing property.

Fifth and finally, Boeing's no-camera rule limits the risk of Boeing becoming a target of terrorist attack. Harris testified that Boeing has "documented evidence" of surveillance by potentially hostile actors "to determine vulnerabilities" on Boeing property, and "[u]ncontrolled photography" could inadvertently disclose such vulnerabilities. . . .

Camera use has occasionally occurred in Boeing facilities in circumstances where Boeing has addressed the above concerns in various ways. . . . Although Boeing does not search tour participants for camera-enabled devices, and tour guides do not confiscate personal camera-enabled devices from individuals who may have used them during a tour, . . . tour participants are briefed beforehand regarding what is and is not permitted during the tour, and Boeing security personnel review tour participants' photos and video footage afterwards. [Boeing produced a time-lapse video of the 777 production line for public release, but it was able to ensure that the video did not reveal confidential or proprietary information and was safe to release to the public.]

The judge rejected Boeing's justifications for its restrictions on the use of camera-enabled devices on Boeing property. He found those justifications contradicted by Boeing's "contrary practice of allowing free access to its manufacturing processes" by releasing to the public a time-lapse video of the 777 production line and by permitting "unfettered photography" during VIP tours. Applying prong one of *Lutheran Heritage*, the judge found that Boeing violated Section 8(a)(1) of the Act by maintaining its no-camera rule because the judge concluded that employees would reasonably construe the no-camera rule to prohibit Section 7 activity. . . .

II. DISCUSSION

A. *Lutheran Heritage Is Overruled*

. . . For the following reasons, we overrule the *Lutheran Heritage* "reasonably construe" standard.

First, the *Lutheran Heritage* "reasonably construe" standard is contrary to Supreme Court precedent because it does not permit *any* consideration of the legitimate justifications that underlie many policies, rules and handbook provisions. These justifications are often substantial, as illustrated by the instant case. More importantly, the Supreme Court has repeatedly required the Board to take these justifications into account. A five-member Board recognized this in *Lafayette Park Hotel*, where it quoted the Supreme Court's decision in *Republic Aviation v. NLRB* [324 U.S. 793 (1945)] and held:

> Resolution of the issue presented by . . . contested rules of conduct involves "working out an adjustment between the undisputed right of self-organization assured to employees under the Wagner Act and the equally undisputed right of employers to maintain discipline in their establishments. . . . Opportunity to organize and proper discipline are both essential elements in a balanced society."

[326 NLRB 824, 825 (1998) (quoting *Republic Aviation*, 324 U.S. 793, 797–798 (1945)).]

Nor does *Republic Aviation* stand alone. The Supreme Court elsewhere has similarly required the Board to weigh the interests advanced by a particular work requirement or restriction before the Board concludes that its potential adverse impact on employee rights warrants a finding of unlawful interference with NLRA rights. See [*NLRB v. Great Dane Trailers, Inc.*, 388 U.S. 26, 33–34 (1967)] (referring to the Board's "duty to strike the proper balance between . . . asserted business justifications and the invasion of employee rights in light of the Act and its policy"); [*NLRB v. Erie Resistor Corp.*, 373 U.S. 221, 229 (1963)] (referring to the "delicate task" of "weighing the interests of employees in concerted activity against the interest of the employer in operating his business in a particular manner and of balancing . . . the intended consequences upon employee rights against the business ends to be served by the employer's conduct"). . . .

Second, the *Lutheran Heritage* "reasonably construe" standard is contradicted by NLRB case law. For example, the Board has recognized that it is lawful for an employer to adopt no-solicitation rules prohibiting *all* employee solicitation—including union-related solicitation—during working time, and no-distribution rules prohibiting *all* distribution of literature—including union-related literature—in work areas. Employers may also lawfully maintain a no-access rule that prohibits off-duty employees from accessing the interior of the employer's facility and outside work areas, even if they desire access to engage in protected picketing, handbilling, or solicitation. Similarly, employers may lawfully adopt "just cause" provisions and attendance requirements that subject employees to discipline or discharge for failing to come to work, even though employees have a Section 7 right to engage in protected strikes. Each of these rules fails the *Lutheran Heritage* "reasonably construe" test because each one clearly prohibits Section 7 activity. Yet each requirement has been upheld by the Board, based on a determination that legitimate employer interests and justifications outweighed any interference with Section 7 rights.

Third, in many cases involving facially neutral policies, rules and handbook provisions, the Board *has explicitly* balanced employees' Section 7 rights against legitimate employer interests rather than narrowly examining the language of a disputed rule solely for its potential to interfere with the exercise of Section 7 rights, as the *Lutheran Heritage* "reasonably construe" test requires. As noted above, in *Lafayette Park Hotel* the Board expressly acknowledged that "[r]esolution of the issue presented by . . . contested rules of conduct involves 'working out an adjustment between the undisputed right of self-organization assured to employees under the Wagner Act and the equally undisputed right of employers to maintain discipline in their establishments.'' . . . .

Fourth, *Lutheran Heritage* is predicated on false premises that are inconsistent with the Act and contrary to the Board's responsibility to promote certainty, predictability and stability. Several considerations are relevant here:

- Because the Act protects so many potential concerted activities (including the right to refrain from such activities), a wide variety of facially neutral rules can be interpreted, under some hypothetical scenario, as potentially limiting some type of Section 7 activity.

- *Lutheran Heritage* requires employers to eliminate all ambiguities from all policies, rules and handbook provisions that might conceivably touch on some type of Section 7 activity, but this disregards the fact that generalized provisions related to employment—including those relating to discipline and discharge—have been deemed acceptable throughout the Act's history.

. . . .

The broader premise of *Lutheran Heritage*, which is even more seriously flawed, is the notion that employees are better served by *not* having employment policies, rules and handbooks. After all, when parties are held to a standard that cannot be attained, the natural and predictable response is that they will give up trying to create written rules, policies and employee handbooks. . . . This would impose substantial hardship on employers that strive for consistency and fairness when making such decisions, and employees would not know what standards of conduct they must satisfy to keep their jobs. . . .

Fifth, the *Lutheran Heritage* "reasonably construe" test imposes too many restrictions on the Board itself. By making the legality of a rule turn on whether employees would "reasonably construe" its language to prohibit *any* type of Section 7 activity, *Lutheran Heritage* requires a "one-size-fits-all" analysis that gives equal weight to every potential intrusion on Section 7 rights, however slight it might be and however remote the possibility that employees would actually engage in that type of protected activity. The "reasonably construe" test also permits no consideration of the justifications for a particular rule, which in turn prevents the Board from treating some justifications as warranting greater weight than others. . . .

Sixth, when applying the *Lutheran Heritage* "reasonably construe" standard, the Board has not given sufficient consideration to unique characteristics of particular work settings and different industries. . . . The "reasonably construe" standard also prevents the Board from taking into consideration specific events that reveal the importance of a particular policy, rule, or handbook provision. For example, in *William Beaumont Hospital*[, 363 NLRB No. 162 (2016)], a full-term newborn infant had unexpectedly died, and the ensuing investigation of that tragic event showed that the infant's death resulted in part from inadequate communication among the hospital's personnel. In addition, when a highly regarded obstetrics nurse resigned, the hospital learned that two other obstetrics nurses had been mean, nasty, intimidating, negative, and bullying. Id., slip op. at 8 (Member Miscimarra, concurring in part and dissenting in part). These events revealed the importance of the interests served by the hospital's rule against conduct that impedes "harmonious interactions and relationships." Nevertheless, a Board majority in *William Beaumont Hospital*, applying prong one of the *Lutheran Heritage* standard, found this rule unlawful, reasoning that since some inharmonious interactions are protected by the NLRA, employees would reasonably construe the rule to prohibit Section 7 activity. Id., slip op. at 2.

Finally, *Lutheran Heritage* has caused extensive confusion and litigation for employers, unions, employees and the Board itself. The "reasonably construe" standard has defied all reasonable efforts to apply and explain it. Indeed, even with the benefit of hindsight, it is still difficult to understand Board rulings that uphold some facially neutral rules while invalidating others. Taking, for example, a sampling of cases dealing with rules regarding civility in the workplace, it is difficult to view the different outcomes reached by the Board as anything other than arbitrary.

- In *Lafayette Park Hotel*, it was *lawful* to have a rule prohibiting "conduct that does not support the . . . Hotel's goals and objectives," even though this arguably encompassed conduct that did not support the Hotel's goal of remaining nonunion, i.e., union organizing. However, it was deemed unreasonable to assume, without more, that remaining nonunion was one of the goals encompassed by the rule.

- In *Lafayette Park Hotel* . . . it was *unlawful* to maintain a rule prohibiting "false, vicious, profane or malicious statements toward or concerning the . . . [employer] or any of its employees" because such statements could occur in the context of activities protected under Section 7.

- In *Adtranz ABB Daimler-Benz Transportation v. NLRB*, [253 F.3d 19, 27 (D.C. Cir. 2001),] the court found it was *lawful* to have a rule prohibiting "abusive or threatening language to anyone on company premises," which the court found merely required employees to "comply with generally accepted notions of civility." The court deemed this "quite different" from *Lafayette Park Hotel* and a similar Board case, in which the Board found that it was *unlawful* to maintain rules "threatening to punish 'false' statements without evidence of malicious intent."

- In *Lutheran Heritage*, it was *lawful* to maintain rules prohibiting "verbal abuse," "abusive or profane language," and "harassment." Although *Lutheran Heritage* renders unlawful every rule that an employee would "reasonably construe" to prohibit Section 7 activity, the Board stated that a rule would not be unlawful merely because it *could* be interpreted that way."

- In *Palms Hotel & Casino*, [344 NLRB 1363 (2005),] it was *lawful* to have a rule prohibiting "conduct which is . . . injurious, offensive, threatening, intimidating, coercing, or interfering with" other employees because the rule was not "so amorphous that reasonable employees would be incapable of grasping the expectation that they comport themselves with general notions of civility and decorum in the workplace."

- In *Flamingo Hilton-Laughlin*, [330 NLRB 287 (1999),] it was *unlawful* to have a rule prohibiting "loud, abusive or foul language" because this was so broad that it "could reasonably be interpreted as barring lawful union organizing propaganda."

- In *2 Sisters Food Group*, [357 NLRB 1816 (2011),] it was *unlawful* to maintain a rule subjecting employees to discipline for "inability or unwillingness to work harmoniously with other employees" because the employer did not "define what it means to 'work harmoniously' (or to fail to do so)," and the rule was "sufficiently imprecise that it could encompass any disagreement or conflict among employees, including those related to discussions and interactions protected by Section 7."

- In *The Roomstore*, [357 NLRB 1690 (2011),] it was *unlawful* to maintain a rule prohibiting "[a]ny type of negative energy or attitudes." Similarly, in *Claremont Resort & Spa*, it was *unlawful* to maintain a rule prohibiting "[n]egative conversations about associates and/or managers" because the employer did not "clarif[y] any potential ambiguities in its rule by providing examples."

. . . .

These examples reveal that to a substantial degree, the *Lutheran Heritage* "reasonably construe" standard has led to arbitrary results. . . .

B. The New Standard Governing Maintenance of Facially Neutral Rules, Employment Policies, and Employee Handbook Provisions

In cases in which one or more facially neutral policies, rules, or handbook provisions are at issue that, when reasonably interpreted, would potentially interfere with Section 7 rights, the Board will evaluate two things: (i) the nature and extent of the potential impact on NLRA rights, *and* (ii) legitimate justifications associated with the requirement(s). [W]e emphasize that *the Board* will conduct this evaluation, consistent with the Board's "duty to strike the *proper balance* between . . . asserted business justifications and the invasion of employee rights in light of the Act and its policy."

When engaging in the above analysis, the Board will place particular emphasis on the following considerations.

First, this is an area where the Board has a special responsibility to give parties certainty and clarity. Most work rules, employment policies, and employee handbook provisions exist for the purpose of permitting employees to understand what their employer expects and requires. Therefore, the chaos that has reigned in this area has been visited most heavily on employees themselves. In the best case, under *Lutheran Heritage* nobody (not even Board members themselves) can reliably predict what rules are permissible and what rules are unlawful under the NLRA. In the worst case, employees may be subjected to intimidation, profanity, harassment, or even workplace violence because their employers rightfully believe the NLRB is likely to overturn reasonable standards regarding respect and civility in the workplace, or such standards will be upheld only after many years of NLRB litigation. Henceforth, consistent with the Board's responsibility to interpret the Act, we will engage in the above analysis and we will delineate three categories of employment policies, rules and handbook provisions:

- *Category 1* will include rules that the Board designates as *lawful* to maintain, either because (i) the rule, when reasonably interpreted, does not prohibit or interfere with the exercise of NLRA rights; or (ii) the potential adverse impact on protected rights is outweighed by justifications associated with the rule. Examples of Category 1 rules are the no-camera requirement in this case, the "harmonious interactions and relationships" rule that was at issue in *William Beaumont Hospital*, and other rules requiring employees to abide by basic standards of civility.

- *Category 2* will include rules that warrant individualized scrutiny in each case as to whether the rule, when reasonably interpreted, would prohibit or interfere with the exercise of NLRA rights, and if so, whether any adverse impact on NLRA-protected conduct is outweighed by legitimate justifications.

- *Category 3* will include rules that the Board will designate as *unlawful* to maintain because they would prohibit or limit NLRA-protected conduct, and the adverse impact on NLRA rights is not outweighed by justifications associated with the rule. An example would be a rule that prohibits employees from discussing wages or benefits with one another.

... [T]he above three categories will represent a classification of results from the Board's application of the new test. The categories are not part of the test itself. The Board will determine, in future cases, what types of additional rules fall into which category. Although the legality of some rules will turn on the particular facts in a given case, we believe adherence to the analysis we announce here will ultimately provide far greater clarity and certainty to employees, employers and unions regarding whether and to what extent different types of rules may lawfully be maintained. Although the Board's cumulative experience with certain types of rules may prompt the Board to re-designate particular types of rules from one category to another, one can expect such circumstances to be relatively rare.

Second, when deciding cases in this area, the Board may differentiate among different types of NLRA-protected activities (some of which might be deemed central to the Act and others more peripheral), and the Board must recognize those instances where the risk of intruding on NLRA rights is "comparatively slight." Similarly, the Board may distinguish between substantial justifications—those that have direct, immediate relevance to employees or the business—and others that might be regarded as having more peripheral importance. In some instances, the impact of a particular rule on NLRA rights may be self-evident, or the justifications associated with particular rules may be apparent from the rule itself or the Board's experience with particular types of workplace issues. Parties may also introduce evidence regarding a particular rule's impact on protected rights or the work-related justifications for the rule. The Board may also draw reasonable distinctions between or among different industries and work settings. We may also take into consideration particular events that may shed light on the purpose or purposes served by a challenged rule or on the impact of its maintenance on protected rights.

Third, when a facially neutral rule, reasonably interpreted, would *not* prohibit or interfere with the exercise of NLRA rights, maintenance of the rule is lawful without any need to evaluate or balance business justifications, and the Board's inquiry into maintenance of the rule comes to an end. . . . Conversely, when a rule, reasonably interpreted, *would* prohibit or interfere with the exercise of NLRA rights, the mere existence of some plausible business justification will not automatically render the rule lawful. Again, the Board must carefully evaluate the nature and extent of a rule's adverse impact on NLRA rights, in addition to potential justifications, and the rule's maintenance will violate Section 8(a)(1) if the Board determines that the justifications are outweighed by the adverse impact on rights protected by Section 7.

Fourth, when the Board interprets any rule's impact on employees, the focus should rightfully be on the employees' perspective. This is consistent with established Board and court case law, and it is especially important when evaluating questions regarding alleged interference with protected rights in violation of Section 8(a)(1). As the Board stated in *Cooper Thermometer Co.*, 154 NLRB 502, 503 fn. 2 (1965), Section 8(a)(1) legality turns on "whether the employer engaged in conduct, which, it may reasonably be said, *tends to interfere with the free exercise of employee rights under the Act*" (emphasis added).

Fifth . . . the Board may find that an employer may lawfully *maintain* a particular rule, notwithstanding some possible impact on a type of protected Section 7 activity, even though the rule cannot lawfully be *applied* against employees who engage in NLRA-protected conduct. For example, if the Board finds that an employer lawfully maintained a "courtesy and respect" rule, but the employer invokes the rule when imposing discipline on employees who engage in a work-related dispute that is protected by Section 7 of the Act, we may find that the discipline constituted unlawful interference with the exercise of protected rights in violation of Section 8(a)(1).

C. *Retroactive Application of the New Standard*

[The Board found it appropriate to apply the standard it announced retroactively to the instant case and to all other pending cases.]

D. Application of the New Standard to Boeing's No-Camera Rule

To determine the lawfulness of Boeing's no-camera rule under the standard we adopt today, the Board must determine whether the no-camera rule, when reasonably interpreted, would potentially interfere with the exercise of Section 7 rights, and if so, the Board must evaluate two things: (i) the nature and extent of the no-camera rule's adverse impact on Section 7 rights, *and* (ii) the legitimate business justifications associated with the no-camera rule. Based on our review of the record and our evaluation of the considerations described above, we find that the no-camera rule in some circumstances may potentially affect the exercise of Section 7 rights, but this adverse impact is comparatively slight. We also find that the adverse impact is outweighed by substantial and important justifications associated with Boeing's maintenance of the no-camera rule. Accordingly, we find that Boeing's maintenance of its no-camera rule does not constitute unlawful interference with protected rights in violation of Section 8(a)(1) of the Act. Although the justifications associated with Boeing's no-camera rule are especially compelling, we believe that no-camera rules, in general, fall into Category 1, types of rules that the Board will find lawful based on the considerations described above.

. . . .

E. Response to the Dissents

. . . .

First, our dissenting colleagues argue against our abandonment of *Lutheran Heritage* based on the mistaken premise that the Board, prospectively, will never declare unlawful the maintenance of work rules that interfere with the exercise of Section 7 rights. Under the standard adopted today, the Board will continue to carefully evaluate the Section 8(a)(1) legality of work rules alleged to be unlawful. . . . Moreover, even when the Board concludes that a challenged rule was lawfully maintained, the Board will independently evaluate situations where, in reliance on the rule, an employer disciplines an employee who has engaged in NLRA-protected activity; and the Board may conclude that the discipline violated Section 8(a)(1) even though the rule's maintenance was lawful. . . .

Second, our colleagues' adherence to *Lutheran Heritage*'s "reasonably construe" standard prompts them to focus on a challenged rule's potential effect on the exercise of Section 7 rights to the exclusion of everything else. In this regard, the dissenting opinions reflect stereotypes regarding workplace conduct and protected activity that fail to adequately address problems have become more prominent in recent years—indeed, in recent weeks. . . . Without question, the NLRA confers vitally important protection on employees by giving them the right to engage in, and refrain from, concerted activities undertaken for the purpose of mutual aid or protection. However, nobody can doubt that employees have equivalent rights—guaranteed by federal, state, and local laws and regulations—to have protection from unlawful workplace harassment and discrimination based on sex, race, national origin, age, disability and numerous other impermissible considerations; protection from workplace assaults and life-threatening violence; and protection from workplace fatalities, accidents and injuries caused by inappropriate employee conduct. Employers have an obligation to maintain work rules and policies to assure these rights. The Board's past decisions have disregarded entirely the overwhelming number of employees and others whose interests are *protected* by rules that the Board has invalidated based on *Lutheran Heritage*. . . .

Third, there is no merit in our dissenting colleagues' protest that we cannot or should not overrule *Lutheran Heritage* in this case without inviting *amicus* briefing, nor is there merit in their contention that the Board is required to engage in rulemaking regarding the issues addressed in today's decision. . . .

We likewise reject any suggestion that the Board lacks authority to resolve issues based on a legal standard that has not been expressly raised the parties. . . .

[The dissent of Member Pearce is omitted.]

■ MEMBER MCFERRAN, dissenting in part.

The Board's approach to employer work rules is worth getting right. Those rules are virtually everywhere, and they surely affect nearly every employee and employer covered by the National Labor Relations Act. For more than 13 years, the Board has applied the analytical framework adopted in *Lutheran Heritage* for assessing whether challenged work rules would reasonably tend to chill employees in the exercise of their Section 7 rights. Even though no court has ever rejected this test, despite many opportunities, it is not surprising that a newly-constituted majority is nonetheless revisiting precedent. What *is* surprising is the arbitrary and capricious process the majority has followed in its rush to replace the current test and the alarmingly flawed result of that process.

No party and no participant in this case—which involves a single, no-photography rule—has asked the Board to overrule *Lutheran Heritage*. Nor has the Board asked anyone whether it should. Over the minority's objection, the Board majority has refused to notify the public that it was contemplating a break with established precedent. It has refused to invite amicus briefing from interested persons, even though this has become the Board's wise norm in the years following *Lutheran Heritage*. Without the benefit of briefs from the parties or the public, the majority invents a comprehensive new approach to work rules that goes far beyond any issue presented in this case and, indeed, beyond the scope of *Lutheran Heritage* itself. This is secret rulemaking in the guise of adjudication, an abuse of the administrative process that leaves Board law not better, but demonstrably worse: The majority has devised a new test that is more complicated, more unpredictable, and much less protective of the statutory rights of employees than the standard it replaces. Indeed, it simply fails to address the labor-law problem before the Board: that employees may be chilled from exercising their statutory rights by overbroad employer rules.

I.

. . . .The judge correctly held that Boeing's rule was unlawfully overbroad under the controlling test. In short, Boeing's rule is closer to the no-photography and/or no-recording rules that the Board has struck down than it is to the rule that the Board has upheld. Of course, Boeing and amicus National Association of Manufacturers disagree on the correct result here under *Lutheran Heritage* and the Board's relevant precedent applying that standard. But what no party to this case has argued is that the Board should or must reverse *Lutheran Heritage* and apply some new test. The majority overrules precedent entirely on its own initiative. That step is suspect—as is the process followed by the majority.

The Board is certainly not responding to the invitation or the order of a federal appellate court. No court has rejected the *Lutheran Heritage* test in the 13 years since it was decided. . . .

It is not the case, in turn, that the Board has somehow failed to consider and address criticisms of *Lutheran Heritage*. Only last year, the Board carefully explained why the dissenting view of then-Member Miscimarra was unpersuasive. *William Beaumont Hospital*, 363 NLRB No. 162, slip op. at 3–6 (2016). Today's majority opinion is based on that dissent, with all of its demonstrated flaws. . . .

Of course, the Board has a new majority. But the change in the composition of the Board is not a reason for us to revisit our earlier decisions—as the Board itself has held, repeatedly, since the mid-1950's.

Just as troubling as the majority's decision to reverse precedent sua sponte is the manner in which it has proceeded to that result. In an unexplained and unwarranted break with the Board's practice of the last several years, the majority has refused to notify the public and the parties that a reversal of *Lutheran Heritage* was under consideration and has refused to solicit briefs from the parties and the public. . . . Since at least the 1950's, the Board has solicited briefing in some major cases. In the last decade, this has become the Board's routine practice in significant cases, particularly those where the Board is contemplating reversal of longstanding precedent.

In refusing to seek briefs, the Board has deprived itself of the benefits of public participation in agency policymaking. And it has done so arbitrarily. . . .

Today's decision—although it was reached entirely without public participation—looks very much like rulemaking, not adjudication. The Board majority does not decide the rules issue actually presented by the parties in this case—the legality of Boeing's no-photography policy under *Lutheran Heritage*—but instead adopts a comprehensive new approach to rules issues generally and even designates two particular *categories* of rules ("no-camera" rules perhaps and "rules requiring employees to abide by basic standards of civility" for sure) as always "lawful to maintain," regardless of the context or the circumstances presented. To be clear, no "civility" rule whatsoever is at issue in this case. In the process, the majority overrules not just *Lutheran Heritage*, but also [*Rio All-Suites Hotel & Casino*, 362 NLRB No. 190 (2015),] involving a no-photography rule, and the Board's 2016 decision in *William Beaumont Hospital*, supra, as well as all prior decisions (unidentified) in which the Board "has held that it violates the Act to maintain rules requiring employees to foster 'harmonious interactions and relationships' or to maintain basic standards of civility in the workplace."

The scope of today's decision demonstrates that the Board is going far beyond the adjudication of a single case. It is making policy and reaching more broadly even than *Lutheran Heritage* did. At the same time, the Board has deliberately and arbitrarily excluded the public from participating in the policymaking process. . . .

II.

The arbitrary process followed by the majority has led, not surprisingly, to an arbitrary result. The majority reverses and replaces *Lutheran Heritage* based on a fundamental, even willful, misunderstanding of the labor-law problem that the *Lutheran Heritage* doctrine is intended to address. That misunderstanding is reflected in the majority's persistent mischaracterization of *Lutheran Heritage* and its progeny—in the face of judicial authority—and it results in a "solution" that creates significant challenges in interpretation and implementation while leaving the key statutory consideration facing the Board largely unaddressed. . . .

A.

The problem before the Board is how to address the fact that some work rules maintained by employers will discourage employees subject to the rules from engaging in activity that is protected by the National Labor Relations Act. An employee who may be disciplined or discharged for violating a work rule may well choose not to do so—whether or not a federal statute guarantees her right to act contrary to her employer's dictates. Not surprisingly, then, it is well established (as the *Lutheran Heritage* Board observed) "that an employer violates Section 8(a)(1) when it maintains a work rule that reasonably tends to chill employees in the exercise of their Section 7 rights." 343 NLRB at 646, citing *Lafayette Park Hotel*, 326 NLRB 824, 825 (1998). The aspect of the *Lutheran Heritage* test that the majority attacks is its approach to a subset of employer work rules that do "not explicitly restrict activity protected by Section 7" of the Act, were not "promulgated in response to union activity," and have not been "applied to restrict the exercise of Section 7 rights." 343 NLRB at

647. For such rules, the *Lutheran Heritage* Board explained, the "violation is dependent upon a showing . . . [that] employees would reasonably construe the language to prohibit Section 7 activity." Id.

Thirteen years after this standard was adopted, the majority belatedly concludes that the Board was not permitted to do so, insisting that the "*Lutheran Heritage* 'reasonably construe' standard is contrary to Supreme Court precedent because it does not permit *any* consideration of the legitimate justifications that underlie many policies, rules and handbook provisions." This premise is simply false.

The Board has never held that legitimate business justifications for employer work rules may not be considered—to the contrary. As the Board recently explained in *William Beaumont*, supra, responding to then-Member Miscimarra's dissent, the claim made by the majority here:

> reflects a fundamental misunderstanding of the Board's task in evaluating rules that are alleged to be unlawfully *overbroad*. . . .
>
> [T]he appropriate inquiry is whether the rules would reasonably tend to chill employees in the exercise of their Section 7 rights.
>
> That a particular rule threatens to have a chilling effect does not mean, however, that an employer may not address the subject matter of the rule and protect his legitimate business interests. Where the Board finds a rule unlawfully overbroad, the employer is free to adopt a more narrowly tailored rule that does not infringe on Section 7 rights. . . .
>
> When, in contrast, the Board finds that a rule is *not* overbroad— that employees would not "reasonably construe the language to prohibit Section 7 activity" (in the *Lutheran Heritage Village* formulation)—it is typically because the rule is tailored such that the employer's legitimate business interest in maintaining the rule will be sufficiently apparent to a reasonable employee . . . . [citing *First Transit, Inc.*, 360 NLRB 619, 620–621 (2014).] Here, too, the *Lutheran Heritage Village* standard demonstrably does take into account employer interests.

363 NLRB No. 162, slip op. at 4 (emphasis in original; quotation marks and footnotes omitted).

No court, meanwhile, has ever understood *Lutheran Heritage*, as the majority does, to prohibit the Board from considering an employer's legitimate business interests. . . .

Oddly, the majority follows up its claim that *Lutheran Heritage* prohibits the Board from considering an employer's legitimate interests by asserting that "in many cases involving facially neutral policies, rules and handbook provisions, the Board *has explicitly* balanced employees' Section 7 rights against legitimate employer interests rather than narrowly examining the language of a disputed rule solely for its potential to interfere with the exercise of Section 7 rights, as the

Lutheran Heritage 'reasonably construe' test requires." Of course, the cited cases—including a decision applying *Lutheran Heritage* to uphold a no-photography rule (*Flagstaff Medical Center*, supra)—simply demonstrate that *Lutheran Heritage* does not impose the prohibition that the majority attributes to it. *Lutheran Heritage*, by its terms, does not preclude the Board from considering employer interests. . . .

The majority's mischaracterization of *Lutheran Heritage* is enough to demonstrate that its reconsideration of the decision is arbitrary and capricious. Before an agency changes a policy, it surely must have a reasonable understanding of what its prior policy actually is.

Apart from the matter of employer interests, however, the majority attributes to *Lutheran Heritage* other features that are simply conjured up. According to the majority, *Lutheran Heritage* "requires employers to eliminate all ambiguities from all policies, rules and handbook provisions that might conceivably touch on some type of Section 7 activity." But the *Lutheran Heritage* Board rejected precisely [this] notion . . . . According to the majority, "[a]nother false premise of *Lutheran Heritage* is the notion that employers drafting facially neutral policies, rules and handbook provisions *can* anticipate and avoid all potential interpretations that may conflict with NLRA-protected activities." But *Lutheran Heritage* actually says just the opposite, observing that "[w]ork rules are necessarily general in nature and are typically drafted by and for laymen, not experts in the field of labor law." Id. at 648. Finally, the majority insists that the "broader premise of *Lutheran Heritage* . . . is the notion that employees are better served by *not* having employment policies, rules and handbooks." There is no support at all for this claim— and certainly no support for the claim that *Lutheran Heritage* has in any way caused employers to abandon, or fail to adopt, any lawful policy, rule, or handbook. . . .

B.

In addition to fundamentally mischaracterizing the *Lutheran Heritage* test itself, the majority attacks the way the test has been applied, taking the language of particular work rules out of context and then insisting that the Board's case law is inconsistent and unpredictable. The *William Beaumont* Board addressed this same charge when it was previously leveled by then-Member Miscimarra:

> Certainly, cases involving allegedly overbroad employer rules and implicating the *Lutheran Heritage Village* standard may raise difficult issues, complicated, too, by the need to harmonize the Board's decisions over time. But this challenge is not a function of the Board's legal standard. Rather, it is inherent in the remarkable number, variety, and detail of employer work rules (and the larger documents in which they appear), drafted with differing degrees of skill and levels of legal sophistication. Already 30 years ago, one legal scholar described the "bureaucratization of work" as having "enmeshe[d] the worker

in a 'web of rules.'' This phenomenon, whatever drives it, is largely out of the Board's hands.

363 NLRB No. 162, slip op. at 5 (footnotes omitted).

The Board's decisions under *Lutheran Heritage*, for all their number and variety, do, in fact, yield clear, guiding principles that allow employers and employees to grasp what sorts of rules are prohibited and what sorts are permitted. The Board has uniformly found that confidentiality rules prohibiting the disclosure of "employee" or "personnel" information, without further clarification, would be reasonably construed by employees to restrict Section 7 activity. The Board has also provided guidelines for employers seeking to address attendance matters and, in so doing, has found that employees would reasonably construe rules prohibiting them from "walking off" the job as unlawfully prohibiting Section 7 strike activity, while they would construe rules that, on their face, only prevent an employee from taking unauthorized leave or breaks and do not expressly restrict concerted activity as being lawful. . . . Even in the often challenging context of so-called civility rules, our precedent establishes that an employer may maintain rules seeking to prevent disparagement, so long as any such rules are focused on its products or services and do not cover disparaging statements more generally such that employees would reasonably construe the prohibition to include matters protected by Section 7. . . And, finally, the Board has long been tolerant of language that seeks to regulate severe or extreme behavior, or conduct which is reasonably associated with actions that fall outside of the Act's protections. . . .

C.

It is hard to know precisely what the majority's new standard for evaluating work rules *is*. The majority opinion is a jurisprudential jumble of factors, considerations, categories, and interpretive principles. To say, as the majority does, that its approach will yield "certainty and clarity" is unbelievable, unless the certainty and clarity intended is that work rules will almost never be found to violate the National Labor Relations Act. Indeed, without even the benefit of prior discussion, the majority reaches out to declare an entire, vaguely-defined category of workplace rules—those "requiring employees to abide by basic standards of civility"—to be always lawful. That today's decision narrows the scope of Section 7 protections for employees is obvious. Put somewhat differently, the majority solves the problem addressed by *Lutheran Heritage*—how to guard against the chilling effect of work rules on the exercise of statutory rights—by deciding it is no real problem at all where a rule does not explicitly restrict those rights and was not adopted in response to Section 7 activity.

1.

To begin, the majority effectively abandons the key premise of *Lutheran Heritage*: that . . . an employer's work rules should be evaluated from the perspective of the employees subject to the rules—and protected by the statute. The majority emphasizes that *the Board* [its emphasis] will conduct this evaluation." One might ask, "Who else would?" But what the majority means is quite clear: going forward, the Board's primary focus will not be on the potential chilling effect of work rules on employees, but rather on the interests of employers in imposing rules on their employees. This new focus—a sharp break from the Board's long-established approach—is unreasonable.

We are dealing here with Section 8(a)(1) of the Act, which makes it an unfair labor practice for an employer "to interfere with, restrain, or coerce employees in the exercise of the rights guaranteed in [Section 7]" of the Act. When the Board evaluates an employer's statements under Section 8(a)(1), it does so " 'from the standpoint of employees over whom the employer has a measure of economic power." ' The Supreme Court itself has made clear that the Board *must* adopt this perspective:

> Any assessment of the precise scope of employer expression, of course, must be made in the context of its labor relations setting. Thus, an employer's rights cannot outweigh the equal rights of the employees to associate freely, as those rights are embodied in [Section] 7 and protected by [Section] 8(a)(1). . . . *And any balancing of those rights must take into account the economic dependence of the employees on their employers, and the necessary tendency of the former, because of that relationship, to pick up intended implications of the latter that might be more readily dismissed by a more disinterested ear.*

NLRB v. Gissel Packing Co., 395 U.S. 575, 617 (1969) (emphasis added). . . .

2.

Coupled with its unwarranted, and impermissible, break from the premise of *Lutheran Heritage* is the majority's false promise of "certainty and clarity." The majority begins by announcing that there are "three categories of employment policies, rules and handbook provisions," essentially the always-lawful, the sometimes-lawful, and the never-lawful. So long as the sometimes-lawful category includes many or most rules, of course, the majority's new framework does very little to create "certainty and clarity"—and that is before taking into account the majority's statement that even these categories are fluid: "[t]he Board's cumulative experience with certain types of rules," the majority observes, "may prompt the Board to re-designate particular types of rules from one category to another." So much for certainty.

What about the sometimes-lawful rules ("Category 2"), which "warrant individualized scrutiny in each case"? Under the majority's new framework, the Board will apply a balancing test that differentiates on the one hand among "different types of NLRA-protected activities (some of which might be deemed central to the Act and others more peripheral)" and, on the other hand, among different "substantial justifications" for work rules, "those that have direct, immediate relevance to employees or the business" versus "others that might be regarded as having more peripheral importance." In this exercise, the Board may consider several factors, including "reasonable distinctions between or among different industries and work settings." To pretend that this ill-defined, multi-factor balancing test will yield "certainty and clarity" is laughable.

The majority offers no hint at all as to precisely which "NLRA-protected activities" are entitled to more weight and which to less weight. Nor, similarly, does it actually identify which particular employer justifications are weightiest. Which industries and which work settings might warrant particular work rules (and which not) is also almost entirely unclear. How, then, are employees to know how the Board's balancing test will come out beforehand, when they are deciding to engage in Section 7 activity that may cost them their jobs, for violating their employer's rule? And, for that matter, how are employers to know whether their work rules will survive the Board's scrutiny and why?

Thirteen years of experience under *Lutheran Heritage*—resulting in some guidance (however imperfect) for employees and employers, as already explained—is now largely discarded. It seems obvious that years of litigation under the Board's *new* approach will be required before employees and employers have even a clue as to what Board law permits and what it prohibits—unless, as suggested, the Board means to give employers far more scope to adopt rules that trench on employees' statutory rights. In that case, there will be certainty, but at the expense of the policies of the National Labor Relations Act.

3.

On that score, consider the majority's holding today that "rules requiring employees to abide by basic standards of civility" are *always* lawful. These are "Category 1" rules, under the majority's new scheme. For these rules, in contrast to "Category 2" rules, it makes absolutely no difference what Section 7 rights are at stake, what justification the employer might offer (or fail to offer), what industry the employer is in, what the "work setting" is, or what "particular events . . . may shed light on the purpose or purposes served by a challenged rule or on the impact of its maintenance on protected rights." Instead, the majority holds that all employers everywhere may always demand that employees "abide by basic standards of civility." That approach—foregoing "individualized scrutiny" altogether—is arbitrary and capricious, particularly as adopted in an adjudication where no such work rule is even before the Board.

First, the majority makes no genuine attempt to *define* the "basic standards of civility." What are those standards—and what are they, in particular, in a workplace setting? . . . Second, the majority seems oblivious to the possibility that common forms of protected concerted activity . . . may reasonably be understood as uncivil. Does walking off the job to protest unsafe working conditions conform to "basic standards of civility"? Or distributing literature that, in impolite language, criticizes an employer's failure to pay employees what they are owed and urges employees to resist? The majority's apparent decision to permit all employers to maintain whatever "civility" rules they wish simply ignores the reality of the labor disputes that can arise in various workplaces and move employees to act to defend themselves—just as federal labor law aims to encourage. With respect to uncivil language, for example, the Supreme Court has observed that "[l]abor disputes are ordinarily heated affairs; the language that is commonplace there might well be deemed actionable per se in some state jurisdictions."

It adds insult to injury for the majority to assert that recognizing the potential for statutorily-protected conflict in the workplace amounts to endorsing "stereotypes regarding workplace conduct and protected activity that fail to adequately address problems [that] have become more prominent in recent years." Nothing in the Board's *Lutheran Heritage* jurisprudence prevents an employer from adopting tailored rules that genuinely serve to protect employees from illegal discrimination or harassment in the workplace—and the majority points to no decision in which the Board has invalidated such a rule. Indeed, in *Lutheran Heritage* itself, the Board upheld a rule prohibiting "[h]arassment of other employees, supervisors and any other individuals in any way." Nothing in the majority's new test, meanwhile, makes it better suited to "address problems [that] have become more prominent in recent years—indeed, in recent weeks"—to the contrary, many aspects of the majority's approach today could have precisely the opposite effect. Categorically approving any and all rules that permit discipline or termination for violating norms of "civility" is the most obvious example. Workers facing harassment or assault often have to act "uncivilly" to protect their safety and their rights. Knowing that their employer has promulgated a workplace rule to make it crystal clear that raising a fuss can be a fireable offense hardly makes it easier on victims reluctant to speak up about assault or harassment.

> . . . .

The majority suggests that maintaining the sort of "civility" rules that it champions (as opposed to clearly lawful rules directly prohibiting harassment or assault) will foster a workplace where employees are less likely to experience discrimination, harassment, or violence. I would suggest instead that when such "civility" rules are unlawfully overbroad, they tend to perpetuate hostile environments and cultures of discrimination, to the detriment of workers, by making employees scared to speak up, and forcing them to choose between being "good" and following the rules, or joining together with colleagues to speak up and report inappropriate behavior.

There can be no doubt, then, that employees who contemplate engaging in basic types of protected concerted activity will be discouraged from doing so by the sort of "civility" rules that the majority give blanket authorization to today. It is no answer to say that employers can only maintain such rules, but cannot enforce them against Section 7 activity. The employee who is chilled from exercising her rights will never have the rule enforced against her, but the harm to the policies of the Act will be the same. The majority seems not to grasp this basic point.

* * *

The issues that the Board must decide in this context are not easy, and perfection cannot be fairly demanded from the Board or any other administrative agency. But the majority's decision fails so badly to address the problem before it, and the process by which it was reached was so flawed, that the Board's new approach seems unlikely to survive judicial review.

III.

. . . . I would decide this case under established law, as reflected in the *Lutheran Heritage* standard, and I would find that Boeing's no-photography rule was unlawfully overbroad. Such a finding, of course, does *not* mean that Boeing is prohibited from adopting a no-photography rule. Rather, Boeing would be free to adopt a more narrowly-tailored rule that did not impermissibly infringe on the Section 7 rights of its employees. . . .

PROBLEMS FOR DISCUSSION

1.   In recent years, the Board has overturned many of its precedents as its membership has changed. Indeed, sometimes the Board has gone back-and-forth multiple times in a relatively short period. Do you agree with Member McFerran that this change in course is different, and, from an institutional perspective, deeply problematic? If so, why? Because the court jettisoned the *Lutheran Heritage* test *sua sponte* and in the absence of critical circuit court decisions? Because it failed to call for public participation through briefing and otherwise? If the majority had done things differently—e.g., asked the parties and the public to address the issue or undertaken a formal rule-making process—do you think a significantly distinct framework would have emerged, assuming the Board's makeup remained the same? Or do you think it would have made little or no difference?

2.   Central to the disagreement between the majority and dissent is how to balance employees' Section 7 rights against employers' legitimate interests. While the Board members disagree sharply over the extent to which *Lutheran Heritage* provided for consideration of employer justifications, isn't this disagreement, at its core, really about how much deference or weight to give to employer interests? After all, Member McFerran cites to decisions applying *Lutheran Heritage* that expressly discussed employer justifications, and an inquiry into overbreadth and tailoring itself must account for such justifications. In other words, competing frameworks aside, how much does the majority opinion (at various points) simply boil down to greater sympathy for the interests employers are claiming to protect?

3.   The majority argues that the *Lutheran Heritage* approach has produced inconsistent results and failed to offer clear guidance. Member McFerran disagrees. But even if the majority is correct, is the framework it adopts likely to fare any better in this regard? As Member McFerran suggestions, how the new framework is to be applied is unclear, and much depends on how often future judges and Boards will decide that particular facially neutral policies fall into Category 2. For example, try your hand at applying the *Boeing* framework to the various types of rules discussed in the Note on Company Rules that follows (page 105 of the casebook). While Boeing itself *might* determine the outcome with regard to the recording devices provisions, what about the other types of employee policies the Note mentions? Does your analysis depend on the particulars of the employer rule and the employer justification? If so, how is the *Boeing* framework less fact sensitive and more predictive than the one in *Lutheran Heritage*?

4.   The majority also emphasizes the need for employers to have the power to regulate civility in the modern workplace, pointing to imperatives such as preventing harassment and discrimination. Member McFerran bitterly contests what she perceives as a new limitation so at odds with Section 7 rights that it threatens to unravel them. Indeed, when, if ever, is concerted activity for mutual aid or protection—at least of the kind that may give rise to a labor dispute or a charge—likely to be entirely harmonious or without acrimony? If meaningful but harmonious concerted activity is rare, then how does one draw the lines between permissible and impermissible broad workplace civility rules? Does the framework the majority articulates help?

5.   The Board majority opines that *Lutheran Heritage* is "predicated on fake premises that are inconsistent with the Act." The dissent points out that for the most part the courts of appeals have found *Lutheran Heritage* to be consistent with the act. How does the majority reconcile that fact with the above assertion?

6.   Employee Cassandra Lowe brought a class action against her employer under the Fair Labor Standards Act and state minimum wage law asserting that she and all others similarly situated had been compelled to work "off the clock" and so were deprived of overtime pay. The Company has emailed a group of twenty co-workers in her unit ordering them in two regards: (1) that as the company was being sued they were not "to comment on the lawsuit and, if anyone contacted them about the lawsuit, they should consult the company's in-house lawyer; and (2) that they must preserve and protect any information in their possession relating to the case, including:

- All documents which contain communications pertaining to any allegation by Ms. Lowe that [the Company] treated him unfairly with regard to his employment with [the Company];
- All communications with Ms. Lowe;
- All communications concerning Ms. Lowe.

The email also instructed employees that the litigation hold applied to all files, including those on "home computer(s) (if used for work)" and any "other type of portable email devices (*i.e.*, PDAs; Blackberrys; iPhones; iPads)."

Under *Boeing*, has the Company committed any unfair labor practice? Advice Memorandum in Uber Technologies Inc., Case 19–CA–199000 (Oct. 2, 2018).

Page 116. Add following the discussion of *Lechmere*:

On June 14, 2019, the Board handed down a decision reversing precedent of long-standing regarding the access of union organizers to employees in areas on the employer's premises that are open to the general public. UPMC Presbyterian Hospital, 368 NLRB No. 2 (2019). The facts were stated in detail in Member McFerran's partial dissent. The Hospital

> operates a cafeteria inside one of its hospitals, which was patronized by both employees and nonemployees. It did not normally monitor who was present in the cafeteria. Nothing was posted either inside or outside the cafeteria indicating who could patronize it.

> [T]wo union representatives sat with employees at two tables in the cafeteria, ate lunch, and discussed the union's organizing campaign. Union flyers and union pins (but no authorization cards) were on the tables. There is no evidence that either union representative distributed the flyers and pins to anyone, and no evidence that either representative solicited any employees to join or support the union. While the union representatives and the employees were sitting at their tables, they were approached by the Respondent's security manager, Gerald Moran. Moran had observed neither solicitation, nor distribution, although he was responding to unverified reports of such conduct.

> Moran asked one of the nonemployee union representatives what she was doing there. The union representatives admitted they were nonemployees; one of them stated that they were talking about the union and that they were allowed to be present. Moran stated to the group that he was responding to a complaint about "unauthorized" individuals in the cafeteria. He told the group that only patients, patient visitors, and employees were allowed in the cafeteria. Moran then told the group that the union representatives, along with two employees who did not furnish identification to prove they were employees, would have to leave because they did not have "any hospital business." When one of the union representatives asked Moran if a nearby patron who was there only as the guest of an employee (and so, under the purported rule barring guests of employees, was not entitled to use the cafeteria) would also be asked to leave, Moran said "maybe," but that he was dealing with them first.

Slip op at 12–13 (footnotes omitted). When the union organizers refused to leave, the Hospital called the police, the organizers were caused to leave, an unfair labor practice charge issued, and the ALJ found a violation of section 8(a)(1).

The Board's Republican majority agreed that the ALJ's decision conformed to extant Board law, which it proceeded to reverse. First, Board law had long recognized a "public space" exception to restrictions on access of non-employee union organizers, *i.e.* to areas, such as a restaurant, that were accessible to members of the public. Second, the Board had also required access where an otherwise permissible non-solicitation prohibition had been applied discriminatorily, *i.e.* by restriction on "the content of the conversation." Slip opinion at 4. The Board abandoned the first and modified the second.

On the first, after discussing the caselaw and emphasizing that the courts of appeals had not tended to accept the "public space" exception, the majority opined:

> [T]o the extent that Board law created a "public space" exception that requires employers to permit nonemployees to engage in *promotional or organizational activity* in public cafeterias or restaurants absent evidence of inaccessibility or activity-based discrimination, we overrule those decisions. . . . [W]e find that an employer does not have a duty to allow the use of its facility by nonemployees *for promotional or organizational activity.* The fact that a cafeteria located on the employer's private property is open to the public does not mean that an employer must allow any nonemployee access for any purpose. Absent discrimination between nonemployee union representatives and other nonemployees—i.e., "disparate treatment where by rule or practice a property owner" bars access to nonemployee union representatives seeking to engage in certain activity while "permit[ting] similar activity in similar relevant circumstances" by other nonemployees—the employer may decide what types of activities, if any, it will allow by nonemployees on its property.

Slip op. at 5 (footnotes omitted) (italics added).

On the second, the Board majority glossed the requirement that the discriminatory treatment that would work to allow the organizers to be present must be "promotional or organizational" in nature:

> The Respondent's [Hospital] practice has been to prohibit nonemployees from engaging in promotional activities, including solicitation and distribution, in its public cafeteria. As set forth above, although the Respondent did not police the cafeteria for nonemployees, it did respond to reports of promotional activity in the cafeteria, and if upon investigation such conduct was occurring, the Respondent would ask the nonemployee to leave the cafeteria. . . . We . . . hold that an employer may prohibit nonemployee union representatives from engaging in promotional activity, including solicitation or

distribution, in its public cafeteria so long as it applies the practice in a nondiscriminatory manner by prohibiting other nonemployees from engaging in *similar* activity. [Italics added.]

Member McFerran prefaced her lengthy dissent on those issues thusly:

> Since at least the 1940's, the National Labor Relations Act has been interpreted, by the Board and by the Supreme Court, to prohibit employers from discriminatorily denying union organizers access to their property. Today, abruptly reversing judicially-approved Board precedent that it misreads, the majority throws that longstanding principle into doubt, by permitting the employer here to expel union representatives from a hospital cafeteria that is open to the public, based entirely on their union affiliation. This was discrimination in its clearest form, and the Board has never before tolerated anything like it.

She zeroed in on the majority's treatment of discrimination and its cognate deployment of a neologism—of *promotional* activity. On the former,

> [B]y the time of the Supreme Court's 1956 decision in *Babcock & Wilcox*, Board decisions had found that an employer violated the Act by denying access to nonemployee union organizers where it had previously admitted teachers and entertainers, vendors, and religions organizations and social societies. The admitted groups can hardly be described as "similar' to union organizers, but excluding union organizers while admitting such other persons was nevertheless deemed discriminatory. *Phillips Petroleum Co.*, 92 NLRB 1344, 1345 (1951), provides one illustrative example. There, the Board found that an employer unlawfully discriminated against union organizers by prohibiting them from using a meeting hall that had been previously used for social gatherings, safety meetings, and church services. The Board observed:
>
>> While it is true that the [employer] may not be under an obligation to provide such a meeting place, once having provided it, the [employer] cannot thereafter arbitrarily and for no valid reason select the [u]nion for special treatment by denying its use. *Discrimination of this nature is here admitted.*

Id. at 1349 (emphasis added). Slip. Op. at 6 (citation omitted).

Member McFerran connected this to the standard the Majority applied to the facts:

> The majority apparently believes that by virtue of her identity, a union representative's contact with employees necessarily constitutes solicitation—or at least prohibitable

"promotional activity"—even if (as here) it amounted to no more than a conversation about union-related matters with off-duty employees seated together at a table over lunch. Board law has never defined solicitation—a term of art in labor law for many decades—so broadly [footnote]. In effect, then, the majority invites employers to post "No Union Representatives Allowed" signs on property that is open to all other members of the public.

Put another way: while longstanding Board law makes clear that it would be unlawful to bar union organizers from a cafeteria simply for talking about the union, the majority's new conceptualization of the discrimination exception clearly permits such exclusion, because that is precisely what happened here.

Slip. Op. at 16 (footnote omitted). The footnote on the meaning of "solicitation" pointed out that,

"solicitation 'for a union is not the same thing as talking about a union meeting or whether a union is good or bad,' but rather is conduct, such as the presentation of a union-authorization card for signature, that 'prompts an immediate response from the individual or individuals being solicited and therefore presents a greater potential for interference with employer productivity if the individuals involved are supposed to be working.'" *Wal-Mart Stores,* 340 NLRB 637, 638 (2003), enf. denied in relevant part 400 F.3d 1093 (8th Cir. 2005).

PROBLEMS FOR DISCUSSION

1. For section 8(a)(1) purposes, is there a difference between a parking lot at a shopping mall and its food court? If so, what is it?

2. The Board majority also refused to enforce the ALJ's finding of unlawful surveillance of union activity: the Hospital's security personnel did not stand near the tables where the organizers were located; their observation of the employees' activities were "not out of the ordinary." Member McFerran did not address this issue.

Under *UPMC Presbyterian Hospital*, it would seem to be the case that a pro-union organizer may lunch with an employee in a cafeteria on the employer's premises that is open to the general public if she engages in no solicitation or union "promotion"? But, if "promotion" would render the organizer subject to eviction, how can the employer's agent tell that a conversation—absent any public display of union literature or the like—is in fact "promotional" without closely monitoring what is said? Would monitoring for this purpose violate § 8(a)(1)?

3. As Member McFerran pointed, "solicitation" has a well-defined meaning in labor law. "Promotion" is a neologism. If the organizer were to say to an employee in the cafeteria, "Have you experienced problems at work that you've brought to the management's attention," would that statement be "promotional" so to allow eviction? Or, "How did management respond to these problems?" Or, "Do you know the union has negotiated contracts to deal with just these problems?"

Page 118. Add to the end of Problems for Discussion:

8.   Four union representatives distributed leaflets in front of the employer's facility. Although they initially may have been standing on the employer's property, after they were asked to do so, they moved back to the adjacent public right-of-way. Thereafter, when the employer asked them to leave the right-of-way, the representatives refused, saying they had a right to be there. The employer was found to have violated Section 8(a)(1) by attempting to remove the representatives from the right-of-way. However, while leafletting in the right-of-way, the representatives also made minor forays onto the edges of the employer's property. Along the way, the employer threatened to summon and summoned the police, purportedly to protect its property rights. Does the employer's summoning of the police in these circumstances constitute interference with Section 7 rights in violation of Section 8(a)(1), or does it constitute a reasonable attempt to protect its property rights? *See* NLRB v. ImageFirst Uniform Rental, 910 F.3d 725 (3rd Cir. 2018).

Page 139. Add to end of Problems for Discussion:

On August 1, 2018, in the context of a case concerning *Purple Communications*, the Board invited amicus briefs to address the following questions:

1.   Should the Board adhere to, modify, or overrule *Purple Communications*?

2.   If you believe the Board should overrule *Purple Communications*, what standard should the Board adopt in its stead? Should the Board return to the holding of *Register Guard* or adopt some other standard?

3.   If the Board were to return to the holding of *Register Guard*, should it carve out exceptions for circumstances that limit employees' ability to communicate with each other through means other than their employer's email system (e.g., a scattered workforce, facilities located in areas that lack broadband access)? If so, should the Board specify such circumstances in advance or leave them to be determined on a case-by-case basis?

4.   The policy at issue in this case applies to employees' use of the Respondent's "[c]omputer resources." Until now, the Board has limited its holdings to employer email systems. Should the Board apply a different standard to the use of computer resources other than email? If so, what should that standard be? Or should it apply whatever standard the Board adopts for the use of employer email systems to other types of electronic communications (E.g., instant messages, texts, postings on social media) when made by employees using employer-owned equipment?

Rio All-Suites Hotel, Case 28–CA–060841 (Aug. 1, 2018). Member McFerran dissented.

2.   ELECTION PROPAGANDA

(a) Threats of Reprisal

Page 156. Add at end of Problem 4:

See also Hogan Transports, Inc., 363 N.L.R.B. No. 196 (2016) (Company President's statement to employees that he believed its primary customer would be reluctant to continue with it were the employees to unionize, confirming the consequent likelihood of job loss, was a threat violative of § 8(a)(1)) (Member Miscimarra dissented).

Page 169. Add to Problems for Discussion:

6.   The Union filed a petition seeking to represent the Employer's twenty janitorial employees and floor techs working at the Army National Guard Readiness Center in Arlington, Virginia. The election was scheduled for October 18, 2016. On October 17, 2016, Vice President Michael Payne and Contract Operations Director Jimmy Vickers had conversations with a majority of the voting unit employees similar to the following recorded conversation Payne had with employee Samantha Ulloa.

> Payne: So if the Union wins, I want to let you know a few things that will probably happen, okay, because we have the same Union at the Pentagon, okay.
>
> Ulloa: Yes.
>
> Payne: First thing they will require you to do is join the Union.
>
> Ulloa: Yes.
>
> Payne: And if you don't, you will not be able to work here. Have they told you that?
>
> Ulloa: No.
>
> Payne: Okay, so if you don't join, you can't work here. Part of that agreement, then, is we will take $37 a month out of your paycheck, and we will give it to the Union on your behalf. They will require us to do that. They will also take 5 cents an hour for every hour that you work, and we will pay that to them as well, okay? So if they win, then we have what's called a collective bargaining agreement. The Union and Didlake will sit down and negotiate the terms and conditions of that contract.
>
> Ulloa: Yes.
>
> Payne: And those terms and conditions are wages, benefits, work rules for the workplace, and those sort of things, so all of that is an unknown. It will have to be negotiated, okay?
>
> Ulloa: Okay.
>
> Payne: Everything may just stay the same, they may go up, or they may go down. It's a gamble. We don't know where all that goes until

we sit down and negotiate with the Union, so we want to make sure that you're aware of it. If they win, you have to join as a condition of your employment to be here, and you will be paying the union dues. Those are the three things that we know for sure. All the other things will become negotiation.

Ulloa: Okay.

Payne and Vickers misstated the law when they characterized union membership and the payment of dues as a "condition of employment" if the Union won the election, since, under Section 8(a)(3), an employee cannot be compelled to pay dues absent an agreement between an employer and a labor organization requiring dues as a condition of employment. The Union lost the election 10–9, and seeks to have to results overturned and a new election ordered. Is the employer's statement a threat under the test set out in *Gissel*, as predicting a dire consequence in a matter within its control? Or is it a misstatement of fact governed by *Midland National*? If the latter, would it warrant a new election? Didlake, Inc., 367 NLRB No. 125 (2019).

3.   OTHER FORMS OF INTERFERENCE, RESTRAINT OR COERCION

Page 179. Add to Problems for Discussion:

6.   Mitchell McConnell worked for Spundyne, Inc., and was leader of the union's successful drive to organize the Spundyne workforce against the Company's strong opposition. The plant manager passed Mr. McConnell's work station and saw his laptop open to a personal website in violation of company policy. He sought out Mr. McConnell and found him asleep behind packing crate. He fired McConnell on the spot. On the union's complaint, the General Counsel filed a charge of violation of section 8(a)(3). In preparation for the hearing, Spundyne's Director of Human Resources interviewed two of McConnell's co-workers in his office. They were told that Mr. McConnell had filed an unfair labor practice which was to be heard and that the Company discharged McConnell for using a computer for personal purposes and for sleeping on the job. They were asked if they had ever seen him doing either of those things and to particularize the date and circumstances. They were not told that the interview was voluntary nor that there would be no reprisal if they refused to answer or for what they said. Has the company violated § 8(a)(1)? Tachiggtrie Properties, Ltd. v. NLRB, 896 F.3d 880 (8th Cir. 2018).

Page 182. Add at the end of Problem 3:

Care One at Madison Ave, LLC v. NLRB, 832 F.3d 351 (D.C. Cir. 2016).

C.   DISCRIMINATION

Page 228. In Judicial Review of Board fact-findings add after the reference to *Slusher*:

See also David Saxe Pdtns., LLC v. NLRB, 888 F.3d 1305 (D.C. Cir. 2018) (on the responsibility of the Board to explain reasons for differing with ALJ credibility determination).

D. REMEDIES FOR UNFAIR LABOR PRACTICES

Page 249. Add to Problems for Discussion:

3.　An employer has unilaterally reduced the work hours of bargaining unit members in violation of § 8(a)(5). The affected employees are entitled to make whole relief. Were they to have been discharged they would be under a duty to mitigate, *i.e.* to seek employment, and any interim earnings would be deducted. But they were not discharged, their work hours were reduced. Are they under a duty to mitigate? *I.e.* must interim earnings be deducted? NLRB v. Community Health Services, Inc., 812 F.3d 768 (10th Cir. 2016).

Page 250. Add at end of "A Note on 'Notice' and 'Access' Remedies":

The Board's remedial authority was addressed in depth by the District of Columbia Circuit in HTH Corp. v. NLRB, 823 F.3d 668 (D.C. Cir. 2016). The Company was a serious labor law recidivist. Two of the challenged Board-ordered remedies were held to be before the court, having been raised earlier before the Board as required by § 10(e): (1) the award of litigation expenses to the Board's General Counsel and to the union; and, (2) the reading to assembled employees the Board's remedial notice by the Company's Regional Vice President, apparently the principal architect of its unfair labor practices, or, at the Company's option, by a Board agent. All members of the panel agreed that the Board lacks the authority to award attorney fees asserted either as authorized by the statute, as within the Board's "interest authority," or as in exercise of some notion of good faith, though they differed on which of these were to be considered. The "notice reading" remedy proved more vexing.

Judge Williams dwelled on the evil of compelled speech by the designated corporate officer, making it clear in considered dictum that he'd hold that remedy to be beyond the Board's power; but, he opined, the opt-out allowing a Board agent to read the notice was permissible. Judge Henderson disagreed. She saw nothing amiss in requiring the designated corporate officer to read the Board's remedial notice; but she was critical of the opt-out which, she reasoned, put the Board's imprimatur of approval on the union and its activities:

> [W]hen a Board agent stands up to castigate an employer in front of unionized employees, those employees are inevitably left with a perception of the Board as a union enforcer, not neutral arbiter. A referee calling a foul is one thing; a referee calling a foul while wearing one team's uniform is quite another. In short, *who* reads the notice matters. (Italics in original.)

In her view, however, the propriety of the opt-out was not before the court as it had not been objected to before the Board under § 10(e). Judge Rodgers concurred with Judge Williams on the ground that precedent supported the opt-out remedy.

QUESTIONS FOR DISCUSSION

1. Judge Williams' opinion explores the weltered history of the "notice reading" remedy, reiterating the view expressed by various judges, including then Judge Ruth Bader Ginsburg, that such compelled speech was "incompatible with the democratic principles of the dignity of man." He echoed this view and with brio:

> What is the subtext communicated by the sort of scene the Board would mandate? What is communicated to the assembled workers and the perpetrator himself? "You see before you one of your managers, who normally has a responsibility to make important choices as to your work. But who is he? Not merely is he a lawbreaker, but he is a pathetic creature who can, at the behest of federal officials be forced to spout lines they have put in his mouth. He is not even a parrot, who can choose when to speak; he is a puppet who speaks on command words that he may well abominate. We have successfully turned him into a pathetic semblance of a human being."

> Note that this analysis is directed exclusively to compelled utterance. No attention is given to compelled audition; *i.e.*, the assumption seems to be that as an employer has the prerogative to compel audition, that prerogative can be exploited by the Board to provide a forum for the Board-ordered speech. (The Order provided that the Company will "convene the bargaining until employees during working times" to hear the reading of the notice.) Unexplored is whether government can compel not utterance, but audition. *See generally*, Charles Black, *He Cannot But Hear: The Plight of the Captive Auditor*, 53 Colum. L. Rev. 960, 966 (1953) ("coerced and unreplying attention to the words of another is known immemorially as . . . a badge of servility"). If compelled audition infringes democratic principles of human dignity, should the Board be allowed that power? Should an employer? *Cf.* Question 8 on page 998.

2. As noted, the court held unanimously that the Board lacked any authority to require the Employer to reimburse the Board and the Union for their litigation expenses. Where an Employer is found to have bargained in bad faith, does the Board have the power under § 10(c) to order the Employer to compensate the Union for its negotiating costs; that is, to put the Union on the financial footing it had prior to the Employer's course of bad faith bargaining? If so, by what measure? *I.e.* had the Employer bargained in good faith the Union still would have incurred bargaining costs. Camelot Terrace, Inc. v. NLRB, 824 F.3d 1085 (D.C. Cir. 2016).

II. SELECTION OF THE REPRESENTATIVE FOR THE PURPOSES OF COLLECTIVE BARGAINING

B. APPROPRIATE BARGAINING UNIT

2. CRITERIA FOR UNIT DETERMINATIONS

Page 272. Add to Questions for Discussion:

5. Dortmund, Inc., is a general contractor. Its employees work in two areas, which it calls the "labor" side and the "contractor" side. The labor side of the business consists of two mechanics, who maintain Dortmund's vehicles, one warehouse worker, and laborers who work in crews for Dortmund's customers doing painting, masonry, carpentry, installation, and snow removal. The contractor side consists of workers who do recycling work under Dortmund's contracts with several recycling facilities. The degree of customer control over Dortmund's workers and the conditions of their work— rates of pay, hours, duties—vary from customer to customer. There is no interchange among these employees. A union has petitioned to represent a "wall-to-wall" bargaining unit of all Dortmund's employees. It seeks no smaller unit or units. Dortmund has objected that the wall-to-wall unit petitioned-for shares no community of interest beyond having a common employer. It argues that the unit is inappropriate; but, it proposes no unit or units of its own. How should the Board rule? NLRB v. Tito Contractors, Inc., 847 F.3d 724 (D.C. Cir. 2017).

Page 277. Add at end of the discussion of *Specialty Healthcare*:

The *Specialty Healthcare* approach—that once the unit petitioned-for is determined to be appropriate by "community of interests" standards, the party seeking a larger unit must prove that those employees share an "overwhelming" community of interests with those petitioned-for—had been judicially approved. *E.g.* FedEx Freight, Inc. v. NLRB, 816 F.3d 515 (8th Cir. 2016) (dock workers do not share an overwhelming community of interests with drivers); Nestle Dreyer's Ice Cream Co. v. NLRB, 821 F.3d 489 (4th Cir. 2016) (production workers do not share an overwhelming community of interests with maintenance workers); NLRB v. FedEx Freight, Inc., 832 F.3d 432 (3d Cir. 2016) (dock workers do not share an overwhelming community of interests with drivers).

However, in *PCC Structurals, Inc.*, 365 NLRB No. 160 (2017), by vote of three to two the Republican majority of the Labor Board overruled *Specialty Healthcare & Rehabilitation Center*, 357 NLRB 934 (2011). *Specialty Healthcare* had held that if the unit petitioned-for was an appropriate unit as determined by the traditional community-of-interest test, the burden shifted to the party seeking a larger unit, unusually the employer, to prove that excluded employees enjoyed an "overwhelming" community-of-interest with the employees petitioned-for.

In this case, *Specialty Healthcare* had been applied by the Regional Director to decide that 100 welders in a wall-to-wall complement of 2,565 production workers constituted an appropriate bargaining unit. The welders had common skills and training particular to them and were functionally integrated among themselves: they performed the same tasks and had minimal interchange with other employees. However, they were not grouped in the same administrative unit or department—they were scattered about separate departments, and did not share common supervision. They shared common working conditions, work rules and policies with production workers, but, welders were at the high end of the pay scale and work with distinctive equipment, had distinct qualifications and training.

The majority held first that *Specialty Healthcare* was an "unwarranted departure" from longstanding Board standards which contemplated that the Board apply the community of interest standard to all employees, both those in the petitioned-for unit and those outside it, *i.e.* when a smaller than wall-to-wall unit was sought whether *their* interests were "*sufficiently distinct*" to warrant separate unit treatment. (Emphasis in original.) Thus, to the majority, *Specialty Healthcare* accorded "extraordinary deference" to the unit petitioned-for.

Second, the *Specialty Healthcare Standard* drives toward making the petitioned-for unit controlling in cases where industry standards drive in quite the opposite direction, *e.g.* in one case according unit status to only the fragrance counter workers of a large department store.

Third, the standard flies in the face of the statutory provisions requiring the Board to decide the unit "in each case" and not to make the extent of organization controlling.

Fourth, the test disregards or discounts the section 7 rights of those the union would exclude from the unit save when their community of interests are "overwhelming":

> All statutory employees have Section 7 rights, including employees that have been excluded from the petitioned-for unit. And the two core principles at the heart of Section 9(a)—the principles of exclusive representation and majority rule—require bargaining-unit determinations that protect the Section 7 rights of all employees. Henceforth, the Board's determination of unit appropriateness will consider the Section 7 rights of employees *excluded* from the proposed unit *and* those included in that unit, regardless of whether there are "overwhelming" interests between the two groups.

(Slip Op. at 8) (italics in original).

Fifth, the majority did not read the acceptance of *Specialty Healthcare* by the courts of appeals as an unqualified endorsement of it. It rejected the dissenting Members' claim that the majority was requiring that the *most* appropriate unit be determined contrary to the statutory requirement that the Board determine only *an* appropriate unit. It stressed, in remanding the case to the Regional Director, that a smaller unit petitioned-for could be approved, as an appropriate unit under traditional community of interest standards.

The two dissenting Members criticized the Board for: (1) rushing to overturn a precedent without adequate public input, of not adhering to the Board's decade-long practice of soliciting *amicus* participation in cases where a change in policy was under consideration; (2) reaching out to decide an issue not presented; and (3) ignoring the fact that eight courts of appeals have rejected the employer arguments against *Specialty Healthcare* that the majority now accepts. The dissenters rejected the weight the majority placed on the qualification "in each case". They reasoned that the requirement actually allowed for the use of discretion the majority rejects; and they disagreed that the prior approach made the extent of organization controlling.

The dissenters also turned to the weight the majority attached to the neglect of the interests of those not petitioned-for. As they saw it, under the majority's view

> the statutory right of employees to seek union representation, as a self-defined group, is contingent on the imputed desires of employees outside the unit who have expressed no view on representation at all—with the employer serving as their self-appointed proxy. Of course, the extent of employees' freedom of association (which, by definition, includes the freedom *not* to associate) is not a matter for *employers* to decide.

(Slip. Op. at 21) (italics in original).

They point out that majority "points to no case in which employees claim that their *interest in being included* in a unit has been ignored". (Slip op. at 23) (emphasis added).

Turning to the attack, the dissenters argue that the majority's approach will frustrate the policy of the Act as failing to "assure employees the fullest freedom" of self-organization as required by § 9(a), which, they opine, is why the law refuses to command the Board to find only the most appropriate unit.

QUESTIONS FOR DISCUSSION

1.   Review the practical considerations that bear on unit determination set out on pages 262–263 of the casebook. Which of those bear on or will are most implicated by the abandonment of *Specialty Healthcare*?

2.   The *PCC Structurals* majority states that under the Board's traditional—*i.e.* pre-*Specialty Healthcare*—approach when a smaller unit that shared a distinct community of interest was sought, the burden had been placed on the petitioner, usually the union, to show why their separate community of interest should outweigh the interests shared with the larger employee group. Given the statutory command in § 9(b) that unit determination is to be made "in order to assure employees the fullest freedom

in exercising the right" to be collectively represented, is it be contrary to the purpose of the Act for the Board to reverse the burden of persuasion.

3. The *PCC Structurals* majority insists that *Specialty Healthcare* disregards "the interests" of the employees whom the union does not seek to represent. What are those interests? How are they disregarded?

4. Consider Problem 2, pages 277–78 of the casebook. Apply *PCC Structurals*. Does the result differ from what it would be in 2011? Is the result consistent with the Act?

Page 278. Add at end of Problem 2:

See also FedEx Freight, Inc. v. NLRB, 839 F.3d 636 (7th Cir. 2016).

Page 278. Add to the end of the *Macy's, Inc.* citation in Problem 3:

enf'd 824 F.3d 557 (2d Cir. 2016) (approving the Board's decision in *Specialty Healthcare*).

4.   MULTIEMPLOYER AND COORDINATED BARGAINING

Page 301. Add the following Questions for Discussion:

5. In *Hy Brand Industrial Contractors, Ltd.,* 365 NLRB No. 156 (2017), the Republican majority overruled *Browning-Ferris* even though that decision had no application to the case before it. However, the Board's Designated Agency Ethics Official determined that Member Emanuel should not have participated in the decision inasmuch as his former law firm represented the staffing agency in *Browning-Ferris*. The Board thereafter struck that part of the decision: "the overruling of the *Browning-Ferris* decision is of no force or effect." Hy-Brand Industrial Contractors, Inc. (Feb. 26, 2018).

On September 14, 2018, the Board published a notice of proposed rulemaking for notice and comment. The notice reviewed the history of the Board's standards for joint employment starting with a 1949 decision which found no joint employment status by virtue of integration alone and ending with *Browning-Ferris*. It proposed to adopt the following:

> An employer, as defined by Section 2(2) of the National Labor Relations Act (the Act), may be considered a joint employer of a separate employer's employees only if the two employers share or codetermine the employees' essential terms and conditions of employment, such as hiring, firing, discipline, supervision, and direction. A putative joint employer must possess and actually exercise substantial direct and immediate control over the employees' essential terms and conditions of employment in a manner that is not limited and routine.

83 Fed. Reg. 46681, 46696 (Sept. 14, 2018). Member McFerren dissented. Three months later the United States Court of Appeals for the District of Columbia Circuit sustained the Board, *Browning-Ferris Indus. v. NLRB*, 911 F.3d 1195 (D.C. Cir. 2018). Control could be retained even if not exercised, and the control retained could be indirect. Nevertheless, the court remanded the case back to the Board to refine two matters. First, the Board neglected to distinguish those matters governing terms and conditions of employment

from employer decisions that "set the objectives, basic ground rules, and expectations for a third-party contractor" which would not render the lead contractor to be a joint employer. Whether Browning-Ferris "influences or controls the basic contours of a contracted-for service—such as requiring four lines' worth of sorters plus supporting seven cleaners and housekeepers— would not count. . . ." *Id.* at 1220–21. Second, in holding that the contractor would be required to bargain with the employees' union only about those terms and conditions over which it possessed sufficient control the Board failed to indicate what terms and conditions the contractor would have to control in order to make bargaining meaningful. 911 F.3d at 1221–22. Senior Circuit Judge Randolph dissented on both the merits and on the ground that the matter was to be disposed of in the already commenced rulemaking.

Page 304. Add following the discussion of *M.B. Sturgis*:

On July 11, 2016, the Labor Board handed down a 3 to 1 decision in *Miller & Anderson, Inc.*, 364 NLRB No. 39 (2016). The Board began by explaining as follows:

> Anyone familiar with the Act's history might well wonder why employees must obtain the consent of their employers in order to bargain collectively. After all, Congress passed the Act to compel employers to recognize and bargain with the designated representatives of appropriate units of employees, even if the employers would prefer not to do so. But most recently in *Oakwood Care Center*, 343 NLRB 659 (2004) ("*Oakwood*"), the Board held that bargaining units that combine employees who are solely employed by a user employer and employees who are jointly employed by that same user employer and an employer supplying employees to the user employer constitute multi-employer units, which are appropriate only with the consent of the parties. Id. at 659. The *Oakwood* Board thereby overruled *M.B. Sturgis, Inc.*, 331 NLRB 1298 (2000) ("*Sturgis*"), which had held that the Act permits such units without the consent of the user and supplier employers, provided the employees share a community of interest. *Sturgis*, 331 NLRB at 1304–1308.

Slip op. at 1.

The Board then overruled *Oakwood* and returned to *M.B. Sturges*:

> Employer consent is not necessary for units that combine jointly employed and solely employed employees of a single user employer. Instead, we will apply the traditional community of interest factors to decide if such units are appropriate. . . . We also agree with the *Sturgis* Board's clarification that there is no statutory impediment to processing petitions that seek units composed only of the employees supplied to a single user, or that seek units of all the employees of a supplier employer and name only the supplier employer.

Slip op. at 2.

Member Miscimarra dissented.

C. REVIEW OF REPRESENTATION PROCEEDINGS

Page 315. Add at the end of Problem 2:

See also Kelly v. Pearce, 178 F. Supp. 3d 172 (S.D. N.Y. 2016) *and* Novelis Corp. v. NLRB, 885 F.3d 100 (2d Cir. 2018).

III. SECURING BARGAINING RIGHTS THROUGH UNFAIR LABOR PRACTICE PROCEEDINGS

Page 329. Add at end of Problem 2:

Compare the majority opinion in *Sysco Grand Rapids, LLC*, 367 NLRB No. 111 (2019) with member McFerran's partial dissent on the issuance of a *Gissel* bargaining order.

Page 355. Add to Problems for Discussion:

5. On May 9, 2016, the Board's General Counsel, pointing to the "peril for employers in determining whether there has been an actual loss of majority support," proposed that the Board adopt a rule allowing the withdrawal of recognition only on the "results of RM or RD election." This would not change the current state of the law requiring an employer to demonstrate "a good-faith reasonable uncertainty" about majority support. GC 16–03 (May 9, 2016). Should the Board adopt such a rule?

PART THREE

NEGOTIATION OF THE COLLECTIVE BARGAINING AGREEMENT

I. EXCLUSIVE REPRESENTATION AND MAJORITY RULE

Page 363. Replace Problem 4 with the following case:

Total Security Management Illinois 1, LLC
364 N.L.R.B. No. 106 (2016).

■ By CHAIRMAN PEARCE and MEMBERS MISCIMARRA, HIROZAWA, and McFERRAN.

The issue in this case is whether the Respondent acted unlawfully when it discharged three employees without first giving the Union notice and an opportunity to bargain about the discharges. The judge found the discharges unlawful, relying on *Alan Ritchey, Inc.*, 359 NLRB 396 (2012), which held that an employer is obligated to provide notice and an opportunity to bargain before imposing certain types of discipline, including discharge, on employees represented by a union but not yet covered by a collective-bargaining agreement. [However, the composition of the Board in *Alan Ritchey* included two persons whose appointments had been challenged as constitutionally infirm and ultimately found invalid in *NLRB v. Noel Canning*, 134 S. Ct. 2550 (2014) (*see* Main Text, pp. 49–50).]

[After examining the issue de novo,] we again hold that, like other terms and conditions of employment, discretionary discipline is a mandatory subject of bargaining and that employers may not unilaterally impose serious discipline, as defined below. Nevertheless, based on the unique nature of discipline and the practical needs of employers, the bargaining obligation we impose is more limited than that applicable to other terms and conditions of employment. We will apply today's holding prospectively and dismiss the allegations in this case, but we will provide guidance regarding the remedies that would be appropriate in later cases.

Background

The complaint alleges that the Respondent, a provider of security planning and security services, violated Section 8(a)(5) and (1) of the Act by discharging three unit employees without prior notice to or bargaining with International Union, Security, Police and Fire Professionals of America (the Union or SPFPA), which represents the employees. The parties submitted, and the judge accepted, a stipulated record that establishes that the relevant facts are undisputed and the issue presented to us is the legal question whether the Respondent's acknowledged failure to bargain with the Union before discharging the three employees was unlawful.

Analysis

The primary question before us is whether an employer has a duty to bargain before disciplining individual employees, when the employer does not alter broad, preexisting standards of conduct but exercises discretion over whether and how to discipline individuals. The issue arose in this case, as it typically will, after the employees voted to be represented by a union, but before the employer and union had entered into a complete collective-bargaining agreement or other agreement governing discipline.

The Board has long held, in a variety of other contexts, that once employees choose to be represented, an employer may not continue to act unilaterally with respect to terms and conditions of employment—even where it has previously done so routinely or at regularly scheduled intervals. If the employer has exercised and continues to exercise discretion in regard to the unilateral change at issue, e.g., the amount of an annual wage increase, it must first bargain with the union over the discretionary aspect. See, e.g., *Oneita Knitting Mills*, 205 NLRB 500 (1973). Other than in *Alan Ritchey*, supra, the Board has never clearly and adequately explained how (and to what extent) this established doctrine applies to the discipline of individual employees. We now conclude that an employer must provide its employees' bargaining representative notice and the opportunity to bargain before exercising its discretion to impose certain discipline on individual employees, absent an agreement with the union providing for a process, such as a grievance-arbitration system, to address such disputes. . . .

A.   Facts

The parties stipulated to the following facts:

- The Union was certified as the exclusive representative of a bargaining unit that included security guards Jason Mack, Winston Jennings, and Nequan Smith on August 21, 2012.
- The Respondent discharged Mack, Jennings, and Smith on March 12, 2013.
- The Respondent exercised discretion in discharging each of the employees; it did not apply any uniform policy or practice regarding discipline for their asserted misconduct.
- The Respondent did not provide the Union notice or an opportunity to bargain over any of the discharges before implementing them.

- At the time of the March 12 discharges, the Respondent and the Union had not reached an initial collective-bargaining agreement or another binding agreement governing discipline.

- The Respondent did not have a reasonable, good-faith belief, at the time of the discharges, that any of the three employees' continued presence on the job presented a serious, imminent danger to the Respondent's business or personnel or that any of them engaged in unlawful conduct, posed a significant risk of exposing the Respondent to legal liability for the employee's conduct, or threatened safety, health, or security in or outside the workplace.

B. Discipline Unquestionably Works a Change in Employees' Terms and Conditions of Employment

Section 8(a)(5) of the Act makes it an unfair labor practice for an employer "to refuse to bargain collectively with the representatives of [its] employees . . . ." In *NLRB v. Katz*, 369 U.S. 736 (1962), the Supreme Court approved the Board's determination that an employer violates Section 8(a)(5) by making unilateral changes to the terms and conditions of employment of employees represented by a union. *Katz* held that such a change "is a circumvention of the duty to negotiate which frustrates the objectives of § 8(a)(5) much as does a flat refusal" to bargain. Id. at 743 (footnote omitted).

The imposition of discipline on individual employees alters their terms or conditions of employment and implicates the duty to bargain if it is not controlled by preexisting, nondiscretionary employer policies or practices. That conclusion flows easily from the terms of the Act and established precedent. When an employee is terminated—whether for lack of work, misconduct, or other reasons—the termination is unquestionably a change in the employee's terms of employment. As the Board has held:

> Under Sections 8(a)(5) and 8(d), it is unlawful for an employer to refuse to bargain with respect to mandatory subjects of bargaining. *Fibreboard Paper Products v. NLRB*, 379 U.S. 203, 209–210 (1964). Termination of employment constitutes such a mandatory subject.

N.K. Parker Transport, Inc., 332 NLRB 547, 551 (2000); see *NLRB v. Advertisers Mfg. Co.*, 823 F.2d 1086, 1090 (7th Cir. 1987) ("Laying off workers works a dramatic change in their working conditions" and thus "[l]ayoffs are not a management prerogative [but] a mandatory subject of collective bargaining"). Similarly, when an employee is demoted or suspended without pay, the action represents a change in terms and conditions of employment. See, e.g., *Pillsbury Chemical Co.*, 317 NLRB 261, 261 fn. 2 (1995) (holding that employee's demotion and substantial wage reduction "rendered [employee's working] conditions so difficult or unpleasant" that constructive discharge was demonstrated). Finally, in *Carpenters Local 1031*, 321 NLRB 30 (1996), the Board held that the suggestion in some prior Board decisions that "a change in terms or conditions of employment affecting only one employee does not constitute a violation of Section 8(a)(5) . . . is erroneous as a matter of law," and the Board overruled all such prior cases. Id. at 32.

Not every unilateral change that affects terms and conditions of employment triggers the duty to bargain. Rather, the Board asks "whether the changes had a *material, substantial, and significant impact* on the employees' terms and conditions of employment." *Toledo Blade Co.*, 343 NLRB 385, 387 (2004) (emphasis added). We draw on this basic principle today. Serious disciplinary actions such as suspension, demotion, and discharge plainly have an inevitable and immediate impact on employees' tenure, status, or earnings. Requiring bargaining *before* these sanctions are imposed is appropriate, as we will explain, because of the impact on the employee and because of the harm caused to the union's effectiveness as the employees' representative if bargaining is postponed. Just as plainly, however, other actions that may nevertheless be referred to as discipline and that are rightly viewed as bargainable, such as oral and written warnings, have a lesser impact on employees, viewed as of the time when action is taken and assuming that they do not themselves automatically result in additional discipline based on an employer's progressive disciplinary system. Bargaining over these lesser sanctions . . . may properly be deferred until after they are imposed.

C. The Board Has Consistently Held that Discretionary Changes in Terms and Conditions of Employment Cannot Be Unilateral

The Board has recognized that an employer's obligation to maintain the status quo sometimes entails an obligation *to make* changes, when those changes are an established part of the status quo. Thus, if an employer has an established practice of granting employees a 1-percent increase in wages on the anniversary of their hire date, an employer not only does not violate its duty to bargain by making that change unilaterally, it violates its duty if it *fails* to do so. *Southeastern Michigan Gas Co.*, 198 NLRB 1221 (1972), affd. 485 F.2d 1239 (6th Cir. 1973). "The cases make it crystal clear that the vice involved in both the unlawful increase situation and the unlawful refusal to increase situation is that the employer has *changed* the existing conditions of employment. It is this *change* which is prohibited and which forms the basis of the unfair labor practice charge." *NLRB v. Dothan Eagle, Inc.*, 434 F.2d 93, 98 (5th Cir. 1970) (emphasis in original). And if the change is consistent with established practice in some respects but also involves an exercise of discretion by the employer, the employer must bargain over the discretionary aspects of the change.

Oneita Knitting Mills, 205 NLRB 500 (1973), illustrates this proposition. There, the Board held that an employer violated Section

8(a)(5) by unilaterally granting merit wage increases to represented employees, even though it had a past practice of granting such increases. . . . *Katz* itself involved an employer's grant of merit increases that were "in no sense automatic, but were informed by a large measure of discretion." *NLRB v. Katz*, 369 U.S. at 746.

In the decades since *Katz* and *Oneita Knitting*, across a range of terms and conditions of employment, the Board has applied the principle that even regular and recurring changes by an employer constitute unilateral action when the employer maintains discretion in relation to the criteria it considers. . . .

. . . Consistency with these precedents and their underlying principles demands that we apply the *Oneita Knitting* approach to require bargaining before discretionary discipline (in the form of a suspension, demotion, discharge, or analogous sanction) is imposed, just as we do in cases involving discretionary layoffs, wage changes, and other changes in core terms or conditions of employment, where bargaining is required before an employer's decision is implemented. Accordingly, where an employer's disciplinary system is fixed as to the broad standards for determining whether a violation has occurred, but discretionary as to whether or what type of discipline will be imposed in particular circumstances, we hold that an employer must maintain the fixed aspects of the discipline system and bargain with the union over the discretionary aspects (if any), e.g., whether to impose discipline in individual cases and, if so, the nature of discipline to be imposed. The obligation to provide notice and an opportunity to bargain is triggered before a suspension, demotion, discharge, or analogous sanction is imposed, but after imposition for lesser sanctions, such as oral or written warnings.

This conclusion is strongly supported by the Board's reasoning in *Washoe Medical Center*, 337 NLRB 202 (2001). *Washoe* was the Board's only substantive discussion of the obligation to bargain over discretionary discipline prior to *Fresno Bee*, 337 NLRB 1161 (2002), on which the Respondent and dissent rely and which we discuss in more detail below. In *Washoe*, the Board affirmed the judge's dismissal of 8(a)(5) charges arising out of individual acts of discipline, on the ground that the union there had not sought to engage in pre-imposition bargaining. Significantly, however, the Board expressly declined to rely on the alternative rationale articulated by the judge, a rationale tracking that of the judge in *Fresno Bee*. In refusing to apply that analysis, the *Washoe* Board stated:

> In light of the Board's holding in *Oneita Knitting Mills* . . . we reject the judge's comment . . . that "[I]t is not sufficient that the General Counsel show only some exercise of discretion to prove the alleged violation; the General Counsel must also demonstrate that imposition of discipline constituted a change in Respondent's policies and procedures." [Footnote omitted.]

337 NLRB at 202 fn. 1.

In fact, the *Washoe* Board applied the holding in *Oneita Knitting*, not only to reject the judge's suggestion that the employer had no duty to bargain over individual acts of discipline absent a change in its disciplinary policies, but also to reject a parallel argument concerning the assignment of initial wage rates to new employees. . . . Although the discussion in *Washoe* concerned starting wage rates, its reasoning applies with equal force to other significant employment terms.

The Respondent and dissent argue that the Board held in *Fresno Bee*, 337 NLRB 1161 (2002), that an employer has no pre-imposition duty to bargain over discretionary discipline. There, the Board, without comment, affirmed a judge's dismissal of 8(a)(5) charges arising out of the imposition of individual discipline. The General Counsel, drawing on the principles and precedent that we discuss here, had argued that the employer "exercised considerable discretion in disciplining its employees and is therefore required to notify and, upon request, bargain to impasse with the Union over each and every imposition of discipline." 337 NLRB at 1186. The judge rejected this argument, but her rationale for doing so misapplied the Board's case law and failed to explain why discipline should be treated as fundamentally different from other employer unilateral changes in terms and conditions of employment.

As her decision reveals, the judge's error was to conclude that because the employer had not changed its disciplinary *system*, the imposition of discipline with respect to individual employees, even if it involved the exercise of discretion, did not amount to a unilateral change. . . .

Under our case law, the judge's conclusion in *Fresno Bee* was a non sequitur. As we have explained, the lesson of well-established Board precedent is that the employer has both a duty to maintain an existing policy governing terms and conditions of employment *and* a duty to bargain over discretionary applications of that policy. . . .

The dissent argues that *NLRB v. J. Weingarten, Inc.*, 420 U.S. 251 (1975), in which the Supreme Court agreed with the Board's holding that an employee has a Section 7 right to union representation in investigatory interviews that the employee reasonably believes may lead to discipline, precludes the bargaining obligation we impose today. Properly understood, however, the rights and duties adopted here are in harmony with those addressed by *Weingarten*. In affirming the Board's recognition of the right to union representation in certain investigatory interviews, the Court agreed with the Board's qualification that the employer had no obligation to bargain with the union representative. Id. at 259–260. But the Board's representations and the Court's ruling addressed the investigatory interview only. That is, the limited right confirmed in *Weingarten* applies only to an employer's investigation—an investigation that may or may not lead to discipline affecting an employee's terms and conditions of employment—and arises only when the employer seeks to interview the employee as part of such an investigation. In other words, an investigation by itself is not, and may not result in, a change in employees' terms and conditions of employment and thus does not constitute discipline or trigger a bargaining obligation.

Weingarten, which is grounded in Section 8(a)(1), seeks to ensure that employers carrying out investigations do not restrain or coerce employees in the exercise of their Section 7 rights to engage in concerted activity for mutual aid or protection. . . . For this reason, the *Weingarten* right is held by the employee, not by the union. It must be asserted by the employee, not by a union representative, and it can be waived by the employee. In contrast, the obligation to refrain from unilateral action regarding mandatory subjects of bargaining is grounded in Section 8(a)(5). Moreover, the two rights arise at different points in time: the *Weingarten* right arises during an investigation into whether discipline is merited, while the right to notice and an opportunity to bargain arises after such an investigation results in a preliminary determination that discipline is warranted, but prior to its imposition. Thus, although the *Weingarten* Court agreed with the Board that an employer's *refusal to bargain* with a union in an investigatory meeting that may lead to discipline does not violate Section 8(a)(1), the Court, contrary to the dissent's contention, expressed no view concerning whether the employer's unilateral decision to discipline an employee violates Section 8(a)(5) by denying the employees' chosen representative the right to participate in good-faith bargaining over mandatory subjects of bargaining.

It is our view that the well-established *Weingarten* right and the bargaining obligation adopted here work in conjunction to ensure that the participants' rights are respected at each stage of the disciplinary process. . . .

As *Weingarten* established, the employer must permit the union to be present at an investigatory interview with an employee, should the employer decide to conduct one, if the employee reasonably believes that the investigation could lead to discipline and requests the union's presence. The employer need not bargain with the union at that interview, however. (As *Weingarten* further established, if the employer is unwilling to allow the union to be present at the investigatory interview, the employer may forgo the interview.)

Under today's decision, after the employer has preliminarily decided (with or without an investigatory interview) to impose serious discipline, it must provide the union with notice and an opportunity to bargain over the discretionary aspects of its decision *before* proceeding to impose the discipline. As explained below, at this stage, the employer need *not* bargain to agreement or impasse, if it commences bargaining promptly. In exigent circumstances, as defined, the employer may act prior to bargaining provided that, immediately afterward, it provides the union with notice and an opportunity to bargain about the disciplinary decision and its effects. Finally, if the employer has properly implemented its disciplinary decision without first reaching agreement or impasse, the employer must bargain with the union to agreement or impasse *after* imposing discipline.

D.   An Obligation to Bargain Prior to Imposing Discipline Is Not an Unreasonable Burden

We recognize that an obligation to bargain prior to imposing discipline may, in some cases, delay the employer's action or change the decision that it would have reached unilaterally. With regard to the latter, it is our view that permitting the employee to address the proposed discipline through his or her representative in bargaining is likely to lead to a more accurate understanding of the facts, a more even-handed and uniform application of rules of conduct, often a better and fairer result, and a result the employee is more able to accept. . . .

With regard to possible delay that a bargaining obligation may cause in implementing discipline, we have sought in our decision today to minimize the burden on employers in that regard to the greatest extent possible consistent with our duty to protect Section 7 rights, including the right of employees to be represented by their chosen representative.

First, as explained above, the pre-imposition obligation attaches only with regard to the discretionary aspects of those disciplinary actions that have an inevitable and immediate impact on an employee's tenure, status, or earnings, such as suspension, demotion, or discharge. Thus, most warnings, corrective actions, counselings, and the like will not require pre-imposition bargaining, assuming they do not automatically result in more serious discipline, based on an employer's progressive disciplinary system, that itself would require such bargaining.

Second, where the pre-imposition duty to bargain exists, the employer's obligation is simply to provide the union with notice and an opportunity to bargain before discipline is imposed. This entails sufficient advance notice to the union to provide for meaningful discussion concerning the grounds for imposing discipline in the particular case, as well as the grounds for the form of discipline chosen, to the extent that this choice involved an exercise of discretion. It will also entail providing the union with relevant information, if a timely request is made, under the Board's established approach to information requests. (Again, we note that, in this context, the scope of the duty to provide information is limited to information relevant to the subject of bargaining: the discretionary aspects of the employer's disciplinary policy.) The aim is to enable the union to effectively represent the employee by, for example, providing exculpatory or mitigating information to the employer, pointing out disparate treatment, or suggesting alternative courses of action. But the employer is not required to bargain to agreement or impasse at this stage; rather, if the parties do not reach agreement, the employer may impose the selected disciplinary action and then continue bargaining to agreement or impasse. Moreover, the employer has no duty to bargain over those aspects of its disciplinary decision that are controlled by nondiscretionary elements of existing policies and procedures. Thus, the less discretion an employer exercises, the less bargaining will be required of the employer.

Third, an employer may act unilaterally and impose discipline without providing the union with notice and an opportunity to bargain in any situation that presents exigent circumstances: that is, where an employer has a reasonable, good-faith belief that an employee's continued presence on the job presents a serious, imminent danger to the employer's business or personnel. The scope of such exigent circumstances is best defined going forward, case by case, but it would surely encompass situations where (for example) the employer reasonably and in good faith believes that an employee has engaged in unlawful conduct that poses a significant risk of exposing the employer to legal liability for the employee's conduct, or threatens safety, health, or security in or outside the workplace. Thus, our holding today does not prevent an employer from quickly removing an employee from the workplace, limiting the employee's access to coworkers (consistent with the employer's legal obligations) or equipment, or taking other necessary actions to address exigent circumstances when they exist.

Finally, an employer need not await an *overall* impasse in bargaining before imposing discipline, so long as it exercises its discretion within existing standards. Considering the practicalities of discipline, we hold that so long as the employer continues to apply existing standards and procedures for discipline, the employer's duty is simply to bargain over the discretionary aspect of the discipline, in accord with today's decision. After fulfilling its pre-imposition responsibilities as described above, the employer may act, but it must continue to bargain concerning its action, including the possibility of rescinding it, until reaching agreement or impasse. We believe such a rule appropriately defines the statutory duty to bargain in good faith in this area critical to both employers and employees.

Thus, the narrow scope of the bargaining obligation and the limited nature of the duty to bargain are tailored to minimize their effect on an employer's ability to effectively manage its workforce. For example, in a workplace where the employer has an established practice of disciplining employees for absenteeism, the decision to impose discipline for such conduct will not give rise to an obligation to bargain over whether absenteeism is generally an appropriate grounds for discipline. Instead, bargaining will be limited to the specific case at hand: for example, if the employer consistently suspends employees for absenteeism but the length of the suspension is discretionary, bargaining will be limited to the latter issue. Our expectation is that bargaining over the limited topics that implicate employer discretion will yield expeditious results, and that it will, in fact, be the norm that parties will reach agreement without testing the limits of the pre-imposition bargaining period. If our expectation proves inaccurate, any constraint on the employer's ability to effectuate its desired discipline will be limited, as we have made clear, because we impose no duty to bargain to impasse prior to imposing discipline.

To hold otherwise, as the dissent would, and permit employers to exercise unilateral discretion over discipline after employees select a representative—i.e., to proceed as before despite the fact that the employees have chosen to be represented—would demonstrate to employees that the Act and the Board's processes implementing it are ineffectual, and would render the union (typically, newly certified or recognized) that represents the employees impotent. . . . An employer's unilateral exercise of discretion in imposing serious discipline without first giving the union notice and an opportunity to bargain would send employees the same signal as the imposition of unilateral layoffs.

Recognition that discretion is inherent—in fact, unavoidable—in most kinds of discipline confirms that a bargaining obligation attaches to the exercise of such discretion. Granting merit increases, as in *Katz*, *Oneita Knitting*, and subsequent cases, is also inherently discretionary, as are many decisions regarding economic layoffs. Nonetheless, we require bargaining over those inherently discretionary decisions. The inevitability of discretion in most decisions to discipline does not support treating it differently from other forms of unilateral change; indeed, it makes bargaining over disciplinary actions that much more critical.

E.   Application to This Case

. . . .

The discharges of Jason Mack, Winston Jennings, and Nequan Smith plainly had material, substantial, and significant impacts on their terms and conditions of employment. In addition, as the Respondent has stipulated, the discharges were discretionary and it imposed them without notice to or bargaining with the Union, which had been certified as the affected employees' exclusive representative. No collective-bargaining agreement or other agreement addressing grievance processing regarding the employees had been agreed to by the Respondent and the Union. As further stipulated, at the time of the discharges, the Respondent did not have a reasonable, good-faith belief that any of the three employees' continued presence at the job presented a serious, imminent danger to the Respondent's business or personnel or that any of them engaged in unlawful conduct, posed a significant risk of exposing the Respondent to legal liability for the employee's conduct, or threatened safety, health, or security in or outside the workplace. Pursuant to our analysis above, the discharges at issue are covered by the obligation to bargain before imposition, an obligation that the Respondent did not meet.

[The Majority then held that retroactive application would be inappropriate in this case because it is not essential to achieving the benefits of the Board's decision and will foreseeably impose unexpected burdens on employers.]

F.   Application to Future Cases

Because we apply today's holding prospectively, we will dismiss the complaint and order no remedy. But, in the interest of administrative efficiency, we provide guidance to Board personnel and labor practitioners, who will apply this decision in the first instance in forthcoming cases, about the appropriate remedies for unfair labor practices arising under today's decision.

If a respondent violates Section 8(a)(5) by failing to provide notice to the union and an opportunity to bargain before it imposes discretionary discipline, the Board's standard remedies for an unlawful unilateral change should be granted. Thus, the remedy should not be limited to a cease-and-desist order, an affirmative order to bargain before changing employees' terms and conditions of employment by imposing discretionary discipline, and notice-posting. Rather, make-whole relief would also be appropriate, including reinstatement and backpay, as explained below. A respondent may, however, raise an affirmative defense that the discipline was "for cause" as that term is used in Section 10(c) of the Act, and, therefore, that reinstatement and backpay may not be awarded. We explain below what must be shown to support such a defense.

[The Majority went on to clarify that, in cases in which the respondent failed to provide notice and an opportunity to bargain before imposing discipline but the parties have bargained in good faith to impasse after the discipline, backpay will be ordered for the pre-discipline bargaining violation (from the date of the discipline until the date on which the parties reached impasse). In so doing, the Majority rejected the argument that Section 10(c) precludes such relief. However, a respondent may raise an affirmative defense that reinstatement and backpay may not be awarded because the discipline was "for cause" within the meaning of Section 10(c).] . . . In order to do so, the respondent must show that: (1) the employee engaged in misconduct, and (2) the misconduct was the reason for the suspension or discharge. In response, the General Counsel and the charging party may contest the respondent's showing, and may also seek to show, for example, that there are mitigating circumstances or that the respondent has not imposed similar discipline on other employees for similar misconduct. If the General Counsel and charging party make such a showing, the respondent must show that it would nevertheless have imposed the same discipline. [T]he respondent retains the burden of persuasion in this analytical framework. . . .

■ MEMBER MISCIMARRA, concurring in part and dissenting in part.

I disagree with my colleagues' decision in this case, which creates entirely new requirements and restrictions regarding discipline. These new requirements include a Board-imposed moratorium on discipline whenever employees are represented—which I refer to as a "discipline bar"—and my colleagues invent a new type of "discipline bargaining" governed by complicated rules, qualifications and exceptions. There is no legal support for these requirements, with the sole exception of one short-lived decision, *Alan Ritchey, Inc.*, 359 NLRB 396 (2012), which set forth, nearly verbatim, the same rationale my colleagues rely on here. . . .

Most troubling and disappointing is the fact that so many fundamental labor law principles—all well-established—are being cast aside by my colleagues. The new obligations take a wrecking ball to eight decades of NLRA case law. My problems with the new discipline bar and discipline bargaining requirements do not stem from their novelty. Rather, these new obligations cannot be squared with existing legal principles. Indeed, they are contradicted by the Board's own representations to the Supreme Court in *NLRB v. J. Weingarten, Inc.*, where the Board clearly indicated that employers and unions have no obligation to engage in bargaining before imposing discipline.

My colleagues resolve these contradictions by overhauling a broad range of existing principles as they pertain to a single subject: discipline imposed on represented employees. My colleagues grossly understate the extent to which their new requirements are contrary to existing law. These new requirements upend existing principles governing conventional decision and effects bargaining, they require bargaining over actions that effect no change in the manner in which the employer has disciplined employees in the past, they contradict existing law that disfavors single-issue negotiations, and they disregard the Board's longstanding position regarding the waiver of collective-bargaining rights. I also believe these new requirements are precluded by express provisions in the National Labor Relations Act (NLRA or Act)—specifically, Section 8(d), which prohibits the Board from imposing substantive terms on parties under the guise of enforcing Section 8(a)(5) bargaining requirements, and Section 10(c), which prohibits the Board from ordering backpay or reinstatement for any employee who was suspended or discharged for " "cause," with the General Counsel bearing the burden of proving the absence of " "cause"—and by Supreme Court decisions limiting the Board to "remedial" relief. The Supreme Court may very well have anticipated the instant case when it stated, in *Republic Steel Corp. v. NLRB*, that Congress never intended to give the Board "virtually unlimited discretion" to impose "punitive measures," "penalties" or "fines" based on what "the Board may think would effectuate the policies of the Act."

I am not a champion of an employer's right to impose discipline on employees, and I do not seek to minimize the role played by unions in relation to discipline. My concern here is that these new requirements are not faithful to existing legal principles, and I believe they disregard important constraints that our statute places on the Board. However, it is also relevant to point out that represented employees and unions have substantial protection in discipline cases, as reflected in Section 8(a)(1) (which prohibits discipline motivated by hostility towards protected concerted activities); Section 8(a)(3) (which prohibits discipline motivated by antiunion discrimination); Section 8(a)(5) (which makes disciplinary standards and procedures a mandatory subject of bargaining whenever bargaining is requested by the union, and which prohibits any unilateral "change" in disciplinary standards and procedures); the *Weingarten* right to request the presence of a union representative whenever an employee reasonably believes an investigative meeting may result in discipline; and potential collective-bargaining agreement (CBA) provisions regarding discipline, grievances, and arbitration. It is noteworthy that the requirements announced by my colleagues substantially exceed what parties have typically included in their own CBAs, which rarely, if ever, require bargaining over discipline before it is imposed, and they nearly always treat discipline as a management prerogative, subject to the existence of " "cause," and the union's right to pursue post-discipline challenges in grievance arbitration.

How does one explain everybody's failure to realize, until now, that the NLRA imposes an obligation to have bargaining between employers and unions regarding every decision to impose discipline on represented employees? Employee discipline is hardly a new development in our statute's 80-year history. In my view, it is not plausible to believe these new requirements have support in our statute but somehow escaped the attention of Congress, the Supreme Court, other courts, and previous Boards for the past 80 years.

. . . .

QUESTIONS FOR DISCUSSION

1.   The Majority discusses the various benefits of the approach to the bargaining obligation it adopts as well as how its limits protect important employer prerogatives. As for the former, are you convinced that a duty to bargain but not to impasse (before the discipline is imposed) genuinely protects unit members? With regard to the latter, might the complexity of the framework the Majority adopts, the allocation of the burden with regard to cause, and the uncertainty in application undermine an employer's ability to act on its legitimate interests? If you are troubled either way, what would be better approach to strike a balance between competing interests here?

2.   Member Miscimarra criticizes the Majority for fashioning a new approach to bargaining obligations regarding employee discipline eighty years after the Act's enactment. Do you find this argument persuasive? Does it matter whether the Majority is correct that, prior to *Alan Ritchey*, the Board had never confronted this precise issue directly? Member Miscimarra is now the Chairman of a soon-to-be-reconstituted Board. It may be interesting to observe whether this new Board will act consistent with this critique—that is, hesitant to craft new approaches to seemly persistent controversies over interpretation and application of the Act.

3. The vast majority of collective bargaining agreements contain both an arbitration and a no-strike provision. They also usually contain a prohibition on dismissal without just cause which could be pursued to arbitration. *See Lincoln Mills* in the Main Volume at page 775. In the absence of a no-strike pledge a Union is free to strike over the dismissal of an employee which it believes to be unjustified. Assess the claim that the burden of bargaining with the union about the dismissal is undue in light of the Union's possession of this lawful option.

4. Although criticized as inappropriate and burdensome by Member Miscimarra and employer advocates, the *Alan Rickey* proceeding, which provides another opportunity for assessment of facts and deliberation over potential disciplinary action, can have utility beyond facilitating bargaining and protecting employee rights. One example can be found in *Cellco Partnership v. NLRB*, 892 F.3d 1256 (D.C. Cir. 2018), in which it was not until revelations emerged during the *Alan Rickey* meeting that it became clear that the employee subject to potential discipline for dishonesty had been telling the truth throughout the investigation, and another employee, whom management had previously believed, had in fact been untruthful.

II. THE DUTY TO BARGAIN IN GOOD FAITH

Page 394. At the end of the Problems for Discussion:

7. The Hospital of Barstow operates an acute-care facility. The Union initiated an organizing campaign to represent Barstow's nurses, and, thereafter, Barstow and the Union entered into a consent election agreement. The nurses voted in favor of the union. Following the Regional Directors rejection of Barstow's election challenges and certification of the election, Barstow and the Union commenced bargaining. After discussions of several bargaining subjects and tentative agreement on a handful of issues, Barstow refused to put forward further proposals until the Union presented its proposals on every issue over which the parties were bargaining. When the Union did not present its proposals in full, Barstow declared an impasse and ceased bargaining. Has Barstow violated its duty to bargain in good faith? *See* Hospital of Barstow, Inc. v. NLRB, 897 F.3d 280 (D.C. Cir. 2018).

Page 398. At the end of the section preceding Problems for Discussion:

Both the Board and courts have recognized that the union is entitled to information regarding non-bargaining unit employees and employment positions if the can demonstrate the relevance of this information to its bargaining or other duties. In *Teachers College v. NLRB*, 902 F.3d 296 (D.C. Cir. 2018), the court upheld under a substantial evidence standard the Board's determination that the union is entitled to information from the employer regarding non-unit employees in the context of an ongoing grievance proceeding addressing whether the employer had transferred work to employees outside of the bargaining unit in violation of the CBA. Although the court emphasized that the union must do more than offer a bare assertion of relevance, it articulated a minimum, "discovery-type standard," under which a showing that information is of probable or potential relevance is sufficient to give rise to an obligation to disclose. Here, the court agreed with the Board that the union had clearly met this standard, having done its own initial information gathering of job descriptions and postings, prepared a chart identifying and describing thirty-four positions it believed to encompass unit work, and limited its information request to these listed positions.

Page 405. Add at the end of the paragraph preceding the Problems for Discussion:

In *AT&T Services, Inc.*, 366 NLRB No. 48 (2018), the Board again concluded that the employer violated Section 8(a)(5) and (1) by failing and refusing to furnish the Union with the information it requested as to bargaining unit employees' results on an employer-administered test which could affect the employees' entitlement to layoff protection. In so doing, the Board rejected the employer's claim that disclosure would place the test's integrity genuinely at risk or that other confidentiality concerns akin those credited in *Detroit Edison* would be implicated.

Page 418. Add at the end of Problem 2:

The Burnham Hospital has made a collective bargaining agreement with the Nurses Union. It is the parties' first agreement, and was made for the period July 1, 2016 to June 30, 2017. It included the following:

> 20.3 Base Rate Increase During Term of Agreement. For the duration of this Agreement, the Hospital will adjust the pay of Nurses on his/her anniversary date. Such pay increases for Nurses not on probation, during the term of this Agreement will be three (3) percent.

The parties commenced bargaining in early May, 2017. In the bargaining session on July 10, 2017, the Hospital informed the Union that it would not adjust the nurses' pay on their anniversary dates in the future. When the Union protested, the Hospital stated that pay raises were "on the table." Has the Hospital violated section 8(a)(5)? Finley Hosp. v. NLRB, 827 F.3d 720 (8th Cir. 2016).

III. SUBJECTS OF COLLECTIVE BARGAINING

Page 455. Add at the end of the discussion of "Waiver":

As the Second Circuit noted, the Circuits are divided on the "contract coverage" vs "clear and unmistakable" test for the waiver of the duty to bargain. As the dissenting judge in Heartland Plymouth Court MI, LLC v. NLRB, 838 F.3d 16, 29–30 (D.C. Cir. 2016) (Millett, C.J., dissenting) pointed out, a majority of circuits, including the Sixth, have supported the Board. But the D.C. Circuit has not. In that case, the court held the Board, by persisting in its position of non-acquiescence before a court it had every reason expect would reject its position, and seeking neither transfer to the Sixth Circuit (which would have had venue) nor *certiorari* from the U.S. Supreme Court, acted in bad faith, oppressive of the respondent Employer. It required the Board to pay the Employer's attorney fees for the appeal. The majority parsed the issue of administrative non-acquiescence closely and found no justification for the Board's conduct. As noted, Judge Millett disagreed.

MORE ON UNILATERAL ACTION

Consider these two situations:

1.   A company has a new bargaining relationship with a union. The parties are bargaining about medical insurance. The Company proposed a medical benefits plan that contains the following provision:

> The Company reserves the right to change or discontinue this Plan in its discretion provided, however, that any change in price or level of coverage shall be announced at the time of annual enrollment and shall not be changed during the Plan year. . . .

It has also proposed a management's rights clause whereby the Company "reserves the right to amend or terminate its Group Benefit Plans, all benefits being subject in every respect to the terms of the applicable Plan documents." The Union agreed.

The collective agreement has expired and the parties are bargaining for a new collective agreement. During the period of bargaining, the medical benefits plan's enrollment period becomes open and the Company unilaterally increases employee costs, of which it informs the Union and enrollees. It has not bargained with the Union about the change.

2.   The facts are the same as (1) above, except that the medical benefits plan had been in effect for some years prior to Union certification and during that period of time the Company had made periodic changes in price and coverage.

Has the Company in either or both of these cases violated Section 8(a)(5) of the Act? *See* E.I. DuPont de Nemours, 364 NLRB No. 113 (2016) *on remand from* E.I. DuPont de Nemours & Co. v. NLRB, 682 F.3d 65 (D.C. Cir. 2012), *overruled* Raytheon Network Centric Systems, 365 NLRB No. 161 (2017).

IV. THE ROLE OF THE STRIKE AND THIRD-PARTY IMPASSE RESOLUTION

A. THE PREMISES OF COLLECTIVE BARGAINING AND THE ROLE OF THE STRIKE

Page 489. Add After "The Role of the Strike":

According to the Bureau of National Affairs (Bloomberg) Labor Data, there were almost 600 strikes in 1990—most would presumably be in the private sector, but the federal government only collects data on strikes involving more than 1,000 workers, so, if these data are what is reported, small walkouts would not be included. The number of strikes declined to just over 100 in 2016, an 87% decrease even as union membership declined by 12% in that period. In other words, the decline of strikes has outpaced by far the decline in union representation. How is this explained? *See* Jacquie Lee, *Union Membership Doesn't Explain Drastic Drop in Strikes*, 22 DLR p. 5 (2017).

PART FOUR

PROTESTS AND PICKETING, STRIKES AND BOYCOTTS

I. RIGHTS OF EMPLOYEE PROTESTERS UNDER THE NLRA

A. PROTECTED AND UNPROTECTED CONCERTED ACTIVITY

Page 526. Add after Problems for Discussion:

Alstate Maintenance, LLC
367 N.L.R.B. No. 68 (2019).

[Trevor Greenidge was a skycap at Kennedy International Airport. Most of the skycap income comes from passengers' tips. On July 17, 2013, Greenidge was working with three other skycaps outside the entrance to terminal one. He was approached by his supervisor, Cebon Crawford, who informed Greenidge that Lufthansa had requested skycaps to assist with a soccer team's equipment. Greenidge remarked, "We did a similar job a year prior and we didn't receive a tip for it." When a van containing the team's equipment arrived, the skycaps walked away. Lufthansa's managers on scene asked baggage handlers inside the terminal for help, which they did. Greenidge and his co-workers returned to complete the work and were tipped a total of $83. The terminal manager learned what happened and fired all four. Greenidge's discharge letter said,

> You were indifferent to the customer and verbally make [sic] comments about the job stating you get no tip or it is very small tip. Trevor, you made this comments [sic] in front of other skycaps, Terminal One Mod [manager on duty] and the Station Manager of Lufthansa.

The ALJ held that Greenidge's complaint, for which he was discharged, was neither concerted nor for mutual aid or protection. The Board's three Republican members agreed with the ALJ. They stressed that the skycaps' walkout was not the issue: the General Counsel's theory of the case was concerned only with Greenidge's statement—"We did a similar job a year prior and we didn't receive tips for it"—for which he was discharged.]

A. Greenidge's Comment Was not Concerted Activity

First, the General Counsel does not contend that Greenidge was bringing a truly group complaint to the attention of management, and the record is devoid of evidence of "group activities" upon which to base a finding that Greenidge was doing so. There is no evidence that the tipping habits of soccer players (or anyone else) had been a topic of conversation among the skycaps prior to Greenidge's statement. Neither does Greenidge's use of the word "we" supply the missing "group activities" evidence: it shows only that the skycaps had worked as a group and been "stiffed" as a group, not that they had discussed the incident among themselves. Second, the statement in and of itself does not demonstrate that Greenidge was seeking to initiate or induce group action, and the record contains direct evidence to the contrary. At the hearing, Greenidge testified that his remark was "just a comment" and was not aimed at changing the Respondent's policies or practices (Tr. 75), and the judge credited Greenidge's testimony in this regard, finding that the remark "was simply an offhand gripe about [Greenidge's] belief that French soccer players were poor tippers." Where a statement looks forward to no action at all, it is more than likely mere griping, and we find as much here. Accordingly, *Meyers II* compels affirmance of the judge's finding that Greenidge did not engage in concerted activity.

Nonetheless, counsel for the General Counsel excepts to the judge's finding, contending that Greenidge's comment qualifies as concerted activity because Greenidge made it "in a group setting . . . in the presence of his coworkers and Crawford" and used the first-person plural pronoun "we.". . . [The opinion this parses the Board's decisions. It treats the strongest authority in support of protection, *World Mark by Windham*, 356 NLRB 765 (2011), and overrules it.]

* * *

The fact that a statement is made at a meeting, in a group setting or with other employees present will not automatically make the statement concerted activity. Rather, to be concerted activity, an individual employee's statement to a supervisor or manager must either bring a truly group complaint regarding a workplace issue to management's attention, or the totality of the circumstances must support a reasonable inference that in making the statement, the employee was seeking to initiate, induce or prepare for group action. . . . [R]elevant factors that would tend to support drawing such an inference include that (1) the statement was made in an employee meeting called by the employer to announce a decision affecting wages, hours, or some other term or condition of employment; (2) the decision affects multiple employees attending the meeting; (3) the employee who speaks up in response to the announcement did so to protest or complain about the decision, not merely . . . to ask questions about how the decision has been or will be implemented; (4) the speaker protested or complained about the decision's effect on the work force generally or some portion of the work force, not solely about its effect on the speaker him- or herself; and (5) the meeting presented the first opportunity employees had to address the decision, so that the speaker had no opportunity to discuss it with other employees beforehand. Of course, other evidence that a statement made in the presence of coworkers was made to initiate, induce or prepare for

group action—such as an express call for employees to act collectively—
would also support a finding of concertedness under *Meyers II*.

B.   *Greenidge's Comment Was Not for the Purpose of Mutual Aid or Protection*

[E]ven if Greenidge's remark about soccer players' tipping habits
qualifies as concerted activity, we find that Greenidge did not make it for
the purpose of mutual aid or protection, and therefore the remark still
would have been unprotected.

The judge found that Greenidge's statement concerning customers'
tipping habits "did not relate to the skycap's wages, hours, or other terms
and conditions of employment." Taking the judge's finding as he intended
it—i.e., that tips given to the skycaps by airline passengers are not wages
received from, and controlled by, the Respondent—we agree.[47] The
amount of a tip given by an airline passenger to the skycap handling his
or her luggage at curbside is a matter between the passenger and the
skycap, from which the skycap's employer is essentially detached. . .
Neither was Greenidge's statement aimed at improving the skycaps' lot
as employees through channels outside the immediate employee-
employer relationship, i.e., through recourse to an administrative,

---

[47]   *The Capital Times Company*, 223 NLRB 651 (1976), cited by the dissent, is not to the
contrary. There, the Board stated that for purposes of determining the scope of the duty to
bargain under Sec. 8(d), the statutory term "wages" includes tips. Id. at 652. Thus, if tipped
employees are represented by a union, their employer must bargain on request over matters
related to tips, such as tip-pooling and tip-sharing. . . . But *Capital Times* does not change the
fact that customers furnish tips, not employers, or that arriving airline passengers, and they
alone, decide whether to tip the skycap and, if so, how much, as Greenidge testified. . . . ("[S]ome
people give you $5, some give you 20. It depends. We take whatever we get, sir."); . . . ("[E]ach
individual gets their own tips from each customer that it helps."); Tr. 74 ("Many times we didn't
get a tip").

The dissent also cites *Nellis Cab Co.*, 362 NLRB 1587 (2015), but our colleague's own
discussion of that case shows that it is distinguishable from this one. In *Nellis Cab*, Las Vegas
taxicab drivers staged an extended break to protest the potential issuance of additional taxicab
medallions by the Las Vegas Taxicab Authority—a move that would have put more taxicabs on
the street, which would have meant less income for individual drivers. The Board found the
extended break to be protected concerted activity, even though the Taxicab Authority controlled
the decision whether or not to issue more medallions, because the employer played a role in that
decision. The Board stated that "the taxicab companies obviously could be expected and did seek
to influence Taxicab Authority's decision (for example, at [a] . . . meeting of the Taxicab
Authority, where representatives of taxicab companies spoke in favor of issuing more
medallions)." Id., slip op. at 2. Here, in contrast, the Respondent had no mechanism for, or
history of, exerting pressure on airline passengers to provide skycaps more generous tips—or,
indeed, any tips at all.

The dissent claims that the Respondent did have some control over tips, citing as evidence
that "the skycaps' protest prompted their supervisor to relay their concerns to managers of the
airline terminal." Here our colleague either distorts the record or strays from the General
Counsel's theory of the case. Greenidge's remark did not prompt Crawford to mention the tip
issue to the terminal manager. Crawford mentioned the issue after the terminal manager
questioned him, and the terminal manager questioned Crawford when she saw the skycaps walk
away. But perhaps by "the skycaps' protest," the dissent *means* their act of walking away. In
that case, she abandons the General Counsel's theory of the case, which is that Greenidge's
remark alone constitutes the allegedly protected concerted activity at issue here. The dissent
says that we miss her point, which is that "an employer has the means to address employee
concerns over poor tips." In certain settings, that may be true. For example, a restaurant can
slap a mandatory tip surcharge on every bill, and some do. But that is a very different setting
than the one we are dealing with here.

legislative, or judicial forum. *Eastex, Inc. v. NLRB*, 437 U.S. 556, 565–566 (1978). Thus, the statement did not have mutual aid or protection as its purpose.

Moreover, despite Greenidge's understandable resentment at having received no tip for a time-consuming job the previous year, there is no evidence that he was dissatisfied with the existing tipping arrangements or wanted them to be modified. Indeed, the evidence is to the contrary. Greenidge testified that the tips he receives "help[ ] to make a good bit of change," as much as $150 a day (Tr. 31). And, as stated previously, Greenidge testified that the remark at issue here was "just a comment" and was not aimed at changing the Respondent's policies or practices. Thus, the evidence does not support a finding that Greenidge was seeking "to improve terms and conditions of employment." *Eastex*, supra at 565.

* * *

■ MEMBER MCFERRAN, dissenting.

[L]ongstanding Board and court precedent compels a finding that Greenidge's complaint constituted an attempt to initiate a group objection over tips, and that he was thus engaged in concerted activity for the mutual aid and protection of his fellow skycaps—conduct for which he could not lawfully be fired. Instead, the majority upholds Greenidge's discharge, misreading and overruling (without being asked) a recent Board decision and imposing sharp new restrictions (unsupported by precedent) on what counts as "concerted" and "mutual aid or protection" for purposes of Section 7.

* * *

In order *not* to find concerted activity here, the majority chooses, without any request by a party or invitation for briefing,[18] to unnecessarily overrule a recent Board decision, *WorldMark by Wyndham*, and to improperly recast settled Board precedent. The majority purports to accept and apply the *Meyers I* and *II* lines of cases and their definition of concerted activity—which includes individual conduct intended to induce or initiate group action—but either casts aside or reinterprets those precedents. In their place, the majority adopts a checklist of factors that imposes significant, and unwarranted, restrictions on what counts as concerted activity.

* * *

---

[18] This appears to be another example of procedural overreach by the majority. Yet again, the majority disregards adjudicative norms in order to make new law without giving the parties or the public any notice or opportunity to weigh in. *See, e.g., UPMC*, 365 NLRB No. 153, slip op. at 17 (2017) (Member McFerran, dissenting). Although my colleagues dismiss my "familiar refrain," I remain convinced that the Board, the Act, and reasoned decision-making are all better served if we invite public participation in deciding important labor-law questions—as the Board used to do.

The majority risks frustrating the full realization of that statutory objective by subordinating the fact-sensitive approach at the heart of a *Meyers* analysis to criteria that effectively establish a minimum threshold for finding that an employee's activity is concerted.[23] As the Third Circuit put it, in rejecting an employer's attempt to pick apart an employee's protest based on assertedly missing elements, the majority's factors "espouse an unduly cramped interpretation of concerted activity under [Section] 7—one that assesses concerted activity in terms of isolated points of conduct rather than the totality of the circumstances.". . .

It is not difficult to see, moreover, how the majority's "unduly cramped" factors are likely to exclude from protection what is concerted activity by any reasonable measure.[24] Take the majority's first factor: whether the statement occurred at a meeting called by the employer at which the policy being protested was newly announced. To be sure, that an employee has raised a matter at an official meeting might well *strengthen* an inference of the intent to induce group action. But, as Board and judicial decisions illustrate, employees also initiate protest through spontaneous, informal means that also deserve Section 7 protection. Factor 3—which suggests that employee questions, as opposed to declarative protests, are less likely to be inducements of group action—suffers from the same obvious defect. Asking questions is frequently an indirect way of criticizing and drawing others to oppose a new policy. Likewise, the majority's factor 5—which suggests that an intent to induce group action is absent if the employee previously had an opportunity to, but did not, discuss a matter with his coworkers—unnecessarily excludes the possibility that an employee might not jump at the first opportunity to protest, but instead might take or need time to work up the resolve to confront his employer about a matter of obvious mutual employee concern.

---

[23] The majority states that the factors are not exhaustive. Yet, somewhat contradictorily, my colleagues expressly provide that not *all* of these factors must be present to find an inducement to group action—thus implying that *at least one factor must be present* and that situations not encompassed by these factors will not support an inference of concerted action. Further, my colleagues' application of these factors in the present case makes clear that the absence of any one of these factors will weigh against an inference of concerted intent. For example, my colleagues find that, with respect to Greenidge's comment, there "was no meeting, no announcement by management regarding wages, hours, or other terms and conditions of employment, and absent such an announcement, no protest that, under the totality of the circumstances, would support an inference that an individual was seeking to initiate or induce group action." In other words, the absence of these new criteria is dispositive, despite other circumstances supporting an inference of concert.

[24] My colleagues deem my criticism of their factor-based approach an "alarmist response," because this case is not within the "heartland" of concerted activity. But Sec. 7 rights are the core of the Act, and they should be protected to the full extent Congress intended, not cut back for the sake of predictability (the majority's stated aim). If Sec. 7 were interpreted down to nothing, of course, predictability would be achieved, but at the expense of the purpose of the statute. The majority is similarly incorrect not to recognize that what begins on the "borderline" may well lead to the "heartland." As the Board has observed, "almost any concerted activity for mutual aid or protection has to start with some kind of communication between individuals. . . ."

Applying the majority's factor-based test to Greenidge's case puts its severe limitations in stark relief. The majority ignores the overall picture that the facts in this case depict: spontaneous or not, Greenidge's statement indicated an objective intent to induce group action. As described, prompted by Greenidge's complaint to Supervisor Crawford about the soccer team's previous failure to tip the skycaps—a matter of mutual concern among them—the skycaps initially refused to attend to the team. All of the skycaps acted together, and they were subsequently disciplined as a group for their response to Greenidge's statement. Thus, at each step of the way, the evidence shows that Greenidge's objection cannot reasonably be dismissed as a purely personal concern, as the majority does.[27] Rather, the Board should find that it qualified as "concerted" activity under well-settled Board and court precedent.

B.

Just as it errs with respect to whether Greenidge's protest was concerted, the majority erroneously concludes that the protest was not for "mutual aid or protection." "The concept of 'mutual aid or protection' focuses on the *goal* of concerted activity;" here, Greenidge's obvious concern that the skycaps be compensated fairly for work performed. *Fresh & Easy Neighborhood Market*, supra, 361 NLRB at 153. That the Respondent was not directly responsible for the skycaps' tips does not mean that group action related to tips was not for "mutual aid or protection." In fact, the "mutual aid or protection" element is easily satisfied in this case. By broadly holding that tips are not matters of "mutual aid or protection," my colleagues have unquestionably curtailed the Act's protection for tipped employees who engage in any form of concerted conduct involving this critical aspect of their working conditions.[28]

As the Board observed in *Fresh & Easy Neighborhood Market*, supra, the Supreme Court has endorsed the view that "Congress designed Section 7 'to protect concerted activities for the *somewhat broader* purpose of "mutual aid or protection" as well as for the narrower purposes of "self-organization and collective bargaining.'" 361 NLRB at 154

---

[27] As noted, the majority mistakenly relies on Greenidge's testimony that his remark was "just a comment," as "[a]n employee's subjective motive for taking action is not relevant to whether that action was concerted." *Fresh & Easy Neighborhood Market*, supra, 361 NLRB at 153 (internal citations omitted). Further, whatever Greenidge's subjective intent, his coworkers plainly did not understand it as a purely personal concern to him. Why else did they follow his lead? Query, moreover, whether the majority would find the converse to be true: if an employee is credited as subjectively intending to induce group action, but there is no objective evidence supporting that aim, is the conduct concerted? Compare *Citizens Investment*, supra 342 NLRB at 316 fn. 2 (disavowing any reliance on employee's subjective statement that he intended to engage in concerted activity).

[28] The majority accuses me of inappropriately turning this case into a "referendum" on the Act's protections for tipped employees, because "[n]othing in [the] holding should be read as reducing the Act's protection for employees whose pay is in part comprised of tips." Except, that is exactly what my colleagues are doing—expressly finding that Greenidge's remark was not for mutual aid or protection because he was a worker whose compensation involved tips and his comment was directed toward this aspect of his compensation.

(quoting *Eastex, Inc. v. NLRB*, 437 U.S. 556, 565 (1978)). Thus, the "mutual aid or protection" clause encompasses a wide swath of employee activity that has the potential to "improve their lot as employees." Id. This necessarily includes employees' shared "interests as employees," even if they do not "relate to a specific dispute between employees and their own employer over an issue which the employer has the right or power to affect." *Eastex, Inc. v. NLRB*, supra, 437 U.S. at 563, 566–567. As with "concerted" activity, the concept of "mutual aid or protection" has its limits, but those limits are reached only when there is a highly "attenuated" connection to workplace interests. Id. at 567–568. The present case falls well within that limit.

Greenidge's comment raised an issue of shared interest among all skycaps and other employees: how much they were paid. Tips constituted the lion's share of the skycaps' earnings, a common reality faced by many service workers. Indeed, for many if not most tipped employees, few subjects impinge more dramatically on working conditions than the amount of their tips. The federal minimum wage for tipped workers is $2.13[29] and tips generally make up the remainder of their hourly earnings. For restaurant workers, who make up the largest portion of the tipped work force, tips can make up over half their income (leaving some below the poverty level *even after* accounting for tips).[30] Consequently, for most employees, and certainly for the skycaps in this case, discussions about the amount of tips directly concern their compensation, are integral to their "interests as employees," and are thus for "mutual aid or protection." *Eastex*, supra, at 567. Thus, Greenidge's comment directly implicated the skycaps' interests as employees and fell comfortably within the scope of Section 7's "mutual aid or protection" clause.

The majority's contrary view misunderstands both the broad language of Section 7 and the workplace reality for tipped workers by inexplicably holding that Greenidge's comment was unrelated to terms and conditions of employment, despite overwhelming evidence to the contrary. In particular, there is no merit at all to the majority's argument that the skycaps' tips were solely a matter between them and airline passengers. As discussed, there can be no denying that tips fall within the broad ambit of matters within the shared interests of employees, regardless of whether the tips were within the Respondent's control or even a term or condition of employment. Moreover, tips are clearly an implicit part of skycaps' terms and conditions of employment, as both employers and employees in tip-reliant industries expect and depend upon the fact that tips will supplement direct wages and thus provide for

---

[29] This is the amount the employer must directly pay tipped employees. The difference between the $2.13 minimum wage and the standard $7.25 minimum wage must be made up for in tips, or else the employer will have to make up the difference in order to be in compliance with the federal minimum wage. States often establish their own minimum and tipped-employee minimum wages.

[30] See Irene Tung, National Employment Law Project, *Wait Staff and Bartenders Depend on Tips for More Than Half of Their Earnings*, available at *https://www.nelp.org/publication/wait-staff-and-bartenders-depend-on-tips-for-more-than-half-of-their-earnings/*.

adequate overall compensation. Indeed, the Respondent was legally permitted to pay the skycaps less than the state and federal minimum wage precisely because the skycaps were expected to work for and receive tips. Not surprisingly, the Board has recognized that tips, particularly in customer-service-oriented industries, are properly regarded as a component of wages, and thus are a term and condition of employment, *even when the employer is not the source of those tips.* See generally *The Capitol Times Co.*, 223 NLRB 651–652 (1976), overruled on other grounds by *Peerless Publications*, 283 NLRB 334 (1987). That recognition is grounded in the common sense understanding that the payment of customer tips to an employee actually bears on the employer-employee relationship, not least of all because the employer benefits when employees are rewarded and encouraged to provide good services on the employer's behalf. Id. For this reason, the majority's insistence that the Respondent was "essentially detached" from the skycaps' concern over their tips is baseless.[33]

* * *

QUESTIONS FOR DISCUSSION

1. The *Alstate* majority opines that prior Board precedent "erroneously shields individual action and thereby undermines congressional intent" to the contrary. They cite no evidence of such intent other than the words of Section 7 taken from Section 2 of the Norris-LaGuardia Act. Does the history of these support the categorical claim the majority makes? *See* Robert Gorman & Matthew Finkin, *The Individual and the Requirement of "Concert" Under the National Labor Relations Act*, 130 U. PA. L. REV. 286 (1981).

2. If Greenidge had not expressed a group grievance, why did he say "we"? The Board had attached considerable significance in its caselaw to whether an employee grievance was couched in the first person plural or singular. Those precedents were overruled by *Alstate*. Did the Board place too much weight on a pronoun? How else is a group concern to be expressed?

3. The Board majority says the payment of a tip is entirely a matter between the customer and the worker—"the employer is essentially detached." Is that true? Isn't a payment made by a customer to an employee to reward the employee or doing some act for the customer that is within the employee's scope of employment possibly to encourage the doing of such acts

---

[33] The Supreme Court's decision in *Eastex* also undercuts the majority's position that Greenidge's comment concerned a matter solely between the skycaps and the passengers. *Eastex* itself involved protests concerning federal and state law—matters further afield than customer tips from the employer-employee relationship. The *Eastex* Court nevertheless found that a wide range of factors—including matters not even "relate[d] to a specific dispute between employees and their own employer," id. at 563, 567—are matters of mutual aid or protection. Although Greenidge, unlike the employees in *Eastex*, did not appeal to legislative, judicial, or administrative forums, the Court made clear that the scope of the clause was far broader, including "*much legitimate activity* that could improve their lot as employees." Id. at 566 (emphasis added). Certainly, a verbal protest, directed not at a third-party government entity but at one's own employer, regarding a central workplace concern, is well within the bounds of mutual aid or protection.

in future a bribe? Is the employer "essentially detached" from that transaction? Matthew Finkin, *"The Kindness of Strangers": The Tip and the Minimum Wage in France, Germany, and the United States*, 32 INT'L J. COMP. LAB. L. & INDUS. REL. 3 (2016).

4. It appears that the customer for whom the baggage was being stowed and who would pay the tip was not the soccer players—there is no reference to their being present—but rather Lufthansa, their carrier. The majority discounts the Labor Act significance of Mr. Greenidge's comment insofar as it was directed to his manager who had no control over tips. But it was also made in the presence of Lufthansa's manager, who did. Why was Mr. Greenidge's comment made in Lufthansa's presence not protected?

5. ChumpOn, Inc., is a waste disposal company. Overtime is voluntary and is assigned in order of seniority. An overtime sheet is posted on a bulletin board. Workers wanting to work sign their names. When overtime work is needed the supervisor retrieves this sheet, checks the names by seniority, and assigns the work in order of seniority. The workers have demanded that overtime assignments be equalized; volunteers having the fewest overtime hours could be given it first. The Company has refused; the sign-up system has continued. The sign-up sheet has become universally referred to by workers and supervisors alike as the "whore board." Bob Dylan, 23, has worked as a sorter for 18 months. He has a wife, two children, and one on the way. He needs to work as much overtime as possible for family income. As he clocked out he wrote "Whore Board" on the posted overtime sheet. He has been discharged for defacing company property. Has the Company violated the Labor Act? Should it make a difference whether the workforce was unionized? Why? Constellium Rolled Products Ravenswood, LLC, 366 NLRB No. 131 (2018).

Page 562. Add to Problems for Discussion:

4. Jessica Leo is a software engineer for Aries Services. Aries has sent her a notice that as of the next working day she would be considered an independent contractor. A statement of terms was attached. This included the loss of medical insurance provided employees. A month later, she emailed Aries' CEO stating that she was "not trying to rock the boat or anything, but I am trying to look out for myself and get proper health insurance". Aries then fired her. She filed a charge of violation of sections 8(a)(1) and (3) with the NLRB. You are General Counsel. Will you issue a complaint? NLRB Gen. Counsel Advice Mem. in Libra Services, Inc. (April 23, 2018). Should it make a difference to you that she was the only software engineer employed by Aries? Or that there was a group of software engineers who's status changed, but that Ms. Leo was the only one of them to challenge it? Or whether she had spoken to them before writing the CEO, that they encourage her to do so but declined to join their names to her letter? If any of these make a difference, why?

Page 560. Add following to *Murphy Oil*:

Epic Sys. Corp. v. Lewis[*]
___ U.S. ___, 138 S.Ct. 1612, 200 L.Ed.2d 889 (2018).

■ JUSTICE GORSUCH delivered the opinion of the Court.

* * *

[These three cases involved company policies governing their employees that required them to resort exclusively to the Company-created arbitration system to vindicate most employment law claim they had against the Company. These policies limited employee resort to arbitration only individually. Under these policies two or more employees who claimed to suffer the same legal wrong—misclassification as an independent contractor, denied of overtime pay under federal or cognate state law, and the like—were required to arbitrate only in bilateral arbitrations. They could not join one another in making a common claim against a common wrong. The Labor Board in *Murphy Oil*, set out in the casebook at page 544, held the policy to violate section 8(a)(1) of the Labor Act.]

II

We begin with the Arbitration Act and the question of its saving clause.

Congress adopted the Arbitration Act in 1925 in response to a perception that courts were unduly hostile to arbitration. No doubt there was much to that perception. Before 1925, English and American common law courts routinely refused to enforce agreements to arbitrate disputes. *Scherk v. Alberto-Culver Co.*, 417 U. S. 506, 510, n. 4 (1974). But in Congress's judgment arbitration had more to offer than courts recognized—not least the promise of quicker, more informal, and often cheaper resolutions for everyone involved. *Id.*, at 511. So Congress directed courts to abandon their hostility and instead treat arbitration agreements as "valid, irrevocable, and enforceable." 9 U. S. C. § 2. The Act, this Court has said, establishes "a liberal federal policy favoring arbitration agreements." *Moses H. Cone Memorial Hospital v. Mercury Constr. Corp.*, 460 U. S. 1, 24 (1983) (citing *Prima Paint Corp. v. Flood & Conklin Mfg. Co.*, 388 U. S. 395 (1967)); see *id.*, at 404 (discussing "the plain meaning of the statute" and "the unmistakably clear congressional purpose that the arbitration procedure, when selected by the parties to a contract, be speedy and not subject to delay and obstruction in the courts").

---

[*] Together with No. 16–300, *Ernst & Young LLP et al.* v. *Morris et al.*, on certiorari to the United States Court of Appeals for the Ninth Circuit, and No. 16–307, *National Labor Relations Board* v. *Murphy Oil USA, Inc., et al.*, on certiorari to the United States Court of Appeals for the Fifth Circuit.

Not only did Congress require courts to respect and enforce agreements to arbitrate; it also specifically directed them to respect and enforce the parties' chosen arbitration procedures. See § 3 (providing for a stay of litigation pending arbitration "in accordance with the terms of the agreement"); § 4 (providing for "an order directing that . . . arbitration proceed in the manner provided for in such agreement"). Indeed, we have often observed that the Arbitration Act requires courts "rigorously" to "enforce arbitration agreements according to their terms, including terms that specify *with whom* the parties choose to arbitrate their disputes and *the rules* under which that arbitration will be conducted." *American Express Co. v. Italian Colors Restaurant*, 570 U. S. 228, 233 (2013) (some emphasis added; citations, internal quotation marks, and brackets omitted).

On first blush, these emphatic directions would seem to resolve any argument under the Arbitration Act. The parties before us contracted for arbitration. They proceeded to specify the rules that would govern their arbitrations, indicating their intention to use individualized rather than class or collective action procedures. And this much the Arbitration Act seems to protect pretty absolutely. See *AT&T Mobility LLC v. Concepcion*, 563 U. S. 333 (2011); *Italian Colors, supra*; *DIRECTV, Inc. v. Imburgia*, 577 U. S. ___ (2015). You might wonder if the balance Congress struck in 1925 between arbitration and litigation should be revisited in light of more contemporary developments. You might even ask if the Act was good policy when enacted. But all the same you might find it difficult to see how to avoid the statute's application.

Still, the employees suggest the Arbitration Act's saving clause creates an exception for cases like theirs. By its terms, the saving clause allows courts to refuse to enforce arbitration agreements "upon such grounds as exist at law or in equity for the revocation of any contract." § 2. That provision applies here, the employees tell us, because the NLRA renders their particular class and collective action waivers illegal. In their view, illegality under the NLRA is a "ground" that "exists at law . . . for the revocation" of their arbitration agreements, at least to the extent those agreements prohibit class or collective action proceedings.

The problem with this line of argument is fundamental. Put to the side the question whether the saving clause was designed to save not only state law defenses but also defenses allegedly arising from federal statutes. See 834 F. 3d, at 991–992, 997 (Ikuta, J., dissenting). Put to the side the question of what it takes to qualify as a ground for "revocation" of a contract. See *Concepcion, supra,* at 352–355 (THOMAS, J., concurring); *post,* at 1–2 (THOMAS, J., concurring). Put to the side for the moment, too, even the question whether the NLRA actually renders class and collective action waivers illegal. Assuming (but not granting) the employees could satisfactorily answer all those questions, the saving clause still can't save their cause.

It can't because the saving clause recognizes only defenses that apply to "any" contract. In this way the clause establishes a sort of "equal-treatment" rule for arbitration contracts. *Kindred Nursing Centers L. P. v. Clark*, 581 U. S. ___ (2017) (slip op., at 4). The clause "permits agreements to arbitrate to be invalidated by 'generally applicable contract defenses, such as fraud, duress, or unconscionability.'" *Concepcion*, 563 U. S., at 339. At the same time, the clause offers no refuge for "defenses that apply only to arbitration or that derive their meaning from the fact that an agreement to arbitrate is at issue." *Ibid.* Under our precedent, this means the saving clause does not save defenses that target arbitration either by name or by more subtle methods, such as by "interfer[ing] with fundamental attributes of arbitration." *Id.*, at 344; see *Kindred Nursing, supra,* at (slip op., at 5).

This is where the employees' argument stumbles. They don't suggest that their arbitration agreements were extracted, say, by an act of fraud or duress or in some other unconscionable way that would render *any* contract unenforceable. Instead, they object to their agreements precisely because they require individualized arbitration proceedings instead of class or collective ones. And by attacking (only) the individualized nature of the arbitration proceedings, the employees' argument seeks to interfere with one of arbitration's fundamental attributes.

We know this much because of *Concepcion*. There this Court faced a state law defense that prohibited as unconscionable class action waivers in consumer contracts. The Court readily acknowledged that the defense formally applied in both the litigation and the arbitration context. 563 U. S., at 338, 341. But, the Court held, the defense failed to qualify for protection under the saving clause because it interfered with a fundamental attribute of arbitration all the same. It did so by effectively permitting any party in arbitration to demand classwide proceedings despite the traditionally individualized and informal nature of arbitration. This "fundamental" change to the traditional arbitration process, the Court said, would "sacrific[e] the principal advantage of arbitration—its informality—and mak[e] the process slower, more costly, and more likely to generate procedural morass than final judgment." *Id.,* at 347, 348. Not least, *Concepcion* noted, arbitrators would have to decide whether the named class representatives are sufficiently representative and typical of the class; what kind of notice, opportunity to be heard, and right to opt out absent class members should enjoy; and how discovery should be altered in light of the classwide nature of the proceedings. *Ibid.* All of which would take much time and effort, and introduce new risks and costs for both sides. *Ibid.* In the Court's judgment, the virtues Congress originally saw in arbitration, its speed and simplicity and inexpensiveness, would be shorn away and arbitration would wind up looking like the litigation it was meant to displace.

Of course, *Concepcion* has its limits. The Court recognized that parties remain free to alter arbitration procedures to suit their tastes, and in recent years some parties have sometimes chosen to arbitrate on a classwide basis. *Id.*, at 351. But *Concepcion*'s essential insight remains: courts may not allow a contract defense to reshape traditional individualized arbitration by mandating classwide arbitration procedures without the parties' consent. *Id.*, at 344–351; see also *Stolt-Nielsen S. A. v. AnimalFeeds Int'l Corp.*, 559 U. S. 662, 684–687 (2010). Just as judicial antagonism toward arbitration before the Arbitration Act's enactment "manifested itself in a great variety of devices and formulas declaring arbitration against public policy," *Concepcion* teaches that we must be alert to new devices and formulas that would achieve much the same result today. 563 U. S., at 342 (internal quotation marks omitted). And a rule seeking to declare individualized arbitration proceedings off limits is, the Court held, just such a device.

The employees' efforts to distinguish *Concepcion* fall short. They note that their putative NLRA defense would render an agreement "illegal" as a matter of federal statutory law rather than "unconscionable" as a matter of state common law. But we don't see how that distinction makes any difference in light of *Concepion*'s rationale and rule. Illegality, like unconscionability, may be a traditional, generally applicable contract defense in many cases, including arbitration cases. But an argument that a contract is unenforceable *just because it requires bilateral arbitration* is a different creature. A defense of that kind, *Concepcion* tells us, is one that impermissibly disfavors arbitration whether it sounds in illegality or unconscionability. The law of precedent teaches that like cases should generally be treated alike, and appropriate respect for that principle means the Arbitration Act's saving clause can no more save the defense at issue in these cases than it did the defense at issue in *Concepcion*. At the end of our encounter with the Arbitration Act, then, it appears just as it did at the beginning: a congressional command requiring us to enforce, not override, the terms of the arbitration agreements before us.

III

But that's not the end of it. Even if the Arbitration Act normally requires us to enforce arbitration agreements d choose among congressional enactments" and must instead strive " 'to give effect to both.' " *Morton v. Mancari*, 417 U. S. 535, 551 (1974). A party seeking to suggest that two statutes cannot be harmonized, and that one displaces the other, bears the heavy burden of showing " 'a clearly expressed congressional intention' " that such a result should follow. *Vimar Seguros y Reaseguros, S. A. v. M/V Sky Reefer*, 515 U. S. 528, 533 (1995). The intention must be " 'clear and manifest.' " *Morton, supra*, at 551. And in approaching a claimed conflict, we come armed with the "stron[g] presum[ption]" that repeals by implication are "disfavored" and that "Congress will specifically address" preexisting law when it wishes to suspend its normal operations in a later statute. *United States v. Fausto*, 484 U. S. 439, 452, 453 (1988).

These rules exist for good reasons. Respect for Congress as drafter counsels against too easily finding irreconcilable conflicts in its work. More than that, respect for the separation of powers counsels restraint. Allowing judges to pick and choose between statutes risks transforming them from expounders of what the law *is* into policymakers choosing what the law *should be*. Our rules aiming for harmony over conflict in statutory interpretation grow from an appreciation that it's the job of Congress by legislation, not this Court by supposition, both to write the laws and to repeal them.

Seeking to demonstrate an irreconcilable statutory conflict even in light of these demanding standards, the employees point to Section 7 of the NLRA. That provision guarantees workers "the right to self-organization, to form, join, or assist labor organizations, to bargain collectively through representatives of their own choosing, and to engage in other concerted activities for the purpose of collective bargaining or other mutual aid or protection." 29 U. S. C. § 157. From this language, the employees ask us to infer a clear and manifest congressional command to displace the Arbitration Act and outlaw agreements like theirs.

But that much inference is more than this Court may make. Section 7 focuses on the right to organize unions and bargain collectively. It may permit unions to bargain to prohibit arbitration. Cf. *14 Penn Plaza LLC v. Pyett*, 556 U. S. 247, 256–260 (2009). But it does not express approval or disapproval of arbitration. It does not mention class or collective action procedures. It does not even hint at a wish to displace the Arbitration Act—let alone accomplish that much clearly and manifestly, as our precedents demand.

Neither should any of this come as a surprise. The notion that Section 7 confers a right to class or collective actions seems pretty unlikely when you recall that procedures like that were hardly known when the NLRA was adopted in 1935. Federal Rule of Civil Procedure 23 didn't create the modern class action until 1966; class arbitration didn't emerge until later still; and even the Fair Labor Standards Act's collective action provision postdated Section 7 by years. See Rule 23–Class Actions, 28 U. S. C. App., p. 1258 (1964 ed., Supp. II); 52 Stat. 1069; *Concepcion*, 563 U. S., at 349; see also *Califano v. Yamasaki*, 442 U. S. 682, 700–701 (1979) (noting that the "usual rule" then was litigation "conducted by and on behalf of individual named parties only"). And while some forms of group litigation existed even in 1935, see 823 F. 3d, at 1154, Section 7's failure to mention them only reinforces that the statute doesn't speak to such procedures.

A close look at the employees' best evidence of a potential conflict turns out to reveal no conflict at all. The employees direct our attention to the term "other concerted activities for the purpose of . . . other mutual aid or protection." This catchall term, they say, can be read to include class and collective legal actions. But the term appears at the end of a detailed list of activities speaking of "self-organization," "form[ing], join[ing], or assist[ing] labor organizations," and "bargain[ing] collectively." U. S. C. § 157. And where, as here, a more general term follows more specific terms in a list, the general term is usually understood to " 'embrace only objects similar in nature to those objects enumerated by the preceding specific words.' " *Circuit City Stores, Inc. v. Adams*, 532 U. S. 105, 115 (2001) (discussing *ejusdem generis* canon); *National Assn. of Mfrs. v. Department of Defense*, 583 U. S. ___ (2018) (slip op., at 10). All of which suggests that the term "other concerted activities" should, like the terms that precede it, serve to protect things employees "just do" for themselves in the course of exercising their right to free association in the workplace, rather than "the highly regulated, courtroom-bound 'activities' of class and joint litigation." *Alternative Entertainment*, 858 F. 3d, at 414–415 (Sutton, J., concurring in part and dissenting in part) (emphasis deleted). None of the preceding and more specific terms speaks to the procedures judges or arbitrators must apply in disputes that leave the workplace and enter the courtroom or arbitral forum, and there is no textually sound reason to suppose the final catchall term should bear such a radically different object than all its predecessors.

The NLRA's broader structure underscores the point. After speaking of various "concerted activities" in Section 7, Congress proceeded to establish a regulatory regime applicable to each of them. The NLRA provides rules for the recognition of exclusive bargaining representatives, 29 U. S. C. § 159, explains employees' and employers' obligation to bargain collectively, § 158(d), and conscribes certain labor organization practices, §§ 158(a)(3), (b). The NLRA also touches on other concerted activities closely related to organization and collective bargaining, such as picketing, § 158(b)(7), and strikes, § 163. It even sets rules for adjudicatory proceedings under the NLRA itself. §§ 160, 161. Many of these provisions were part of the original NLRA in 1935, see 49 Stat. 449, while others were added later. But missing entirely from this careful regime is any hint about what rules should govern the adjudication of class or collective actions in court or arbitration. Without some comparably specific guidance, it's not at all obvious what procedures Section 7 might protect. Would opt-out class action procedures suffice? Or would opt-in procedures be necessary? What notice might be owed to absent class members? What standards would govern class certification? Should the same rules always apply or should they vary based on the nature of the suit? Nothing in the NLRA even whispers to us on any of these essential questions. And it is hard to fathom why Congress would take such care to regulate all the other matters mentioned in Section 7 yet remain mute about this matter alone—unless, of course, Section 7 doesn't speak to class and collective action procedures in the first place.

Telling, too, is the fact that when Congress wants to mandate particular dispute resolution procedures it knows exactly how to do so. Congress has spoken often and clearly to the procedures for resolving "actions," "claims," "charges," and "cases" in statute after statute. *E.g.,* 29 U. S. C. §§ 216(b), 626; 42 U. S. C. §§ 2000e–5(b), (f)(3)–(5). Congress has likewise shown that it knows how to override the Arbitration Act when it wishes—by explaining, for example, that, "[n]otwithstanding any other provision of law, . . . arbitration may be used . . . only if " certain conditions are met, 15 U. S. C. § 1226(a)(2); or that "[n]o predispute arbitration agreement shall be valid or enforceable" in other circumstances, 7 U. S. C. § 26(n)(2); 12 U. S. C. § 5567(d)(2); or that requiring a party to arbitrate is "unlawful" in other circumstances yet, 10 U. S. C. § 987(e)(3). The fact that we have nothing like that here is further evidence that Section 7 does nothing to address the question of class and collective actions.

In response, the employees offer this slight reply. They suggest that the NLRA doesn't discuss any particular class and collective action procedures because it merely confers a right to use *existing* procedures provided by statute or rule, "on the same terms as [they are] made available to everyone else." Brief for Respondent in No. 16–285, p. 53, n. 10. But of course the NLRA doesn't say even that much. And, besides, if the parties really take existing class and collective action rules as they find them, they surely take them subject to the limitations inherent in those rules—including the principle that parties may (as here) contract to depart from them in favor of individualized arbitration procedures of their own design.

Still another contextual clue yields the same message. The employees' underlying causes of action involve their wages and arise not under the NLRA but under an entirely different statute, the Fair Labor Standards Act. The FLSA allows employees to sue on behalf of "themselves and other employees similarly situated," 29 U. S. C. § 216(b), and it's precisely this sort of collective action the employees before us wish to pursue. Yet they do not offer the seemingly more natural suggestion that the FLSA overcomes the Arbitration Act to permit their class and collective actions. Why not? Presumably because this Court held decades ago that an identical collective action scheme (in fact, one borrowed from the FLSA) does *not* displace the Arbitration Act or prohibit individualized arbitration proceedings. *Gilmer v. Interstate/ Johnson Lane Corp.,* 500 U. S. 20, 32 (1991) (discussing Age Discrimination in Employment Act). In fact, it turns out that "[e]very circuit to consider the question" has held that the FLSA allows agreements for individualized arbitration. *Alternative Entertainment,* 858 F. 3d, at 413 (opinion of Sutton, J.) (collecting cases). Faced with that obstacle, the employees are left to cast about elsewhere for help. And so they have cast in this direction, suggesting that one statute (the NLRA) steps in to dictate the procedures for claims under a different statute (the

FLSA), and thereby overrides the commands of yet a third statute (the Arbitration Act). It's a sort of interpretive triple bank shot, and just stating the theory is enough to raise a judicial eyebrow.

Perhaps worse still, the employees' theory runs afoul of the usual rule that Congress "does not alter the fundamental details of a regulatory scheme in vague terms or ancillary provisions—it does not, one might say, hide elephants in mouseholes." *Whitman v. American Trucking Assns., Inc.*, 531 U. S. 457, 468 (2001). Union organization and collective bargaining in the workplace are the bread and butter of the NLRA, while the particulars of dispute resolution procedures in Article III courts or arbitration proceedings are usually left to other statutes and rules—not least the Federal Rules of Civil Procedure, the Arbitration Act, and the FLSA. It's more than a little doubtful that Congress would have tucked into the mousehole of Section 7's catchall term an elephant that tramples the work done by these other laws; flattens the parties' contracted-for dispute resolution procedures; and seats the Board as supreme superintendent of claims arising under a statute it doesn't even administer.

Nor does it help to fold yet another statute into the mix. At points, the employees suggest that the Norris-LaGuardia Act, a precursor of the NLRA, also renders their arbitration agreements unenforceable. But the Norris-LaGuardia Act adds nothing here. It declares "[un]enforceable" contracts that conflict with its policy of protecting workers' "concerted activities for the purpose of collective bargaining or other mutual aid or protection." 29 U. S. C. §§ 102, 103. That is the same policy the NLRA advances and, as we've seen, it does not conflict with Congress's statutory directions favoring arbitration. See also *Boys Markets, Inc. v. Retail Clerks*, 398 U. S. 235 (1970) (holding that the Norris-LaGuardia Act's anti-injunction provisions do not bar enforcement of arbitration agreements).

What all these textual and contextual clues indicate, our precedents confirm. In many cases over many years, this Court has heard and rejected efforts to conjure conflicts between the Arbitration Act and other federal statutes. In fact, this Court has rejected *every* such effort to date (save one temporary exception since overruled), with statutes ranging from the Sherman and Clayton Acts to the Age Discrimination in Employment Act, the Credit Repair Organizations Act, the Securities Act of 1933, the Securities Exchange Act of 1934, and the Racketeer Influenced and Corrupt Organizations Act. *Italian Colors*, 570 U. S. 228; *Gilmer*, 500 U. S. 20; *CompuCredit Corp. v. Greenwood*, 565 U. S. 95 (2012); *Rodriguez de Quijas v. Shearson/American Express, Inc.*, 490 U. S. 477 (1989) (overruling *Wilko v. Swan*, 346 U. S. 427 (1953)); *Shearson/American Express Inc. v. McMahon*, 482 U. S. 220 (1987). Throughout, we have made clear that even a statute's express provision for collective legal actions does not necessarily mean that it precludes " 'individual attempts at conciliation' " through arbitration. *Gilmer*, *supra,* at 32. And we've stressed that the absence of any specific statutory discussion of arbitration or class actions is an important and telling clue that Congress has not displaced the Arbitration Act. *CompuCredit, supra,* at 103–104; *McMahon, supra,* at 227; *Italian Colors, supra,* at 234. Given so much precedent pointing so strongly in one direction, we do not see how we might faithfully turn the other way here.

Consider a few examples. In *Italian Colors,* this Court refused to find a conflict between the Arbitration Act and the Sherman Act because the Sherman Act (just like the NLRA) made "no mention of class actions" and was adopted before Rule 23 introduced its exception to the "usual rule" of "individual" dispute resolution. 570 U. S., at 234 (internal quotation marks omitted). In *Gilmer,* this Court "had no qualms in enforcing a class waiver in an arbitration agreement even though" the Age Discrimination in Employment Act "expressly permitted collective legal actions." *Italian Colors, supra,* at 237 (citing *Gilmer, supra,* at 32). And in *CompuCredit,* this Court refused to find a conflict even though the Credit Repair Organizations Act expressly provided a "right to sue," "repeated[ly]" used the words "action" and "court" and "class action," and even declared "[a]ny waiver" of the rights it provided to be "void." 565 U. S., at 99–100 (internal quotation marks omitted). If all the statutes in all those cases did not provide a congressional command sufficient to displace the Arbitration Act, we cannot imagine how we might hold that the NLRA alone and for the first time does so today.

The employees rejoin that our precedential story is complicated by some of this Court's cases interpreting Section 7 itself. But, as it turns out, this Court's Section 7 cases have usually involved just what you would expect from the statute's plain language: efforts by employees related to organizing and collective bargaining in the workplace, not the treatment of class or collective actions in court or arbitration proceedings. See, *e.g., NLRB v. Washington Aluminum Co.,* 370 U. S. 9 (1962) (walkout to protest workplace conditions); *NLRB v. Textile Workers,* 409 U. S. 213 (1972) (resignation from union and refusal to strike); *NLRB v. J. Weingarten, Inc.,* 420 U. S. 251 (1975) (request for union representation at disciplinary interview). Neither do the two cases the employees cite prove otherwise. In *Eastex, Inc. v. NLRB,* 437 U. S. 556, 558 (1978), we simply addressed the question whether a union's distribution of a newsletter in the workplace qualified as a protected concerted activity. We held it did, noting that it was "undisputed that the union undertook the distribution in order to boost its support and improve its bargaining position in upcoming contract negotiations," all part of the union's " 'continuing organizational efforts.' " *Id.,* at 575, and n. 24. In *NLRB v. City Disposal Systems, Inc.,* 465 U. S. 822, 831–832 (1984), we held only that an employee's assertion of a right under a collective bargaining agreement was protected, reasoning that the collective bargaining "process—beginning with the organization of the union, continuing into the negotiation of a collective-bargaining agreement, and extending through the enforcement of the agreement—is a single, collective activity." Nothing in our cases indicates that the NLRA guarantees class and collective action procedures, let alone for claims arising under different statutes and despite the express (and entirely unmentioned) teachings of the Arbitration Act.

That leaves the employees to try to make something of our dicta. The employees point to a line in *Eastex* observing that "it has been held" by other courts and the Board "that the 'mutual aid or protection' clause protects employees from retaliation by their employers when they seek to improve working conditions through resort to administrative and judicial forums." 437 U. S., at 565–566; see also Brief for National Labor Relations Board in No. 16–307, p. 15 (citing similar Board decisions). But even on its own terms, this dicta about the holdings of other bodies does not purport to discuss what *procedures* an employee might be entitled to in litigation or arbitration. Instead this passage at most suggests only that "resort to administrative and judicial forums" isn't "entirely unprotected." *Id.*, at 566. Indeed, the Court proceeded to explain that it did not intend to "address . . . the question of what may constitute 'concerted' activities in this [litigation] context." *Ibid.*, n. 15. So even the employees' dicta, when viewed fairly and fully, doesn't suggest that individualized dispute resolution procedures might be insufficient and collective procedures might be mandatory. Neither should this come as a surprise given that not a single one of the lower court or Board decisions *Eastex* discussed went so far as to hold that Section 7 guarantees a right to class or collective action procedures. As we've seen, the Board did not purport to discover that right until 2012, and no federal appellate court accepted it until 2016. See *D. R. Horton*, 357 N. L. R. B. 2277; 823 F. 3d 1147 (case below in No. 16–285).

* * *

[The Court then discussed deference to the Labor Board as a matter of administrative law under the *Chevron* doctrine and held no deference due.]

IV

The dissent sees things a little bit differently. In its view, today's decision ushers us back to the *Lochner* era when this Court regularly overrode legislative policy judgments. The dissent even suggests we have resurrected the long-dead "yellow dog" contract. *Post,* at 3–17, 30 (opinion of GINSBURG, J.). But like most apocalyptic warnings, this one proves a false alarm. Cf. L. Tribe, American Constitutional Law 435 (1978) (" '*Lochnerizing*' has become so much an epithet that the very use of the label may obscure attempts at understanding").

Our decision does nothing to override Congress's policy judgments. As the dissent recognizes, the legislative policy embodied in the NLRA is aimed at "safeguard[ing], first and foremost, workers' rights to join unions and to engage in collective bargaining." *Post,* at 8. Those rights stand every bit as strong today as they did yesterday. And rather than revive "yellow dog" contracts against union organizing that the NLRA outlawed back in 1935, today's decision merely declines to read into the NLRA a novel right to class action procedures that the Board's own general counsel disclaimed as recently as 2010.

Instead of overriding Congress's policy judgments, today's decision seeks to honor them. This much the dissent surely knows. Shortly after invoking the specter of *Lochner*, it turns around and criticizes the Court for trying *too hard* to abide the Arbitration Act's " 'liberal federal policy favoring arbitration agreements,' " *Howsam v. Dean Witter Reynolds, Inc.*, 537 U. S. 79, 83 (2002), saying we " 'ski' " too far down the " 'slippery slope' " of this Court's arbitration precedent, *post,* at 23. But the dissent's real complaint lies with the mountain of precedent itself. The dissent spends page after page relitigating our Arbitration Act precedents, rehashing arguments this Court has heard and rejected many times in many cases that no party has asked us to revisit. Compare *post,* at 18–23, 26 (criticizing *Mitsubishi Motors Corp. v. Soler Chrysler-Plymouth, Inc.*, 473 U. S. 614 (1985), *Gilmer*, 500 U. S. 20, *Circuit City*, 532 U. S. 105, *Concepcion*, 563 U. S. 333, *Italian Colors*, 570 U. S. 228, and *CompuCredit*, 565 U. S. 95), with *Mitsubishi, supra,* at 645–650 (Stevens, J., dissenting), *Gilmer, supra,* at 36, 39–43 (Stevens, J., dissenting), *Circuit City, supra,* at 124–129 (Stevens, J., dissenting), *Concepcion, supra,* at 357–367 (BREYER, J., dissenting), *Italian Colors, supra,* at 240–253 (KAGAN, J., dissenting), and *CompuCredit, supra,* at 116–117 (GINSBURG, J., dissenting).

When at last it reaches the question of applying our precedent, the dissent offers little, and understandably so. Our precedent clearly teaches that a contract defense "conditioning the enforceability of certain arbitration agreements on the availability of classwide arbitration procedures" is inconsistent with the Arbitration Act and its saving clause. *Concepcion, supra,* at 336 (opinion of the Court). And that, of course, is exactly what the employees' proffered defense seeks to do.

Nor is the dissent's reading of the NLRA any more available to us than its reading of the Arbitration Act. The dissent imposes a vast construction on Section 7's language. *Post,* at 9. But a statute's meaning does not always "turn solely" on the broadest imaginable "definitions of its component words." *Yates v. United States*, 574 U. S. ___ (2015) (plurality opinion) (slip op., at 7). Linguistic and statutory context also matter. We have offered an extensive explanation why those clues support our reading today. By contrast, the dissent rests its interpretation on legislative history. *Post,* at 3–5; see also *post,* at 19–21. But legislative history is not the law. "It is the business of Congress to sum up its own debates in its legislation," and once it enacts a statute " '[w]e do not inquire what the legislature meant; we ask only what the statute means.' " *Schwegmann Brothers v. Calvert Distillers Corp.*, 341 U. S. 384, 396, 397 (1951) (Jackson, J., concurring) (quoting Justice

Holmes). Besides, when it comes to the legislative history here, it seems Congress "did not discuss the right to file class or consolidated claims against employers." *D. R. Horton,* 737 F. 3d, at 361. So the dissent seeks instead to divine messages from congressional commentary directed to different questions altogether—a project that threatens to "substitute [the Court] for the Congress." *Schwegmann, supra,* at 396.

Nor do the problems end there. The dissent proceeds to argue that its expansive reading of the NLRA conflicts with and should prevail over the Arbitration Act. The NLRA leaves the Arbitration Act without force, the dissent says, because it provides the more "pinpointed" direction. *Post,* at 25. Even taken on its own terms, though, this argument quickly faces trouble. The dissent says the NLRA is the more specific provision because it supposedly "speaks directly to group action by employees," while the Arbitration Act doesn't speak to such actions. *Ibid.* But the question before us is whether courts must enforce particular arbitration agreements according to their terms. And it's the Arbitration Act that speaks directly to the enforceability of arbitration agreements, while the NLRA doesn't mention arbitration at all. So if forced to choose between the two, we might well say the Arbitration Act offers the more on-point instruction. Of course, there is no need to make that call because, as our precedents demand, we have sought and found a persuasive interpretation that gives effect to all of Congress's work, not just the parts we might prefer.

Ultimately, the dissent retreats to policy arguments. It argues that we should read a class and collective action right into the NLRA to promote the enforcement of wage and hour laws. *Post,* at 26–30. But it's altogether unclear why the dissent expects to find such a right in the NLRA rather than in statutes like the FLSA that actually regulate wages and hours. Or why we should read the NLRA as mandating the availability of class or collective actions when the FLSA expressly authorizes them yet allows parties to contract for bilateral arbitration instead. 29 U. S. C. § 216(b); *Gilmer, supra,* at 32. While the dissent is no doubt right that class actions can enhance enforcement by "spread[ing] the costs of litigation," *post,* at 9, it's also well known that they can unfairly "plac[e] pressure on the defendant to settle even unmeritorious claims," *Shady Grove Orthopedic Associates, P. A. v. Allstate Ins. Co.,* 559 U. S. 393, 445, n. 3 (2010) (GINSBURG, J., dissenting). The respective merits of class actions and private arbitration as means of enforcing the law are questions constitutionally entrusted not to the courts to decide but to the policymakers in the political branches where those questions remain hotly contested. Just recently, for example, one federal agency banned individualized arbitration agreements it blamed for underenforcement of certain laws, only to see Congress respond by immediately repealing that rule. See 82 Fed. Reg. 33210 (2017) (cited *post,* at 28, n. 15); Pub. L. 115–74, 131 Stat. 1243. This Court is not free to substitute its preferred economic policies for those chosen by the people's representatives. *That*, we had always understood, was *Lochner's* sin.

* * *

[Justice Thomas' concurring opinion is omitted.]

■ JUSTICE GINSBURG, with whom JUSTICE BREYER, JUSTICE SOTOMAYOR, and JUSTICE KAGAN join, dissenting.

The employees in these cases complain that their employers have underpaid them in violation of the wage and hours prescriptions of the Fair Labor Standards Act of 1938 (FLSA), 29 U. S. C. § 201 *et seq.*, and analogous state laws. Individually, their claims are small, scarcely of a size warranting the expense of seeking redress alone. See Ruan, What's Left To Remedy Wage Theft? How Arbitration Mandates That Bar Class Actions Impact Low-Wage Workers, 2012 Mich. St. L. Rev. 1103, 1118–1119 (Ruan). But by joining together with others similarly circumstanced, employees can gain effective redress for wage underpayment commonly experienced. See *id.,* at 1108–1111. To block such concerted action, their employers required them to sign, as a condition of employment, arbitration agreements banning collective judicial and arbitral proceedings of any kind. The question presented: Does the Federal Arbitration Act (Arbitration Act or FAA), 9 U. S. C. § 1 *et seq.,* permit employers to insist that their employees, whenever seeking redress for commonly experienced wage loss, go it alone, never mind the right secured to employees by the National Labor Relations Act (NLRA), 29 U. S. C. § 151 *et seq.,* "to engage in . . . concerted activities" for their "mutual aid or protection"? § 157. The answer should be a resounding "No."

In the NLRA and its forerunner, the Norris-LaGuardia Act (NLGA), 29 U. S. C. § 101 *et seq.*, Congress acted on an acute awareness: For workers striving to gain from their employers decent terms and conditions of employment, there is strength in numbers. A single employee, Congress understood, is disarmed in dealing with an employer. See *NLRB v. Jones & Laughlin Steel Corp.*, 301 U. S. 1, 33–34 (1937). The Court today subordinates employee-protective labor legislation to the Arbitration Act. In so doing, the Court forgets the labor market imbalance that gave rise to the NLGA and the NLRA, and ignores the destructive consequences of diminishing the right of employees "to band together in confronting an employer." *NLRB v. City Disposal Systems, Inc.*, 465 U. S. 822, 835 (1984). Congressional correction of the Court's elevation of the FAA over workers' rights to act in concert is urgently in order.

To explain why the Court's decision is egregiously wrong, I first refer to the extreme imbalance once prevalent in our Nation's workplaces, and Congress' aim in the NLGA and the NLRA to place employers and employees on a more equal footing. I then explain why the Arbitration Act, sensibly read, does not shrink the NLRA's protective sphere.

I

It was once the dominant view of this Court that "[t]he right of a person to sell his labor upon such terms as he deems proper is . . . the same as the right of the purchaser of labor to prescribe [working] conditions." *Adair v. United States*, 208 U. S. 161, 174 (1908) (invalidating federal law prohibiting interstate railroad employers from discharging or discriminating against employees based on their membership in labor organizations); accord *Coppage v. Kansas*, 236 U. S. 1, 26 (1915) (invalidating state law prohibiting employers from requiring employees, as a condition of employment, to refrain or withdraw from union membership).

The NLGA and the NLRA operate on a different premise, that employees must have the capacity to act collectively in order to match their employers' clout in setting terms and conditions of employment. For decades, the Court's decisions have reflected that understanding. See *Jones & Laughlin Steel*, 301 U. S. 1 (upholding the NLRA against employer assault); cf. *United States v. Darby*, 312 U. S. 100 (1941) (upholding the FLSA).

A

The end of the 19th century and beginning of the 20th was a tumultuous era in the history of our Nation's labor relations. Under economic conditions then prevailing, workers often had to accept employment on whatever terms employers dictated. See 75 Cong. Rec. 4502 (1932). Aiming to secure better pay, shorter workdays, and safer workplaces, workers increasingly sought to band together to make their demands effective. See *ibid.*; H. Millis & E. Brown, From the Wagner Act to Taft-Hartley: A Study of National Labor Policy and Labor Relations 7–8 (1950).

Employers, in turn, engaged in a variety of tactics to hinder workers' efforts to act in concert for their mutual benefit. See J. Seidman, The Yellow Dog Contract 11 (1932). Notable among such devices was the "yellow-dog contract." Such agreements, which employers required employees to sign as a condition of employment, typically commanded employees to abstain from joining labor unions. See *id.*, at 11, 56. Many of the employer-designed agreements cast an even wider net, "proscrib[ing] all manner of concerted activities." Finkin, The Meaning and Contemporary Vitality of the Norris-LaGuardia Act, 93 Neb. L. Rev. 6, 16 (2014); see Seidman, *supra*, at 59–60, 65–66. As a prominent United States Senator observed, contracts of the yellow-dog genre rendered the "laboring man . . . absolutely helpless" by "waiv[ing] his right . . . to free association" and by requiring that he "singly present any grievance he has." 75 Cong. Rec. 4504 (remarks of Sen. Norris).

Early legislative efforts to protect workers' rights to band together were unavailing. See, *e.g., Coppage*, 236 U. S., at 26; Frankfurter & Greene, Legislation Affecting Labor Injunctions, 38 Yale L. J. 879, 889–

890 (1929). Courts, including this one, invalidated the legislation based on then-ascendant notions about employers' and employees' constitutional right to "liberty of contract." See *Coppage*, 236 U. S., at 26; Frankfurter & Greene, *supra,* at 890–891. While stating that legislatures could curtail contractual "liberty" in the interest of public health, safety, and the general welfare, courts placed outside those bounds legislative action to redress the bargaining power imbalance workers faced. See *Coppage*, 236 U. S., at 16–19.

In the 1930's, legislative efforts to safeguard vulnerable workers found more receptive audiences. As the Great Depression shifted political winds further in favor of worker-protective laws, Congress passed two statutes aimed at protecting employees' associational rights. First, in 1932, Congress passed the NLGA, which regulates the employer-employee relationship indirectly. Section 2 of the Act declares:

> "Whereas . . . the individual unorganized worker is commonly helpless to exercise actual liberty of contract and to protect his freedom of labor, . . . it is necessary that he have full freedom of association, self-organization, and designation of representatives of his own choosing, . . . and that he shall be free from the interference, restraint, or coercion of employers . . . in the designation of such representatives or in self-organization or in other concerted activities for the purpose of collective bargaining or other mutual aid or protection." 29 U. S. C. § 102.

Section 3 provides that federal courts shall not enforce "any . . . undertaking or promise in conflict with the public policy declared in [§ 2]." § 103.[1] In adopting these provisions, Congress sought to render ineffective employer-imposed contracts proscribing employees' concerted activity of any and every kind. See 75 Cong. Rec. 4504–4505 (remarks of Sen. Norris) ("[o]ne of the objects" of the NLGA was to "outlaw" yellow-dog contracts); Finkin, *supra*, at 16 (contracts prohibiting "all manner of concerted activities apart from union membership or support . . . were understood to be 'yellow dog' contracts"). While banning court enforcement of contracts proscribing concerted action by employees, the NLGA did not directly prohibit coercive employer practices.

But Congress did so three years later, in 1935, when it enacted the NLRA. Relevant here, § 7 of the NLRA guarantees employees "the right to self-organization, to form, join, or assist labor organizations, to bargain collectively through representatives of their own choosing, *and to engage in other concerted activities for the purpose of collective bargaining or other mutual aid or protection.*" 29 U. S. C. § 157 (emphasis added). Section 8(a)(1) safeguards those rights by making it an "unfair labor

---

[1] Other provisions of the NLGA further rein in federal-court authority to disturb employees' concerted activities. See, *e.g.,* 29 U. S. C. § 104(d) (federal courts lack jurisdiction to enjoin a person from "aiding any person participating or interested in any labor dispute who is being proceeded against in, or [who] is prosecuting, any action or suit in any court of the United States or of any State").

practice" for an employer to "interfere with, restrain, or coerce employees in the exercise of the rights guaranteed in [§ 7]." § 158(a)(1). To oversee the Act's guarantees, the Act established the National Labor Relations Board (Board or NLRB), an independent regulatory agency empowered to administer "labor policy for the Nation." *San Diego Building Trades Council v. Garmon*, 359 U. S. 236, 242 (1959); see 29 U. S. C. § 160.

Unlike earlier legislative efforts, the NLGA and the NLRA had staying power. When a case challenging the NLRA's constitutionality made its way here, the Court, in retreat from its *Lochner*-era contractual-"liberty" decisions, upheld the Act as a permissible exercise of legislative authority. See *Jones & Laughlin Steel*, 301 U. S., at 33–34. The Court recognized that employees have a "fundamental right" to join together to advance their common interests and that Congress, in lieu of "ignor[ing]" that right, had elected to "safeguard" it. *Ibid.*

B

Despite the NLRA's prohibitions, the employers in the cases now before the Court required their employees to sign contracts stipulating to submission of wage and hours claims to binding arbitration, and to do so only one-by-one.[2] When employees subsequently filed wage and hours claims in federal court and sought to invoke the collective-litigation procedures provided for in the FLSA and Federal Rules of Civil Procedure,[3] the employers moved to compel individual arbitration. The Arbitration Act, in their view, requires courts to enforce their take-it-or-leave-it arbitration agreements as written, including the collective-litigation abstinence demanded therein.

In resisting enforcement of the group-action foreclosures, the employees involved in this litigation do not urge that they must have

---

[2] The Court's opinion opens with the question: "Should employees and employers be allowed to agree that any disputes between them will be resolved through one-on-one arbitration?" *Ante,* at 1. Were the "agreements" genuinely bilateral? Petitioner Epic Systems Corporation e-mailed its employees an arbitration agreement requiring resolution of wage and hours claims by individual arbitration. The agreement provided that if the employees "continue[d] to work at Epic," they would "be deemed to have accepted th[e] Agreement." App. to Pet. for Cert. in No. 16–285, p. 30a. Ernst & Young similarly e-mailed its employees an arbitration agreement, which stated that the employees' continued employment would indicate their assent to the agreement's terms. See App. in No. 16–300, p. 37. Epic's and Ernst & Young's employees thus faced a Hobson's choice: accept arbitration on their employer's terms or give up their jobs.

[3] The FLSA establishes an opt-in collective-litigation procedure for employees seeking to recover unpaid wages and overtime pay. See 29 U. S. C. § 216(b). In particular, it authorizes "one or more employees" to maintain an action "in behalf of himself or themselves and other employees similarly situated." *Ibid.* "Similarly situated" employees may become parties to an FLSA collective action (and may share in the recovery) only if they file written notices of consent to be joined as parties. *Ibid.* The Federal Rules of Civil Procedure provide two collective-litigation procedures relevant here. First, Rule 20(a) permits individuals to join as plaintiffs in a single action if they assert claims arising out of the same transaction or occurrence and their claims involve common questions of law or fact. Second, Rule 23 establishes an opt-out class-action procedure, pursuant to which "[o]ne or more members of a class" may bring an action on behalf of the entire class if specified prerequisites are met.

access to a judicial forum.[4] They argue only that the NLRA prohibits their employers from denying them the right to pursue work-related claims in concert in any forum. If they may be stopped by employer-dictated terms from pursuing collective procedures in court, they maintain, they must at least have access to similar procedures in an arbitral forum.

C

Although the NLRA safeguards, first and foremost, workers' rights to join unions and to engage in collective bargaining, the statute speaks more embracively. In addition to protecting employees' rights "to form, join, or assist labor organizations" and "to bargain collectively through representatives of their own choosing," the Act protects employees' rights "to engage in *other* concerted activities for the purpose of . . . mutual aid or protection." 29 U. S. C. § 157 (emphasis added); see, *e.g., NLRB v. Washington Aluminum Co.*, 370 U. S. 9, 14–15 (1962) (§ 7 protected unorganized employees when they walked off the job to protest cold working conditions). See also 1 J. Higgins, The Developing Labor Law 209 (6th ed. 2012) ("Section 7 protects not only union-related activity but also 'other concerted activities . . . for mutual aid or protection.' "); 1 N. Lareau, Labor and Employment Law § 1.01[1], p. 1–2 (2017) ("Section 7 extended to employees three federally protected rights: (1) the right to form and join unions; (2) the right to bargain collectively (negotiate) with employers about terms and conditions of employment; *and* (3) the right to work in concert with another employee or employees to achieve employment-related goals." (emphasis added)).

Suits to enforce workplace rights collectively fit comfortably under the umbrella "concerted activities for the purpose of . . . mutual aid or protection." 29 U. S. C. § 157. "Concerted" means "[p]lanned or accomplished together; combined." American Heritage Dictionary 381 (5th ed. 2011). "Mutual" means "reciprocal." *Id.,* at 1163. When employees meet the requirements for litigation of shared legal claims in joint, collective, and class proceedings, the litigation of their claims is undoubtedly "accomplished together." By joining hands in litigation, workers can spread the costs of litigation and reduce the risk of employer retaliation. See *infra,* at 27–28.

Recognizing employees' right to engage in collective employment litigation and shielding that right from employer blockage are firmly rooted in the NLRA's design. Congress expressed its intent, when it enacted the NLRA, to "protec[t] the exercise by workers of full freedom of association," thereby remedying "[t]he inequality of bargaining power" workers faced. 29 U. S. C. § 151; see, *e.g., Eastex, Inc. v. NLRB*, 437 U. S. 556, 567 (1978) (the Act's policy is "to protect the right of workers to act together to better their working conditions" (internal quotation marks

---

[4]   Notably, one employer specified that if the provisions confining employees to individual proceedings are "unenforceable," "any claim brought on a class, collective, or representative action basis must be filed in . . . court." App. to Pet. for Cert. in No. 16–285, at 35a.

omitted)); *City Disposal*, 465 U. S., at 835 ("[I]n enacting § 7 of the NLRA, Congress sought generally to equalize the bargaining power of the employee with that of his employer by allowing employees to band together in confronting an employer regarding the terms and conditions of their employment."). See also *supra,* at 5–6. There can be no serious doubt that collective litigation is one way workers may associate with one another to improve their lot.

Since the Act's earliest days, the Board and federal courts have understood § 7's "concerted activities" clause to protect myriad ways in which employees may join together to advance their shared interests. For example, the Board and federal courts have affirmed that the Act shields employees from employer interference when they participate in concerted appeals to the media, *e.g., NLRB v. Peter Cailler Kohler Swiss Chocolates Co.,* 130 F. 2d 503, 505–506 (CA2 1942), legislative bodies, *e.g., Bethlehem Ship-building Corp. v. NLRB*, 114 F. 2d 930, 937 (CA1 1940), and government agencies, *e.g., Moss Planing Mill Co.,* 103 N. L. R. B. 414, 418–419, enf'd, 206 F. 2d 557 (CA4 1953). "The 74th Congress," this Court has noted, "knew well enough that labor's cause often is advanced on fronts other than collective bargaining and grievance settlement within the immediate employment context." *Eastex*, 437 U. S., at 565.

Crucially important here, for over 75 years, the Board has held that the NLRA safeguards employees from employer interference when they pursue joint, collective, and class suits related to the terms and conditions of their employment. See, *e.g., Spandsco Oil and Royalty Co.,* 42 N. L. R. B. 942, 948–949 (1942) (three employees' joint filing of FLSA suit ranked as concerted activity protected by the NLRA); *Poultrymen's Service Corp.,* 41 N. L. R. B. 444, 460–463, and n. 28 (1942) (same with respect to employee's filing of FLSA suit on behalf of himself and others similarly situated), enf'd, 138 F. 2d 204 (CA3 1943); *Sarkes Tarzian, Inc.,* 149 N. L. R. B. 147, 149, 153 (1964) (same with respect to employees' filing class libel suit); *United Parcel Service, Inc.,* 252 N. L. R. B. 1015, 1018 (1980) (same with respect to employee's filing class action regarding break times), enf'd, 677 F. 2d 421 (CA6 1982); *Harco Trucking, LLC*, 344 N. L. R. B. 478, 478–479 (2005) (same with respect to employee's maintaining class action regarding wages). For decades, federal courts have endorsed the Board's view, comprehending that "the filing of a labor related civil action by a group of employees is ordinarily a concerted activity protected by § 7." *Leviton Mfg. Co. v. NLRB*, 486 F. 2d 686, 689 (CA1 1973); see, *e.g., Brady v. National Football League*, 644 F. 3d 661,

673 (CA8 2011) (similar).[5] The Court pays scant heed to this longstanding line of decisions.[6]

D

In face of the NLRA's text, history, purposes, and longstanding construction, the Court nevertheless concludes that collective proceedings do not fall within the scope of § 7. None of the Court's reasons for diminishing § 7 should carry the day.

1

The Court relies principally on the *ejusdem generis* canon. See *ante,* at 12. Observing that § 7's "other concerted activities" clause "appears at the end of a detailed list of activities," the Court says the clause should be read to "embrace" only activities "similar in nature" to those set forth first in the list, *ibid.* (internal quotation marks omitted), *i.e.,* " 'self-organization,' 'form[ing], join[ing], or assist[ing] labor organizations,' and 'bargain[ing] collectively,' " *ibid.* The Court concludes that § 7 should, therefore, be read to protect "things employees 'just do' for themselves." *Ibid.* (quoting *NLRB v. Alternative Entertainment, Inc.*, 858 F. 3d 393, 415 (CA6 2017) (Sutton, J., concurring in part and dissenting in part); emphasis deleted). It is far from apparent why joining hands in litigation would not qualify as "things employees just do for themselves." In any event, there is no sound reason to employ the *ejusdem generis* canon to narrow § 7's protections in the manner the Court suggests.

The *ejusdem generis* canon may serve as a useful guide where it is doubtful Congress intended statutory words or phrases to have the broad scope their ordinary meaning conveys. See *Russell Motor Car Co. v. United States*, 261 U. S. 514, 519 (1923). Courts must take care, however, not to deploy the canon to undermine Congress' efforts to draft encompassing legislation. See *United States v. Powell*, 423 U. S. 87, 90 (1975) ("[W]e would be justified in narrowing the statute only if such a narrow reading was supported by evidence of congressional intent over and above the language of the statute."). Nothing suggests that Congress envisioned a cramped construction of the NLRA. Quite the opposite, Congress expressed an embracive purpose in enacting the legislation, *i.e.,* to "protec[t] the exercise by workers of full freedom of association." 29 U. S. C. § 151; see *supra,* at 9.

---

[5] The Court cites, as purported evidence of contrary agency precedent, a 2010 "Guideline Memorandum" that the NLRB's then-General Counsel issued to his staff. See *ante,* at 4, 19, 22. The General Counsel appeared to conclude that employees have a § 7 right to file collective suits, but that employers can nonetheless require employees to sign arbitration agreements waiving the right to maintain such suits. See Memorandum GC 10–06, p. 7 (June 16, 2010).

[6] In 2012, the Board held that employer-imposed contracts barring group litigation in any forum—arbitral or judicial—are unlawful. *D. R. Horton*, 357 N. L. R. B. 2277. In so ruling, the Board simply applied its precedents recognizing that (1) employees have a § 7 right to engage in collective employment litigation and (2) employers cannot lawfully require employees to sign away their § 7 rights. See *id.,* at 2278, 2280. It broke no new ground. But cf. *ante,* at 2, 19.

2

In search of a statutory hook to support its application of the *ejusdem generis* canon, the Court turns to the NLRA's "structure." *Ante,* at 12. Citing a handful of provisions that touch upon unionization, collective bargaining, picketing, and strikes, the Court asserts that the NLRA "establish[es] a regulatory regime" governing each of the activities protected by § 7. *Ante,* at 12–13. That regime, the Court says, offers "specific guidance" and "rules" regulating each protected activity. *Ante,* at 13. Observing that none of the NLRA's provisions explicitly regulates employees' resort to collective litigation, the Court insists that "it is hard to fathom why Congress would take such care to regulate all the other matters mentioned in [§ 7] yet remain mute about this matter alone— unless, of course, [§ 7] doesn't speak to class and collective action procedures in the first place." *Ibid.*

This argument is conspicuously flawed. When Congress enacted the NLRA in 1935, the only § 7 activity Congress addressed with any specificity was employees' selection of collective-bargaining representatives. See 49 Stat. 453. The Act did not offer "specific guidance" about employees' rights to "form, join, or assist labor organizations." Nor did it set forth "specific guidance" for any activity falling within § 7's "other concerted activities" clause. The only provision that touched upon an activity falling within that clause stated: "Nothing in this Act shall be construed so as to interfere with or impede or diminish in any way the right to strike." *Id.,* at 457. That provision hardly offered "specific guidance" regarding employees' right to strike.

Without much in the original Act to support its "structure" argument, the Court cites several provisions that Congress added later, in response to particular concerns. Compare 49 Stat. 449–457 with 61 Stat. 142–143 (1947) (adding § 8(d) to provide guidance regarding employees' and employers' collective-bargaining obligations); 61 Stat. 141–142 (amending § 8(a) and adding § 8(b) to proscribe specified labor organization practices); 73 Stat. 544 (1959) (adding § 8(b)(7) to place restrictions on labor organizations' right to picket employers). It is difficult to comprehend why Congress' later inclusion of specific guidance regarding some of the activities protected by § 7 sheds any light on Congress' initial conception of § 7's scope.

But even if each of the provisions the Court cites had been included in the original Act, they still would provide little support for the Court's conclusion. For going on 80 years now, the Board and federal courts— including this one—have understood § 7 to protect numerous activities for which the Act provides no "specific" regulatory guidance. See *supra,* at 9–10.

3

In a related argument, the Court maintains that the NLRA does not "even whispe[r]" about the "rules [that] should govern the adjudication of class or collective actions in court or arbitration." *Ante,* at 13. The employees here involved, of course, do not look to the NLRA for the procedures enabling them to vindicate their employment rights in arbitral or judicial forums. They assert that the Act establishes their right to act in concert using existing, generally available procedures, see *supra,* at 7, n. 3, and to do so free from employer interference. The FLSA and the Federal Rules on joinder and class actions provide the procedures pursuant to which the employees may ally to pursue shared legal claims. Their employers cannot lawfully cut off their access to those procedures, they urge, without according them access to similar procedures in arbitral forums. See, *e.g.,* American Arbitration Assn., Supplementary Rules for Class Arbitrations (2011).

To the employees' argument, the Court replies: If the employees "really take existing class and collective action rules as they find them, they surely take them subject to the limitations inherent in those rules—including the principle that parties may (as here) contract to depart from them in favor of individualized arbitration procedures." *Ante,* at 14. The freedom to depart asserted by the Court, as already underscored, is entirely one sided. See *supra,* at 2–5. Once again, the Court ignores the reality that sparked the NLRA's passage: Forced to face their employers without company, employees ordinarily are no match for the enterprise that hires them. Employees gain strength, however, if they can deal with their employers in numbers. That is the very reason why the NLRA secures against employer interference employees' right to act in concert for their "mutual aid or protection." 29 U. S. C. §§ 151, 157, 158.

4

Further attempting to sow doubt about § 7's scope, the Court asserts that class and collective procedures were "hardly known when the NLRA was adopted in 1935." *Ante,* at 11. In particular, the Court notes, the FLSA's collective-litigation procedure postdated § 7 "by years" and Rule 23 "didn't create the modern class action until 1966." *Ibid.*

First, one may ask, is there any reason to suppose that Congress intended to protect employees' right to act in concert using only those procedures and forums available in 1935? Congress framed § 7 in broad terms, "entrust[ing]" the Board with "responsibility to adapt the Act to changing patterns of industrial life." *NLRB v. J. Weingarten, Inc.,* 420 U. S. 251, 266 (1975); see *Pennsylvania Dept. of Corrections v. Yeskey,* 524 U. S. 206, 212 (1998) ("[T]he fact that a statute can be applied in situations not expressly anticipated by Congress does not demonstrate ambiguity. It demonstrates breadth." (internal quotation marks omitted)). With fidelity to Congress' aim, the Board and federal courts have recognized that the NLRA shields employees from employer interference when they, *e.g.,* join together to file complaints with administrative agencies, even if those agencies did not exist in 1935. See, *e.g., Wray Electric Contracting, Inc.,* 210 N. L. R. B. 757, 762 (1974) (the

NLRA protects concerted filing of complaint with the Occupational Safety and Health Administration).

Moreover, the Court paints an ahistorical picture. As Judge Wood, writing for the Seventh Circuit, cogently explained, the FLSA's collective-litigation procedure and the modern class action were "not written on a clean slate." 823 F. 3d 1147, 1154 (2016). By 1935, permissive joinder was scarcely uncommon in courts of equity. See 7 C. Wright, A. Miller, & M. Kane, Federal Practice and Procedure § 1651 (3d ed. 2001). Nor were representative and class suits novelties. Indeed, their origins trace back to medieval times. See S. Yeazell, From Medieval Group Litigation to the Modern Class Action 38 (1987). And beyond question, "[c]lass suits long have been a part of American jurisprudence." 7A Wright, *supra*, § 1751, at 12 (3d ed. 2005); see *Supreme Tribe of Ben-Hur v. Cauble*, 255 U. S. 356, 363 (1921). See also Brief for Constitutional Accountability Center as *Amicus Curiae* 5–16 (describing group litigation's "rich history"). Early instances of joint proceedings include cases in which employees allied to sue an employer. *E.g., Gorley v. Louisville*, 23 Ky. 1782, 65 S.W. 844 (1901) (suit to recover wages brought by ten members of city police force on behalf of themselves and other officers); *Guiliano v. Daniel O'Connell's Sons*, 105 Conn. 695, 136 A. 677 (1927) (suit by two employees to recover for injuries sustained while residing in housing provided by their employer). It takes no imagination, then, to comprehend that Congress, when it enacted the NLRA, likely meant to protect employees' joining together to engage in collective litigation.[7]

E

Because I would hold that employees' § 7 rights include the right to pursue collective litigation regarding their wages and hours, I would further hold that the employer-dictated collective-litigation stoppers, *i.e.,* "waivers," are unlawful. As earlier recounted, see *supra,* at 6, § 8(a)(1) makes it an "unfair labor practice" for an employer to "interfere with, restrain, or coerce" employees in the exercise of their § 7 rights. 29 U. S. C. § 158(a)(1). Beyond genuine dispute, an employer "interfere[s] with" and "restrain[s]" employees in the exercise of their § 7 rights by mandating that they prospectively renounce those rights in individual employment agreements.[8] The law could hardly be otherwise: Employees' rights to band together to meet their employers' superior strength would be worth precious little if employers could condition employment on

---

[7] The Court additionally suggests that something must be amiss because the employees turn to the NLRA, rather than the FLSA, to resist enforcement of the collective-litigation waivers. See ante, at 14–15. But the employees' reliance on the NLRA is hardly a reason to "raise a judicial eyebrow." Ante, at 15. The NLRA's guiding purpose is to protect employees' rights to work together when addressing shared workplace grievances of whatever kind.

[8] See, *e.g., Bethany Medical Center*, 328 N. L. R. B. 1094, 1105–1106 (1999) (holding employer violated § 8(a)(1) by conditioning employees' rehiring on the surrender of their right to engage in future walkouts); *Mandel Security Bureau Inc.*, 202 N. L. R. B. 117, 119, 122 (1973) (holding employer violated § 8(a)(1) by conditioning employee's reinstatement to former position on agreement that employee would refrain from filing charges with the Board and from circulating work-related petitions, and, instead, would "mind his own business").

workers signing away those rights. See *National Licorice Co. v. NLRB*, 309 U. S. 350, 364 (1940). Properly assessed, then, the "waivers" rank as unfair labor practices outlawed by the NLRA, and therefore unenforceable in court. See *Kaiser Steel Corp. v. Mullins*, 455 U. S. 72, 77 (1982) ("[O]ur cases leave no doubt that illegal promises will not be enforced in cases controlled by the federal law.").[9]

II

Today's decision rests largely on the Court's finding in the Arbitration Act "emphatic directions" to enforce arbitration agreements according to their terms, including collective-litigation prohibitions. *Ante,* at 6. Nothing in the FAA or this Court's case law, however, requires subordination of the NLRA's protections. Before addressing the interaction between the two laws, I briefly recall the FAA's history and the domain for which that Act was designed.

* * *

[Justice Ginsburg recounted the history of the Court's treatment of arbitration agreements under the FAA.]

B

Through the Arbitration Act, Congress sought "to make arbitration agreements as enforceable as other contracts, but not more so." *Prima Paint*, 388 U. S., at 404, n. 12. Congress thus provided in § 2 of the FAA that the terms of a written arbitration agreement "shall be valid, irrevocable, and enforceable, *save upon such grounds as exist at law or in equity for the revocation of any contract.*" 9 U. S. C. § 2 (emphasis added).

---

[9] I would similarly hold that the NLGA renders the collective-litigation waivers unenforceable. That Act declares it the public policy of the United States that workers "shall be free from the interference, restraint, or coercion of employers" when they engage in "concerted activities" for their "mutual aid or protection." 29 U. S. C. § 102; see *supra,* at 5. Section 3 provides that federal courts shall not enforce any "promise in conflict with the [Act's] policy." § 103. Because employer-extracted collective-litigation waivers interfere with employees' ability to engage in "concerted activities" for their "mutual aid or protection," see *supra,* at 8–11, the arm-twisted waivers collide with the NLGA's stated policy; thus, no federal court should enforce them. See Finkin, The Meaning and Contemporary Vitality of the Norris-LaGuardia Act, 93 Neb. L. Rev. 6 (2014).

Boys Markets, Inc. v. *Retail Clerks*, 398 U. S. 235 (1970), provides no support for the Court's contrary conclusion. See *ante,* at 16. In *Boys Markets*, an employer and a union had entered into a collective-bargaining agreement, which provided that labor disputes would be resolved through arbitration and that the union would not engage in strikes, pickets, or boycotts during the life of the agreement. 398 U. S., at 238–239. When a dispute later arose, the union bypassed arbitration and called a strike. *Id.,* at 239. The question presented: Whether a federal district court could enjoin the strike and order the parties to arbitrate their dispute. The case required the Court to reconcile the NLGA's limitations on federal courts' authority to enjoin employees' concerted activities, see 29 U. S. C. § 104, with § 301(a) of the Labor Management Relations Act, 1947, which grants federal courts the power to enforce collective-bargaining agreements, see 29 U. S. C. § 185(a). The Court concluded that permitting district courts to enforce no-strike and arbitration provisions in collective-bargaining agreements would encourage employers to enter into such agreements, thereby furthering federal labor policy. 398 U. S., at 252–253. That case has little relevance here. It did not consider the enforceability of arbitration provisions that require employees to arbitrate disputes only one-by-one. Nor did it consider the enforceability of arbitration provisions that an employer has unilaterally imposed on employees, as opposed to provisions negotiated through collective-bargaining processes in which employees can leverage their collective strength.

Pursuant to this "saving clause," arbitration agreements and terms may be invalidated based on "generally applicable contract defenses, such as fraud, duress, or unconscionability." *Doctor's Associates, Inc. v. Casarotto*, 517 U. S. 681, 687 (1996); see *ante,* at 7.

Illegality is a traditional, generally applicable contract defense. See 5 R. Lord, Williston on Contracts § 12.1 (4th ed. 2009). "[A]uthorities from the earliest time to the present unanimously hold that no court will lend its assistance in any way towards carrying out the terms of an illegal contract." *Kaiser Steel*, 455 U. S., at 77 (quoting *McMullen v. Hoffman*, 174 U. S. 639, 654 (1899)). For the reasons stated *supra,* at 8–17, I would hold that the arbitration agreements' employer-dictated collective-litigation waivers are unlawful. By declining to enforce those adhesive waivers, courts would place them on the same footing as any other contract provision incompatible with controlling federal law. The FAA's saving clause can thus achieve harmonization of the FAA and the NLRA without undermining federal labor policy.

The Court urges that our case law—most forcibly, *AT&T Mobility LLC v. Concepcion*, 563 U. S. 333 (2011)—rules out reconciliation of the NLRA and the FAA through the latter's saving clause. See *ante,* at 6–9. I disagree. True, the Court's Arbitration Act decisions establish that the saving clause "offers no refuge" for defenses that discriminate against arbitration, "either by name or by more subtle methods." *Ante,* at 7. The Court, therefore, has rejected saving clause salvage where state courts have invoked generally applicable contract defenses to discriminate "covertly" against arbitration. *Kindred Nursing Centers L. P. v. Clark*, 581 U. S. ___ (2017) (slip op., at 5). In *Concepcion*, the Court held that the saving clause did not spare the California Supreme Court's invocation of unconscionability doctrine to establish a rule blocking enforcement of class-action waivers in adhesive consumer contracts. 563 U. S., at 341–344, 346–352. Class proceedings, the Court said, would "sacrific[e] the principal advantage of arbitration—its informality—and mak[e] the process slower, more costly, and more likely to generate procedural morass than final judgment." *Id.,* at 348. Accordingly, the Court concluded, the California Supreme Court's rule, though derived from unconscionability doctrine, impermissibly disfavored arbitration, and therefore could not stand. *Id.,* at 346–352.

Here, however, the Court is not asked to apply a generally applicable contract defense to generate a rule discriminating against arbitration. At issue is application of the ordinarily superseding rule that "illegal promises will not be enforced," *Kaiser Steel*, 455 U. S., at 77, to invalidate arbitration provisions at odds with the NLRA, a path-marking federal statute. That statute neither discriminates against arbitration on its face, nor by covert operation. It requires invalidation of *all* employer-imposed contractual provisions prospectively waiving employees' § 7 rights. See *supra,* at 17, and n. 8; cf. *Kindred Nursing Centers*, 581 U. S., at ___, n. 2 (slip op., at 7, n. 2) (States may enforce generally applicable rules so long as they do not "single out arbitration" for disfavored treatment).

C

Even assuming that the FAA and the NLRA were inharmonious, the NLRA should control. Enacted later in time, the NLRA should qualify as "an implied repeal" of the FAA, to the extent of any genuine conflict. See *Posadas v. National City Bank*, 296 U. S. 497, 503 (1936). Moreover, the NLRA should prevail as the more pinpointed, subject-matter specific legislation, given that it speaks directly to group action by employees to improve the terms and conditions of their employment. See *Radzanower v. Touche Ross & Co.*, 426 U. S. 148, 153 (1976) ("a specific statute" generally "will not be controlled or nullified by a general one" (internal quotation marks omitted)).[13]

Citing statutory examples, the Court asserts that when Congress wants to override the FAA, it does so expressly. See *ante,* at 13–14. The statutes the Court cites, however, are of recent vintage.[14] Each was enacted during the time this Court's decisions increasingly alerted Congress that it would be wise to leave not the slightest room for doubt if it wants to secure access to a judicial forum or to provide a green light for group litigation before an arbitrator or court. See *CompuCredit Corp. v. Greenwood*, 565 U. S. 95, 116 (2012) (GINSBURG, J., dissenting). The Congress that drafted the NLRA in 1935 was scarcely on similar alert.

III

The inevitable result of today's decision will be the underenforcement of federal and state statutes designed to advance the well-being of vulnerable workers. See generally Sternlight, Disarming Employees: How American Employers Are Using Mandatory Arbitration To Deprive Workers of Legal Protections, 80 Brooklyn L. Rev. 1309 (2015).

The probable impact on wage and hours claims of the kind asserted in the cases now before the Court is all too evident. Violations of minimum-wage and overtime laws are widespread. See Ruan 1109–1111; A. Bernhardt et al., Broken Laws, Unprotected Workers: Violations of Employment and Labor Laws in America's Cities 11–16, 21–22 (2009).

One study estimated that in Chicago, Los Angeles, and New York City alone, low-wage workers lose nearly $3 billion in legally owed wages each year. *Id.,* at 6. The U. S. Department of Labor, state labor departments, and state attorneys general can uncover and obtain

---

[13] Enacted, as was the NLRA, after passage of the FAA, the NLGA also qualifies as a statute more specific than the FAA. Indeed, the NLGA expressly addresses the enforceability of contract provisions that interfere with employees' ability to engage in concerted activities. See *supra,* at 17, n. 9. Moreover, the NLGA contains an express repeal provision, which provides that "[a]ll acts and parts of acts in conflict with [the Act's] provisions . . . are repealed." 29 U. S. C. § 115.

[14] See 116 Stat. 1836 (2002); 120 Stat. 2267 (2006); 124 Stat. 1746 (2010); 124 Stat. 2035 (2010).

recoveries for some violations. See EPI, B. Meixell & R. Eisenbrey, An Epidemic of Wage Theft Is Costing Workers Hundreds of Millions of Dollars a Year 2 (2014), available at https://www.epi.org/files/2014/wage-theft.pdf. Because of their limited resources, however, government agencies must rely on private parties to take a lead role in enforcing wage and hours laws. See Brief for State of Maryland et al. as *Amici Curiae* 29–33; Glover, The Structural Role of Private Enforcement Mechanisms in Public Law, 53 Wm. & Mary L. Rev. 1137, 1150–1151 (2012) (Department of Labor investigates fewer than 1% of FLSA-covered employers each year).

If employers can stave off collective employment litigation aimed at obtaining redress for wage and hours infractions, the enforcement gap is almost certain to widen. Expenses entailed in mounting individual claims will often far outweigh potential recoveries. See *id.*, at 1184–1185 (because "the FLSA systematically tends to generate low-value claims," "mechanisms that facilitate the economics of claiming are required"); *Sutherland v. Ernst & Young LLP*, 768 F. Supp. 2d 547, 552 (SDNY 2011) (finding that an employee utilizing Ernst & Young's arbitration program would likely have to spend $200,000 to recover only $1,867.02 in overtime pay and an equivalent amount in liquidated damages); cf. Resnik, Diffusing Disputes: The Public in the Private of Arbitration, the Private in Courts, and the Erasure of Rights, 124 Yale L. J. 2804, 2904 (2015) (analyzing available data from the consumer context to conclude that "private enforcement of small-value claims depends on collective, rather than individual, action"); *Amchem Products, Inc. v. Windsor*, 521 U. S. 591, 617 (1997) (class actions help "overcome the problem that small recoveries do not provide the incentive for any individual to bring a solo action prosecuting his or her rights" (internal quotation marks omitted)).[15]

Fear of retaliation may also deter potential claimants from seeking redress alone. See, *e.g.,* Ruan 1119–1121; Bernhardt, *supra*, at 3, 24–25. Further inhibiting single-file claims is the slim relief obtainable, even of the injunctive kind. See *Califano v. Yamasaki*, 442 U. S. 682, 702 (1979) ("[T]he scope of injunctive relief is dictated by the extent of the violation established."). The upshot: Employers, aware that employees will be disinclined to pursue small-value claims when confined to proceeding one-by-one, will no doubt perceive that the cost-benefit balance of underpaying workers tips heavily in favor of skirting legal obligations.

In stark contrast to today's decision,[16] the Court has repeatedly recognized the centrality of group action to the effective enforcement of antidiscrimination statutes. With Court approbation, concerted legal

---

[15] Based on a 2015 study, the Bureau of Consumer Financial Protection found that "pre-dispute arbitration agreements are being widely used to prevent consumers from seeking relief from legal violations on a class basis, and that consumers rarely file individual lawsuits or arbitration cases to obtain such relief." 82 Fed. Reg. 33210 (2017).

[16] The Court observes that class actions can be abused, see *ante,* at 24, but under its interpretation, even two employees would be stopped from proceeding together.

actions have played a critical role in enforcing prohibitions against workplace discrimination based on race, sex, and other protected characteristics. See, *e.g., Griggs v. Duke Power Co.*, 401 U. S. 424 (1971); *Automobile Workers v. Johnson Controls, Inc.*, 499 U. S. 187 (1991). In this context, the Court has comprehended that government entities charged with enforcing antidiscrimination statutes are unlikely to be funded at levels that could even begin to compensate for a significant dropoff in private enforcement efforts. See *Newman v. Piggie Park Enterprises, Inc.*, 390 U. S. 400, 401 (1968) (*per curiam*) ("When the Civil Rights Act of 1964 was passed, it was evident that enforcement would prove difficult and that the Nation would have to rely in part upon private litigation as a means of securing broad compliance with the law."). That reality, as just noted, holds true for enforcement of wage and hours laws. See *supra*, at 27.

I do not read the Court's opinion to place in jeopardy discrimination complaints asserting disparate-impact and pattern-or-practice claims that call for proof on a group-wide basis, see Brief for NAACP Legal Defense & Educational Fund, Inc., et al. as *Amici Curiae* 19–25, which some courts have concluded cannot be maintained by solo complainants, see, *e.g., Chin v. Port Auth. of N. Y. & N. J.*, 685 F. 3d 135, 147 (CA2 2012) (pattern-or-practice method of proving race discrimination is unavailable in non-class actions). It would be grossly exorbitant to read the FAA to devastate Title VII of the Civil Rights Act of 1964, 42 U. S. C. § 2000e *et seq.*, and other laws enacted to eliminate, root and branch, class-based employment discrimination, see *Albemarle Paper Co. v. Moody*, 422 U. S. 405, 417, 421 (1975). With fidelity to the Legislature's will, the Court could hardly hold otherwise.

I note, finally, that individual arbitration of employee complaints can give rise to anomalous results. Arbitration agreements often include provisions requiring that outcomes be kept confidential or barring arbitrators from giving prior proceedings precedential effect. See, *e.g.,* App. to Pet. for Cert. in No. 16–285, p. 34a (Epic's agreement); App. in No. 16–300, p. 46 (Ernst & Young's agreement). As a result, arbitrators may render conflicting awards in cases involving similarly situated employees—even employees working for the same employer. Arbitrators may resolve differently such questions as whether certain jobs are exempt from overtime laws. Cf. *Encino Motor Cars, LLC v. Navarro, ante,* p. ___ (Court divides on whether "service advisors" are exempt from overtime-pay requirements). With confidentiality and no-precedential-value provisions operative, irreconcilable answers would remain unchecked.

* * *

If these untoward consequences stemmed from legislative choices, I would be obliged to accede to them. But the edict that employees with wage and hours claims may seek relief only one-by-one does not come from Congress. It is the result of take-it-or-leave-it labor contracts harking back to the type called "yellow dog," and of the readiness of this Court to enforce those unbargained-for agreements. The FAA demands no such suppression of the right of workers to take concerted action for their "mutual aid or protection." Accordingly, I would reverse the judgment of the Fifth Circuit in No. 16–307 and affirm the judgments of the Seventh and Ninth Circuits in Nos. 16–285 and 16–300.

QUESTIONS FOR DISCUSSION

Justices Gorsuch and Ginsburg approach the task of understanding these laws rather differently: Justice Gorsuch's focus is on the Court's policies under the Arbitration Act, especially as it played out in *Concepcion*. Justice Ginsburg's focus is on the policy of the Labor and Norris-LaGuardia Acts. She relies, for example, on National Licorice Co. v. NLRB, 309 U.S. 350 (1940) (as did the 7th Circuit in *Epic Systems*), which made clear that freely agreed-to contracts that are inconsistent with the Labor Act—that *inter alia* required a discharged worker who contests his discharge to do so only "personally," 309 U.S. 360—violate the Act. Justice Gorsuch does not confront *National Licorice*; in fact, it doesn't mention it.

Consequently, the student might benefit from an engagement with three aspects of the majority opinion: (1) its approach to the meaning of "concerted activity"; (2) its treatment of what more the Labor, and, presumably, the Norris-LaGuardia Act should have said in order for these laws to affect the terms of an employer's arbitration policy governed by the FAA; and (3) the practical prospect of a "procedural morass" that would result from the Court's acceptance of the Board's position.

CONCERTED ACTIVITY FOR MUTUAL AID OR PROTECTION

Read section 7 of the Labor Act (Supplement page 30). It protects the right to "engage in other concerted activities for the purpose of collective bargaining *or other mutual aid or protection*" (italics added). Now read section 2 of the Norris-LaGuardia Act. (Supplement page 5). It "declares" the "public policy of the United States" that employees should have "full freedom of association" and shall be free of restraint in collective representation and in "other concerted activities for the purpose of other mutual aid or protection." Now read section 3: "Any undertaking or promise . . . in conflict with the public policy declared in section 2" shall not be enforceable in any federal court. Justice Gorsuch gives several reasons why these provisions should not be given their plain language meaning.

1. Justice Gorsuch argues that the Labor Act was concerned overwhelmingly—its "bread and butter" (slip. op. at 15)—with unionization and collective bargaining. The "other concerted activities" clause is a "catch all" (he uses the term twice) that cannot be made to trample, like an "elephant" he says, over the terms of an arbitration agreement's restriction to bilateral arbitration. *Eastex* (Casebook page 336) addresses the right of workers to band together in any forum—the

courts, the legislatures, administrative agencies—"to protect their interests as employees." He calls this "dicta". Slip op at 18. Is it?

One of the issues the employees were addressing in that case was the minimum wage. Accordingly, assume that a group of non-unionized workers are circulating a petition—in non-work areas, on non-work time—supporting the passage of a city ordinance to increase the minimum wage to $15/hour. There is no hint of their unionizing. No one has expressed the slightest interest in collective bargaining. Can they be discharged?

2.   Having restricted the scope of the "other concerted activities clause" in the Labor Act, as a "catch all" that only echoes the larger purpose of unionization and collective bargaining, Justice Gorsuch turns to the Norris-LaGuardia Act, where the policy was first crafted. It "adds nothing," he says, as it simply adumbrates the same policy as the Labor Act did. Slip op. at 16. Does it? Or does Justice Gorsuch reason anachronistically: because the Labor Act's primary concern is with unionization and collective bargaining—with "other" concerted activity merely being ancillary to that—such, too, must have been so of the prior act whence that clause came. Is that right?

3.   Norris-LaGuardia is concerned with any "undertaking or promise" by employees by which they eschewed the capacity to engage in concerted activity with their co-workers for their mutual aid or protection. Such is the text's plain language. Was the fundamental thrust of Norris-LaGuardia only those promises or undertakings eschewing unionization or collective bargaining? At this point the student should read Section 4 of the Act (Supplement page 6), for example, subsection (d): a federal court may not enforce an employee's undertaking not to "aid" a person participating in a lawsuit in a labor dispute, which is defined to include "*any* controversy concerning terms or conditions of employment." Sec. 13(c) (italics added). Does this provision relate to unionization and collective bargaining? Does this prohibition include an employer's exacting a worker's promise not to join a coworker in such a lawsuit, as that would mean she was "aiding" in it? If so, does this provision apply as well when the employer requires the workers to arbitrate rather than to go to court? How does Justice Gorsuch deal with the other conduct laid out in section 4 that has nothing to do with unionization or collective bargaining?

4.   The dissent makes a great deal of the Norris-LaGuardia Act's target—the yellow dog contract. Justice Gorsuch dismisses it because the yellow dog contract was solely concerned with union organizing, it had no purchase on arbitration agreements. Slip op at 21–22. Is that right? As the dissent points out, the weight of the argument by the advocates for the Norris-LaGuardia Act concerned the right of workers to join together in a common cause. The debate was couched in terms of a civil liberty: the evil was employer-imposed provisions that prohibited workers from doing that. For example, a contemporary study set out a

taxonomy of yellow dog contracts one of which was the "open shop" contract:

> A typical "open shop" yellow dog was that forced on the employees of the Indianapolis Street Railway Co., in 1914. The document obligated them to obey all rules, present and future, that might be made by the company; not to engage in any strike activities; to submit all grievances to arbitration *individually* and without consultation or agreement with other workers or the union. . . . Theoretically, this contract left the worker free to join a union. But what use would a union be when the worker had already signed away his right to be represented by it in discussing wages, working conditions, and grievances with the company?

Eliot E. Cohen, THE YELLOW DOG CONTRACT 6 (1932) (emphasis in original). How does Justice Gorsuch deal with Congress's understanding of the evil it was addressing in the Norris-LaGuardia Act?

WHAT THESE LABOR LAWS DIDN'T SAY

Justice Gorsuch makes the point in several places that the general— or what he calls the "catch all"—language of concerted activity does not speak with the clarity the Court requires to give one statute the effect of curtailing the reach of another statute, especially one whose reach has expanded in the Court's hands as a matter of its (the Court's) policy. To do so, in his view, the Labor Laws would have had to confront more expressly the bilateral arbitration agreements the FAA protects or somehow guarantee "class or collective action procedures."

1. Section 15 of the Norris-LaGuardia Act provides: "All Acts and parts of Acts in conflict with provisions of this Act are hereby repealed." What reasons does Justice Gorsuch give that this fails to address adequately the resolution of how the Norris-LaGuardia Act is to be read vis-à-vis the FAA?

2. Under the Court's interstate commerce jurisprudence at the time the FAA was enacted, Congress had the power to legislate regarding the contracts of employment of only those employees who actually crossed a state line as part of their work; and all those employments were excluded from the FAA. Circuit City Sales, Inc. v. Adams, 532 U.S. 105 (2001). When the Norris-LaGuardia Act was enacted, such was the state of the law. In 1927, would the Norris-LaGuardia drafting group have seen any need to address the FAA? Should they have? Why?

BILATERALISM AS A "FUNDAMENTAL" ASPECT OF EMPLOYMENT ARBITRATION

Justice Gorsuch says that the challenge mounted in the case is to the "individual nature of the arbitration proceedings" contained in these policies. Slip op at 7. He characterizes the argument as seeking "to interfere with one of arbitration's *fundamental* attributes." *Id.* (emphasis added.) "We know this," he tells us, because the Court has said so. *Id.* (citing AT&T Mobility v. Concepcion, 563 U.S. 333, 341 (2011)). Reshaping "traditional, individualized arbitration" would work a " 'fundamental' change to the arbitration process." *Id.* at 8. Moreover, allowing group or class claims would "sacrifice the principle of advantage of arbitration—its informality"—it would make "the process slower, more costly, and more likely to generate procedural morass. . . ." *Id.* (citing *Concepcion* at 347, 348). The Court later pursued this assertion, 5 to 4, in disallowing a class employee arbitration where the arbitration provision was ambiguous and the lower court had applied the state common law of contract that ambiguities should be resolved contrary to the drafting party. Lamps Plus, Inc. v. Varela, ___ U.S. ___, 139 S. Ct. 1407 (2019).

1.   Historically, the model for the arbitration of employee rights claims is rooted in labor arbitration. A brief *amicus curiae* on behalf of the National Academy of Arbitrators argued that "collective or 'class' claims are common fare in labor arbitration without any loss of simplicity, flexibility, expedition, or informality," citing numerous "class grievances" routinely heard in labor arbitration including claims that sweep in statutory issues, *e.g.,* a "class action for all employees regarding the nonpayment of extra driving time from an employee's home to the Company's branch office," *ADT, LLC*, 133 LA 1821 (Felice, Arb. 2014), that the disallowance of religious exemption from Sunday work violated Title VII of the Civil Rights Act, *Avis Rent-A-Car Sys.*, 107 LA 197 (Shanker, Arb. 1996), that the requirement of a commercial driver's license discriminated against older workers, *The Lion, Inc.*, 198 LA 19 (Kaplan, Arb. 1997), and a good deal more.

The Arbitrators argued that the record, over the decades of class arbitrations, negates the supposition that the hearing of group claims would create a "procedural morass". Is the analogy of labor arbitration to employment arbitration sound? The Court thought so in 14 Penn Plaza LLC v. Pyett, 556 U.S. 247 (2009) discussed in the casebook at page 854. Does Justice Gorsuch deal with the record the arbitrations point to?

2.   With respect to the "procedural morass" that would result were employers disallowed the capacity to require only bilateral arbitration, the arbitrators argued thusly: if two or more workers who have suffered a common wrong cannot challenge that wrong in common but would have to proceed only individually, employers would

> face the prospect of a multiplicity of bilateral arbitrations, each subject separately to discovery of the same documents, depositions of the same managers, presentation of oral testimony on the same practice or decisions made by same people, subject to the same arguments as to events and to the credibility of testimony regarding them, no matter how cumulative or repetitive in the aggregate. Inexorably, this

would be the case if each of these aggrieved employees where to pursue a claim. As no employee would be a party to any other employee's action, each would make his or her case afresh. Were a large number who claim to have suffered the same wrong to bring individual arbitrations—all workers of African descent or all women workers who have been denied promotion by an arguably discriminatory test, all older workers disqualified by a novel job requirement that arguably has a discriminatory impact on grounds of age, those of the company's employees allegedly denied donning and doffing or overtime pay— employers *would* face a procedural morass: line and human resource managers would be required to devote weeks, perhaps months, to repetitive discovery and testimony in as many individual arbitrations as there are claimants.

Is this true? If it is, why would employers restrict their employees to bilateral arbitrations?

A group action was brought by 12,501 Uber drivers claiming misclassification as independent contractors. Because they were bound by an arbitration provision akin to *Epic Sys.*, they were ordered to proceed individually to arbitration. Under the rules of the listing organization a company is required to pay the estimated fees for an arbitration in advance. The plaintiffs then filed as many individual claims in arbitration which faced the Company with $18.7 million in fees. The Company settled these for at least $146 million. Bloomberg Law News (May 13, 2019). In what way is bilateral arbitration to be preferred to the arbitration of group claims?

———————

Page 573. Add to the discussion, in brackets, of *Media General Operations*:

See also NLRB v. Pier Sixty, LLC, 855 F.3d 155 (2d Cir. 2017), in which a Facebook posting was the cause for employee discipline. The Board held the posting to be protected despite its "opprobrious speech": The employee's posting called his boss a "NASTY MOTHER FUCKER" and urged the recipients to "vote YES for the UNION." This, the court said, was "at the outer-bounds of protected, union-related comments," but still within them. In dictum, however, the court expressed dubiety of the Board's liberal standards for speech in the use of social media even when not uttered in the presence of or displayed to customers.

Page 574. Add after the discussion of *Five Star Transportation, Inc.*:

On the determination of whether statements publicly connected to a labor dispute are so "disloyal, reckless, or maliciously untrue" as to lose statutory protection, compare the majority opinion and the dissent in DIRECTV, Inc. v. NLRB, 837 F.3d 25 (D.C. Cir. 2016).

Page 575. Add at the end of Problem 6:

The Board's order was enforced, one judge dissenting on the ground that the posters were impermissibly "disloyal." Miklin Enterprises, Inc. v. NLRB, 818 F.3d 397 (8th Cir. 2016); but, *en banc*, the Eighth Circuit held the posters to be unprotected, 861 F.3d 812 (8th Cir. 2017).

7.   Stanley Oliver is a "trouble man" for OnCall Electric, Inc., and also secretary of the Electrical Workers Local 69 that represents OnCall's workers. A "trouble man" responds to power outages.

A committee of the state senate is investigating whether "smart meters", which monitor customer electric usage without the intervention of a human meter-reader, "have harmful effects on public health". It has allowed members of the public two minutes each to appear before it. Mr. Oliver signed in to appear before the committee. He identified himself as "self Electrical Workers Local (69)." He appeared before the committee and said that in his experience these smart meters "burned up" more than traditional ones and that customers were told incorrectly they would have to pay for the damage.

OnCall, which is in the process of replacing its meters with "smart" ones, fired Mr. Oliver. Dies the discharge violate § 8(a)(3) of the Act? Oncor Electric Delivery Co. LLC v. NLRB, 887 F.3d 488 (D.C. Cir. 2018).

Page 579. Add at the end of Problem 3:

In Wal-Mart Stores, Inc., 364 NLRB No. 118 (2016), the Board found an in-store protest to be protected, applying the considerations laid out in Quietflex Mfg. Co., 344 N.L.R.B. 1055 (2005). Member Miscimarra dissented on the ground that the *Quietflex* factors are inapplicable to what he termed "a modern sit-down strike." He opined:

> The concerns motivating the employees' work stoppage and protest in this case were ongoing. They did not arise spontaneously on the morning of November 2, and there was no "necessary immediacy of action" driving the work stoppage. . . . The employees here had ample opportunity to present their concerns to the Respondent individually through the open-door policy, and they were invited to do so on the morning of the work stoppage. They could have conducted their protest outside the store at any time, as they did after they finally left the store after being repeatedly ordered to return to work or leave the store. The protesters certainly had a protected right to engage in a work stoppage, but their choice to conduct their work stoppage and engage in protest activities (i) inside the Richmond store, (ii) in the customer service area and (iii) briefly, in "Action Alley," the store's main aisle, (iv) in the presence of customers, and (v) for a significant length of time was, in my view, unwarranted and unprotected.

The protest was over a supervisor's mistreatment of a group of temporary remodeling workers—his "racist remarks and threats of physical violence." The employee protest began at 5:24 a.m. and ended at 6:38 a.m. The store opened at 6:00am. The "open door policy," pursuant to which management offered to meet with the protesters was interpreted by management to allow it to entertain only individual grievances, *i.e.* to preclude it from meeting with the protesters as a group. Should the employees' conduct be protected?

Page 579. Add at the end of Problem 4:

On October 3, 2016, the Office of NLRB General Counsel issued Memorandum OM–17–02, a "Model Brief Regarding Intermittent and Partial Strikes." The purpose was explained thusly:

> Employees seeking to improve their working conditions are more frequently engaging in multiple short-term strikes in disputes with employers. The Board's present test for determining whether multiple short-term strikes are protected is difficult to apply to these situations, and exposes employees to potential discipline for activities that should be considered protected under Section 7 of the Act. The General Counsel has therefore decided to ask the Board to clarify and modify the law regarding intermittent and partial strikes.

B. EMPLOYER RESPONSES TO CONCERTED ACTIVITIES

Page 601. Add to the citation at the end of Problem 1:

vacated, Southcoast Hospitals Group, Inc. v. NLRB, 846 F.3d 448 (1st Cir. 2017).

Page 602. Add at the end of the discussion of the *Boeing Company* complaint:

In evaluating the strength of the General Counsel's case, consider Anglo Kenlite Labs., Inc. v. NLRB, 833 F.3d 824 (7th Cir. 2016).

Page 608. Add following *Local 15, IBEW*:

In American Baptist Homes, 364 NLRB No. 13 (2016), a union of non-professional employees at a nursing home notified the employer on July 9 that they would go out on strike from August 2 to August 7. Simultaneously, written unconditional offers to return to work as of that date were submitted. The Employer resisted the strike by hiring temporary replacements, but from August 3 to 6 it began making offers of permanent replacement eventually hiring twenty employees on that basis. The Employer's Executive Director explained that she assumed replacements would be less likely to strike in future; the Employer's attorney stated that the Employer "wanted to teach the strikers and the Union a lesson."

The decision to hire permanent replacements was complained of as violative of § 8(a)(3). The ALJ disagreed. The judge acknowledged that under established precedent the hiring of permanent strike replacements can be an unfair labor practice if done for an "independent unlawful purpose"; but that purpose had to be "unrelated to or extraneous to the strike itself." The Board's two Member majority disagreed. The decision to hire permanent replacements can be unlawful when "motivated for a purpose prohibited by the Act," it need not be "unrelated" or "extrinsic" to the parties bargaining relationship, which the majority found to be the case here. The express purpose was to punish employees for the exercise of their statutory right to strike, which is not protected, citing, *inter alia*, *Erie Resistor* (casebook page 583).

Member Miscimarra dissented and at length: "employers have the right to hire permanent replacements regardless of motive," he opined. It is a weapon given employees to resist strikes under *Mackay Radio*. Any interference in that right, deriving from that which is related to the strike, injects the Board impermissibly into a balancing of the weapons the parties to a labor dispute may deploy, a power the Supreme Court has made clear the Board does not have.

Page 609. Add to Problems for Discussion:

4.   During a strike, several employers broke with it and returned to work. They were "crossovers." When the Union made an unconditional offer to have the strikers return to work, the Company initiated a lockout that included the crossovers. A week later, the Company informed the Union that it would lift the lockout. As it discussed the priority of recall with the Union—the Company had hired both temporary and permanent replacements—the Company notified the crossovers that they could return to work immediately. Has the Company violated § 8(a)(3)? Dresser-Rand Co. v. NLRB, 838 F.3d 512 (5th Cir. 2016). You might care to return to this after discussing Problem 3 on pp. 613–614 of the Main Volume.

II. CONSTITUTIONAL LIMITATIONS ON GOVERNMENT REGULATION

B. PICKETING AND FREEDOM OF COMMUNICATION

Page 653. Add at end of Note following Eliason & Knuth:

The rat has taken on an affectionate appellation—Scabby. Big Sky Balloons advertises its inflatable rats which featured in the Seventh Circuit's dealing with a city ordinance that restricted these displays.

The court held that the ordinance, neutral in content and not discriminatorily applied, could limit Scabby's positioning. Construction & General Laborers' Union No. 330 v. Town of Grande Chute, 915 F.3d 1120 (7th Cir. 2019).

Page 653. Add following Problem for Discussion:

Summit Design + Build is a general contractor for a project in Chicago. Summit has subcontracted the electrical work to Edge Electric. The Electrical Workers Union has written to Summit informing it that Edge fails to pay union area standards and that it would engage in action when Edge is at the job site to pressure Edge to pay area standards. When Edge was at the job site, the Union erected a large yellow banner that read "LABOR DISPUTE: SHAME SHAME," and beneath those words, "SUMMIT DESIGN AND BUILD." The Union also set up a large inflatable fat cat, approximately 10–15 feet tall, clutching a construction worker by the neck. The banner and the cat were located approximately 15 feet from the entrance to the job site.

The NLRB General Counsel has ordered a complaint of violation of § 8(b)(4)(i) and (ii)(B) to issue: that the Region seek to persuade the Board "to reconsider" *Eliason & Knuth*.

> Specifically, the Region should argue: (1) that the Union's erection of a large banner misleadingly claiming a labor dispute with the neutral, as well as the Union's use of a large inflatable cat clutching a construction worker by the neck at a private construction jobsite, was tantamount to unlawful secondary picketing; (2) that the posting of the banner and cat constituted unlawful signal picketing; and (3) that even if this conduct was not tantamount to picketing, it was nevertheless unlawfully coercive and not shielded by the First Amendment because the Union was engaged in labor and/or commercial speech, both of which are entitled to lesser constitutional protection, and also because the banners were knowingly false speech unprotected by the First Amendment.

G.C. Advice Memorandum in Case No. 13–CC–225655 (Dec. 20, 2018).

Page 661. Add to Problem for Discussion:

The collective bargaining agreement between the technical employees union and the Fursorge Clinic, Inc., a proprietary hospital, expired and the bargaining for a successor contract has been hard. Forty to sixty off-duty union supporters have been stationed by the Union on a public sidewalk running parallel to the non-emergency entrance handing out handbills, holding picket signs, singing and chanting for better terms. Two to four employees took handbills and a picket sign each and stood next to the nonemergency entrance on hospital property. The picket signs said, "Respect Our Care" and "Fair Contract Now." They stood still; there was no patrol. They sought to hand out the handbills to those entering and to explain why they were there. There was no disruption. The director of labor relations said the handbillers could stay, but either the picket signs be taken down or those holding them had to relocate to the sidewalk. The Union refused. Clinic security called the police. The police refused to remove the employees as they were neither disruptive nor did they obstruct access. Has the Clinic committed an unfair labor practice? Could the Union communicate to those it wanted to reach as effectively from the sidewalk? If so, is that relevant? Capital Medical Center v. NLRB, 909 F.3d 427 (D.C. Cir. 2018).

Assume the Union was attempting to organize the Clinic and the union representatives engaged in the above activity were not off-duty employees but union organizers. Assume that they did leave the Clinic's premises to leaflet and picket from the sidewalk. If the Clinic called the police would it have committed an unfair labor practice? NLRB v. ImageFirst Uniform Rental Service, Inc., 910 F.3d 725 (3d Cir. 2018).

III. THE NATIONAL LABOR RELATIONS ACT

B. SECONDARY PRESSURE

2. THE 1959 AMENDMENTS: CONSUMER APPEALS

Page 706. Add to Problem for Discussion:

Seven-Seven is a "convenience" store near the interstate. Various soft drinks and food stuffs are supplied to it by Rex Distributors. Rex's workers are represented by the Local 773, Distribution Workers' Union. Under Rex's collective bargaining agreement, salesmen-drivers are paid an 8% commission on goods "receipted to and paid by" the stores they deliver to. Kent Taylor is a Rex salesman driver. He delivered $17,000 of product to Seven-Seven, but failed to have it receipted. Because of that, Seven-Seven has refused to pay for the goods and Rex has not paid him the commission that would be due, over $1,000. The Union has arbitrated Rex's refusal to pay. The arbitrator denied the grievance on the ground that under the collective agreement only commissions on goods paid for must be paid. The Union has begun to picket Seven-Seven urging customers not to shop there and delivery people not to deliver until Seven-Seven pays its bill to Rex. Seven-Seven has sued the Union under § 303(b) of the Labor Act. The Union has moved to dismiss for failure to state a cause of action. How should the court rule? Wartman v. United Food and Commercials Workers Local 653, 871 F.3d 683 (8th Cir. 2017).

3.   HOT CARGO CLAUSES

Page 738. Add to Problems for Discussion:

6.   The parties' collective bargaining agreement contains Art. XXII, headed "Successorship." It provides in pertinent part:

> A.   DEFINITIONS
>
> > 1.   Transfer of Business shall mean the transfer by sale, lease or otherwise ownership of or operational control over a significant portion of the Company's current production functions or facilities to any other individual, partnership or corporation provided, however such term shall not include any such transfer, sale or lease, in whole or in part, which forms part of one or more financing transactions by the Company where the Company retains operational control of the assets transferred, sold or leased.
>
> [. . .]
>
> B.   NOTICE AND REGULATIONS
>
> > 1.   There shall be no Transfer of Business unless at least sixty (60) days prior to the effective date of such Transfer of Business the Company has delivered to the Manager of the [Union] Joint Board a binding written commitment by the Transferee to assume all of the Company's obligations under this Agreement. . . .

The Company has contracted with JDF Industrial Services to provide HVAC maintenance, cleaning, moving, and related services at a facility to which the collective agreement is applicable. The Union has demand production at the written agreement under Art. XXII (B). In response, the Company has filed a charge with the NLRB Regional Office asserting that Art. XXII (B), facially or as applied, violates § 8(e). Does it? Rochester Regional Joint Board, 363 N.L.R.B. No. 179 (2016).

7.   The Union had previously entered into a CBA with the Employer that contained the following subcontracting provision:

> SECTION 7—SUBCONTRACTING AND CONTRACTING OUT WORK
>
> A.   The Company shall have the right to enter into sub-contracts of the work referred to in Section 6 of this Agreement with companies paying wages and benefits similar to this Agreement and providing such sub-contracting is not done for the purpose of laying off employees.

During collective bargaining negotiations concerning a new CBA, the Union proposed that this language be amended to provide for "wages and benefits identical to this Agreement," rather than "similar to this Agreement." The

Employer filed suit, asserting an LMRA Section 303 claim against the Union based on allegations that the subcontracting proposal was unlawful under Section 8(e) and that the Union's strike to compel the Employer to agree to this clause constituted an unfair labor practice under Section 8(b)(4). The Employer argues the Union's proposed language is an "unlawful union signatory" provision because "identical" benefits can only be provided under the CBA. The Union contends that the subcontracting proposal merely seeks the equivalent of union wages, hours, and benefits, and is therefore a facially lawful "union standards" work preservation clause. Which party has the better argument? *See* Charter Communications, Inc. v. Local Union No. 3, IBEW, 338 F. Supp. 3d 242 (S.D.N.Y. 2018).

PART FIVE

ADMINISTRATION OF THE COLLECTIVE AGREEMENT

III. JUDICIAL ENFORCEMENT OF COLLECTIVE AGREEMENTS

Page 793. Add to Problems for Discussion:

5. The Hotel Workers' Union has a collective bargaining agreement (CBA) with Variety Enterprises for its casino and entertainment complex in Biloxi, Mississippi. Article 21 sets out the "Grievance and Arbitration" provision. Section 21.01 defines a "grievance" as "a dispute or difference of opinion between the Union and Variety involving the meaning, interpretation, [and] application [of the CBA] to employees covered by this agreement." The parties also negotiated contractual obligations in the event Variety subcontracted or subleased to third-party operations on its property. Article 29 of the CBA provides that when such is subcontracted,

> (a) all such work shall be performed only by members of the bargaining unit covered by this Agreement, and (b) the Employer shall at all times hold and exercise full control of the terms and conditions of employment of all such employees pursuant to the terms of this Agreement. The provisions of this Article apply to all operations on the Employer's premises covered by this agreement.

Variety leased club space to Brubeck's, a jazz club. Brubeck's hired bargaining unit workers to staff it. Brubeck's closed in six months. The workers were not paid for the last two months' wages and benefits. The Union has filed a grievance against Variety claiming that under Art. 29(b), Variety was liable for Brubeck's wages and benefits. The dispute went to arbitration. Variety argued that the dispute was not arbitrable. The Arbitrator agreed: "As Brubeck's was not a signatory to the CBA Variety was not a guarantor of the wages and benefits due Brubeck's employees. Art. 29(b) meant that Variety would assure that Brubeck's would be in compliance with the CBA and nothing more. The dispute over wages and benefits not paid to Brubeck's employees is not arbitrable." Should the award be enforced? Local Joint Executive Board v. Mirage Casino-Hotel, Inc. 911 F.3d 588 (9th Cir. 2018).

Page 803. Add to Problems for Discussion:

4. The Health Service Workers Union ["Service" Union] represented workers at the Harrisburg Eye & Ear Hospital. In February, the Union filed grievances that several named employees had been denied a variety of benefits in scheduling, overtime, and the like. While the grievances were pending a certification election was run by the NLRB on petition of the Health Care Providers Union ["Providers" Union]. The Providers Union won the election on May 16. On May 23, the Providers Union was certified by the

Board. The next day, the Service Union served notice demanding to arbitrate those outstanding grievances. The Hospital refused. Its lawyer told the Union that as it was no longer the employees' representative the Hospital could not deal with it under § 8(a)(5) and § 9(a). The Service Union replied that, under Board law, the Providers Union may not compel arbitration, as it has no arbitration agreement with the hospital. Unless the now decertified union is able to take these grievances, which arose prior to decertification, to arbitration the grievants will have no remedy. Is the Hospital obligated by § 8(a)(5) to arbitrate with the former union? Children's Hospital of Oakland, 364 N.L.R.B. No. 114 (2016).

Page 811. Add to Problems for Discussion:

5. The collective bargaining agreement between the NFL Players Association and the NFL Management Council sets out a procedure for the imposition of discipline for "conduct detrimental to the integrity of and public confidence in the game of professional football." The NFL Commissioner— the employer's executive officer—is to present charges of misconduct to the player and to a hearing officer of his designation. The Commissioner is to consult the players union on the appointment of the hearing officer, but the appointment is the Commissioner's. The decision of the hearing officer is final and binding.

The Commissioner has presented charges and a sought-for sanction against Tom Brady, quarterback of the New England Patriots, for his involvement in a scheme to deflate footballs during a key game. The Commissioner has designated himself as the hearing officer. He held a hearing and confirmed the discipline he sought. The League moved to confirm the Commissioner's decision under § 301; the Union sought to vacate it. The decision was termed by all parties and by the court as an "arbitration," the Commissioner as the "arbitrator." The district court vacated the award. The Second Circuit reversed, one judge dissenting. The dispute centered on the scope of arbitral discretion under *Enterprise Wheel* and its progeny. National Football League Management Council v. National Football League Players Ass'n, 820 F.3d 527 (2nd Cir. 2016).

Despite the parties' characterization of the proceeding as an "arbitration"—and the court's acquiescence, for that characterization had not been placed in contention before it—did Enterprise Wheel apply? Where a contract provides that disciplinary charges will be presented by an employer to be heard by the employer's representative—in this case, by the same person bringing the charges—for a final and binding decision is such a an "arbitration" within the meaning of *Enterprise Wheel*? *See* Graham v. Scissor-Tail, Inc., 28 Cal.3d 807 (1981); Sam Kane Packing Co. v. Amalgamated Meat Cutters, 477 F.2d 1128, 1136 (5th Cir. 1973). *Cf.* Dr. Bonham's Case, 77 Eng. Rep. 646, 652 (1610).

6. The collective bargaining agreement between Hannover Industrial Demolition, Inc., and the Ironworkers Union provided a grievance procedure culminating in arbitration with the following provision: "The arbitrator shall not have jurisdiction or authority to add on, detract from or alter in any way the provisions of this Agreement." Another section made provision for a pension plan with the eligibility requirements for full-time employees to qualify for participation. These provisions have been in the parties' collective agreements for decades.

In the early 2000s Hannover became extraordinarily profitable: its contracts allow it to own the non-ferrous metals it takes under its industrial demolition projects and the scrap aluminum market had soared. Workers groused over the fact that they were not reaping part of that windfall. In 2005, parties agreed to a bonus to be paid to employees on a formula pegged to the price for scrap aluminum—the Aluminum Price Bonus (APB)—which could amount to several thousand dollars per worker. Eligibility to receive the bonus was subject to intense negotiation. The parties agree to have that turn on eligibility for participation in the pension plan. The pension loomed large in the 2016 negotiations. The parties agreed to restrict eligibility to those hired before July 1, 2017. At no time in these negotiations did the parties mention or acknowledge that that decision would affect eligibility for the APB; it simply never came up.

After the 2017 APB was paid, in 2018, a number of employees hired after July 1, 2017, learned that they would not receive the APB and complained. The Union grieved their exclusion to arbitration. The parties were unable to stipulate the issue presented. Consequently, the arbitrator framed it: "Are employees hired on and after July 1, 2017, entitled to receive the Aluminum Price Bonus?"

The arbitrator held that the exclusion of new hires from the bonus was the product of mutual mistake. Applying "traditional principles of contract law" he awarded that the following italicized lines of text be added to the collective agreement's existing text set out in roman:

> Employees hired on and after the Effective Date are not eligible to participate in the pension plan. *However, the Company shall treat such Employees as if they were accruing Continuous Service under the Retirement Income Plan for Hourly Rated Employees of Industrial Demolition Inc. on the same terms as other Employees, only for purposes of determining eligibility for the Aluminum Price Bonus pursuant to [the CBA].*

The Company has refused to implement the award. The Union has sued to enforce. Should it be enforced? Asarco v. United Steel, Paper & Forestry, 910 F.3d 485 (9th Cir. 2018).

7. Hannover Industrial Demolition, Inc., whose collective bargaining agreement features in Problem 6, above, has a Workplace Violence Policy that prohibits "threatening or intimidating another person . . . and the possession of unauthorized weapons on Company premises including parking lots." Warren Harding, a crew leader, got into a shouting match over work assignment with his supervisor. On investigation, human resource personnel interviewed several co-workers who told them that Harding was hot tempered, argumentative, and given to carrying concealed weapons. They interviewed Harding in the presence of his Union steward and a County Deputy Sheriff. They asked his permission to search his person and his car parked in the Company parking lot. Harding consented. No weapon was found on his person. An assault rifle was found in his car. He was discharged for violation of the Workplace Violence Policy. The discharge was taken to arbitration. The issue submitted was that commonly used; "Was the Grievant Discharged for just cause; and, if not what is the remedy?" The Arbitrator found that Harding had, in fact, violated the policy by storing a firearm in his personal vehicle. However, he determined that the policy was unenforceable because Knox possessed a valid license to carry the weapon under the state's Concealed Carry Act. That statute expressly permitted Harding to store his firearm in his vehicle on private property unless the owner posted a sign "indicating that firearms are prohibited on the property." Because the company had no such sign posted, the arbitrator found that the law "serve[d] to prohibit the Employer from enforcing its rule in the Grievant's case, because he [was] in possession of a concealed carry license." He ordered Harding to be reinstated. The Company refused and the Union has sued to enforce the award. In addition to the provision forbidding the arbitrator from adding to or detracting from the agreement's terms the agreement also contains the following:

> Any provisions of this Agreement found by either party to be in conflict with State or Federal statutes shall be suspended when such conflict occurs and shall immediately thereafter be reopened for amendment to remove such conflict.

Should it be enforced? Ameren Illinois Co. v. IBEW, Local 51, 906 F.3d 612 (7th Cir. 2018). Should it make a difference whether or not the provision quoted above was in the agreement?

IV. THE ROLE OF THE NATIONAL LABOR RELATIONS BOARD AND THE ARBITRATOR DURING THE TERM OF A COLLECTIVE AGREEMENT

A. CONDUCT WHICH ALLEGEDLY VIOLATES BOTH THE CONTRACT AND THE LABOR ACT

Page 857. Add after *Babcock & Wilcox*:

The Ninth Circuit upheld the Board's decision to apply the new deferral standard only prospectively. Beneli v. NLRB, 873 F.3d 1094 (9th Cir. 2017).

On March 15, 2019, the Board issued a Notice and Invitation to File Briefs in *United Parcel Service, Inc.,* Case 06–CA–143062. The questions the parties were invited to address were:

1. Should the Board adhere to, modify, or abandon its existing standard for postarbitral deferral under *Babcock & Wilcox Construction Co.*, 361 NLRB 1127 (2014)?

2. If the Board decides to abandon the *Babcock* standard, should the Board return to the holdings of *Spielberg Mfg. Co.*, 112 NLRB 1080 (1955), and *Olin Corp.*, 268 NLRB 573

(1984), or would some other modification of the Board's
standard for postarbitral deferral be more appropriate?

3. If the Board decides to abandon the *Babcock* standard in
favor of either the *Spielberg/Olin* standard or some other
standard for postarbitral deferral, should it apply the newly
adopted standard retroactively in this case and other
pending cases or prospectively only?

Member McFerran dissented on two grounds: (1) no party had asked
the Board to revisit *Babcock*; and (2) there was inadequate experience
with it to assess its consequences.

Page 858. Add at the very end of the Problem for Discussion:

Verizon's *pet. for rev. granted*, Board's *pet. for enf't den.*, Verizon New
England, Inc. v. NLRB, 826 F.3d 480 (D.C. Cir. 2016) (Judge Henderson
writing separately to reject the Board's new standard regarding the scope of
arbitral authority in interpreting the Labor Act) (Judge Srinivasan writing
separately that the Board could find the majority arbitration panel's decision
"palpably wrong" under the Act).

Hannover Demolition, Inc., is in collective bargaining with the
Ironworkers' Union. The Company has locked out the workers and hired
temporary replacements many of whom are black. Warren Harding
participated in the picketing. While picketing in the strike's third week he
yelled, "Hey, did you bring enough KFC for everybody?" and "Hey anybody
smell that? I smell fried chicken and watermelon." The comments were
directed at a van carrying replacement workers that had just crossed the
picket line. While yelling, Harding's hands were in his pockets; he made no
overt physical movements or gestures. There is no evidence the replacement
workers heard his statements, though dozens in the crowd did. After a
collective agreement was concluded the following week, the lock-out ended
and all the workers were returned to work except Harding. He was
discharged for misconduct. The Union took the discharge to arbitration. The
Arbitrator upheld the discharge: he opined that Harding had engaged in
expressions of bigotry and that sustaining the grievance would be
"tantamount to requiring the Company to violate federal anti-discrimination
law as well as anti-harassment law." Meanwhile, a complaint of violation of
Section 8(a)(3) had issued. The ALJ held the matter was governed by *Clear
Pine Moldings*—discussed on pages 627–28 of the casebook—that "a
discharge for picket line conduct is an unfair labor practice unless it was such
misconduct as tends to coerce on intimidable employees in the exercise of
rights protected under the Act." The ALJ refused to defer to the award. The
matter is now before the Board. How should it rule? Cooper Tire & Rubber
Co. v. NLRB, 866 F.3d 885 (8th Cir. 2017).

**Page 865. Add to the references at the end of the discussion of *14
Penn Plaza*:**

Lawrence v. Sol G. Atlas Realty Co., Inc., 841 F.3d 81 (2d Cir. 2016) (no
clear and unmistakable waiver of right to judicial resort).

Page 866. Add to Problems for Discussion:

5.   Article 13 of the collective bargaining agreement between the City Transit Corp. and the Transport Workers Union sets out a grievance-arbitration procedure. Section 6 provides:

> All disputes, complaints, controversies, claims, and grievances arising between the Employer and the Union or any employees covered by this Agreement with respect to, concerning, or growing out of interpretation, operation, application, performance or claimed breach of any of the terms and conditions of this Agreement or any rights or duties created hereunder or under any federal, state or local law, shall be adjusted in accordance with the following procedure:

Francesco Cifu is a bus driver for City Transport, a member of the bargaining unit. He has commenced a lawsuit against City Transport for the failure to pay overtime in violation of the Fair Labor Standards Act. The Company has moved to compel arbitration. How should the court rule? Alfonso v. Maggie's Paratransit Corp., 203 F.Supp.3d 244 (E.D.N.Y. 2016).

B. THE DUTY TO BARGAIN DURING THE TERM OF AN EXISTING AGREEMENT

Page 898. Add to Problems for Discussion:

3.   H. Knox College has a collective bargaining agreement with the Part Time Faculty Association (PTFA) representing the College's part-time faculty. Article 21 sets out a management rights clause under which the College retains:

> A. The Right to plan, establish, terminate, modify, and implement all aspects of educational policies and practices, including curricula; admission and graduation requirements and standards; scheduling; . . . and the . . . reduction, modification, alteration . . . or transfer of any job, department, program, course, institute, or other academic or non-academic activity and the staffing of the activity, except as may be modified by this Agreement.

> and

> C. The right to . . . establish, modify, and discontinue rules and regulations . . . relating to the performance of work, including workload, scheduling of work and its location . . . except as may be modified by this Agreement.

Article 19 sets out a salary schedule that "represents minimum compensation" for instructors teaching a three credit-hour course and providing that compensation for courses totaling other than three credits would be prorated.

The collective agreement expired on June 30. As the parties negotiated for the ensuing collective agreement, they agreed that the expired collective agreement would remain in effect. In the negotiations the College proposed to change Art. 21 by adding the following as subsection D:

> Article 21 is intended to constitute a clear and unmistakable waiver of any rights the PTFA might otherwise have to bargain over managerial rights and/or the effects or impact on unit members of H. Knox College's decisions with respect to such rights.

The Union has rejected the demand.

Meanwhile, the administration has completed an evaluation of the College's curriculum. It notified the Union and affected faculty that the credit hours assigned to ten courses taught by unit members would be reduced. The Union has demanded to bargain with the College over the effects of that decision. The College has refused. Must the College engage in "effects bargaining"? Would it make a difference if the College were located in the Seventh Circuit or the Sixth Circuit? Columbia College Chicago v. NLRB, 847 F.3d 547 (7th Cir. 2017); *see* the discussion at pages 453–455 of the Main Volume.

PART SIX

SUCCESSORSHIP

Page 926. Add at the end of Problem 2:

Adams & Assoc., Inc., 363 N.L.R.B. No. 193 (2016).

Page 926. Add at the end of Problem 3:

Lily Transp. Co. was enforced, NLRB v. Lily Transp. Co., 853 F.3d 31 (1st Cir. 2017). The court, in an opinion by former Supreme Court Justice David Souter, sustained both the Board's irrebuttable prescription and the adequacy of its explanation for the departure from its antecedent decisions.

Page 926. Add to Problems for Discussion:

4. The Guild has represented a wall-to-wall bargaining unit of workers of *The Newcastle Commercial Intelligencer*, a newspaper. The unit includes all full term and regular part-time employees exclusive of professional, managers, supervisors, and guards. The unit does not include "inserters," people who put advertising inserts between the folds of the Sunday edition. That work is done by a contractor. The newspaper has been sold in a bankruptcy sale. The new owner has offered to interview the incumbent staff for much the same jobs they have been doing but at less pay, with more precarious hours and with fewer benefits. The current complement of workers is 36, of whom 24 worked for the *Commercial Intelligencer*. The Company has decided to take the work of inserters in-house, on a regular part-time basis, and has hired 51 of these. The Guild has demanded that the newspaper bargain with it and to supply staffing and financial information relevant to collective bargaining. Must the newspaper comply? Publi-Inversiones de Puerto Rico, Inc. v. NLRB, 886 F.3d 142 (D.C. Cir. 2018).

5. Trash Mash, Inc., a trash collection company, uses 40 workers supplied by Serviceserf, Inc. Serviceserf's workers are represented by the Trash Collector's Union. Trash Mash is not satisfied with Serviceserf and has decided to have its work done by its own workers. Trash Mash's manager, Taylor Grant, had given 40 job applications and tax forms to one of the collectors, Hoyt Monet, in mid-May. Grant told Monet he'd be paid $11/hr plus benefits and asked him to "spread them [the forms] around." By May 20, Grant had forms from all the workers. He told them to come to the terminal on June 2 and cancelled the contract with Serviceserf. At the beginning of the shift, 4:00 a.m., June 2, Grant told those who were present that "you're all working today" and told them what their wages, benefits, routes and hours were. Five workers walked out. The rest went to work. On June 4, the Union learned about what happened. On June 6, the Union demanded that Trash Mash adhere to the terms of its agreement with Serviceserf and bargain over any change in mandatory bargaining subjects. Must Trash Mash agree to the Union's demands? Creative Vision Resources, LLC v. NLRB, 882 F.3d 510 (5th Cir. 2018).

6.   Assume that Trash Mash was displeased with Serviceserf because it found the work rules in Serviceserf's collective bargaining agreement were too restrictive in terms of scheduling and call-in time to accommodate its customer needs. Would terminating the service contract in order to avoid those union restrictions be an unfair labor practice? NLRB v. CNN America, Inc., 865 F.3d 740 (D.C. Cir. 2017). What if Serviceserf were to be a joint employer with Trash Mash?

Page 926. Add after Problems for Discussion:

A NOTE ON THE "PERFECTLY CLEAR" SUCCESSOR

In Ridgewood Health Care Center, Inc., 367 NLRB No. 110 (2019), the Board confronted manipulation of the number of employees a successor hired from the unionized complement of the predecessor's work force in order to avoid bargaining with the Union. Under prior Board precedent, Galloway School Lines, 321 NLRB 1422 (1996), a successor so doing would have to bargain with the union in establishing initial terms and conditions and continue the status quo ante of the collective bargaining agreement for those hired. The three-member Republican majority overruled that decision as a misreading of *Burns*.

> Expanding that remedy to encompass any successor employer who discriminates to any degree in hiring to avoid the *Burns* majority-based successor obligation goes too far. It effectively eliminates the otherwise customary *Burns* right to set initial employment terms unilaterally even for an employer whose hiring discrimination is limited to a single predecessor employee whose hiring would have established a continuing majority in the successor unit. Imposing the same statutory bargaining obligation as that typically reserved for the exceptional "perfectly clear" successor—and the same remedial obligation to rescind initial employment terms and to make employees whole at the predecessor's contractual wage rates—on employers who undisputedly would have been ordinary *Burns* successors had they not violated Section 8(a)(3) threatens to cross the line from the broad equitable relief permitted under Section 10(c) of the Act to punitive action that the Board is prohibited from taking.

Member McFerran dissented. She pointed out that as the workforce had been assured that over 99% of them would be hired it was a case of "perfectly clear successorship" without reaching out to overrule precedent. She argued that *Galloway* was correct. *Burns* did not apply to the case of new employer's plan to avoid successorship.

From the employees' perspective, the employer discriminatorily refuses to hire a targeted number of their coworkers, refuses to recognize and bargain with their representative, and unilaterally imposes employment terms. The employer has not made a good faith mistake; but rather has intentionally engaged in an unlawful hiring scheme to get rid of the union. The employer's misconduct increases stress and uncertainty for the employees, heightens the risk of labor disputes, and certainly chills union activity. As I will explain, resetting initial employment terms in these circumstances is necessary to effectuate the Act's purposes by establishing stability for the employees, restoring the status quo, and removing an incentive for employers to break the law.

PART SEVEN

Labor and the Antitrust Laws

Page 963. Add at the end of Problem 2:

And, after trial on remand, American Steel Erectors, Inc. v. Local Union 7, Iron Workers, 815 F.3d 43 (1st Cir. 2016) (thoroughly reviewing the law).

PART EIGHT

FEDERALISM AND LABOR RELATIONS

I. PREEMPTION OF STATE LABOR LAW: AN OVERVIEW

Page 1001. Add at the end of Problem 2:

Assume that the chanting, bannering, and leafleting included a demand for the Company to recognize the Union and that the Company filed charges of violation of § (8)(b)(1)(A) and § 8(b)(7) with the NLRB. Is the Company's suit to enjoin trespassing preempted? United Food and Commercial Workers v. Wal-Mart Stores, Inc., 137 A.3d 355 (Md. App. 2016).

Page 1016. Add to Problems for Discussion:

8. The City of Seattle has enacted an ordinance to allow for-hire transportation drivers who are classified as independent contractors to engage in collective bargaining with the "entity that hires, contracts with, or partners with them." Seattle Mun. Code § 6.310.735. Is this ordinance preempted by the National Labor Relations Act? See Chamber of Commerce v. City of Seattle, 890 F.3d 769 (9th Cir. 2018).

II. SPECIFIC APPLICATIONS: REPRESENTATION, BARGAINING AND CONCERTED ACTIVITIES

A. SELECTION OF BARGAINING REPRESENTATIVE

Page 1018. Add to Problems for Discussion:

3. Wisconsin and Georgia have legislated to preclude employees of franchisees from being held to be employees of their franchisee's franchisors. Wisconsin Senate Bill 422 (2015) (enacted 2016); Georgia Senate Bill 277 (effective Jan. 1, 2016). Do these laws apply to the Labor Act? *See* Question for Discussion 4 at p. 301.

B. COLLECTIVE BARGAINING

Page 1030. Add to Problems for Discussion:

7. Utopia City has adopted an ordinance governing hotels in the City providing for a minimum wage of $15.37 an hour. It provides an opt-out for workers covered by a bona fide, non-expired collective bargaining agreement, if the waiver is set forth in that agreement in clear and unambiguous terms. Is the Ordinance preempted? McCray v. Marriott Hotel Servs., Inc., 902 F.3d 1005 (9th Cir. 2018); American Hotel & Lodging Ass'n v. City of Los Angeles, 834 F.3d 958 (9th Cir. 2016); Fil Foods, LLC v. City of Seatac, 357 P.3d 1040 (Wash. 2015).

8.   Would a state law providing for collective bargaining by "for hire drivers" who are independent contractors be preempted by the Labor Act? Chamber of Commerce v. City of Seattle, 890 F.3d 769 (9th Cir. 2018).

9.   Gotham City has adopted an ordinance regulating the car wash industry. The ordinance finds that those enterprises are often fly-by-night with a record of stiffing suppliers, creditors, and workers. The ordinance requires that car washing companies be licensed and sets out conditions for licensure including the posting of a bond to cover the non-payment of bills. The bond is $150,000, but it can be reduced to $30,000 if "the applicant [for the license] satisfies the Department of Consumer Affairs that it "is a party to a current and bona fide collective bargaining agreement, with a collective bargaining representative of its employees, that expressly provides for the timely payment of wages and an expeditious process to resolve disputes concerning nonpayment or underpayment of wages." Is the ordinance preempted by the Labor Act? Ass'n of Car Wash Owners, Inc. v. City of New York, 911 F.3d 74 (2d Cir. 2018).

10.   Gotham City has enacted a "Deductions Law" applicable to fast food enterprises in the city. They are required to administer payroll deduction for consenting employees to have a portion of their wages remitted to non-profit organizations registered with the city's Department of Consumer Affairs. The organization receiving these funds is required to cover the employers' costs of administering the system. "Labor organizations" as defined by the Labor Act, are excluded from participation. (Including them would have required employers to "contribute . . . other support" to a labor organization on violation of Section 8(a)(2).) One non-profit organization approved to receive employee dues deduction is Food Worker Justice. The organization was created from start-up funding and staff were supplied by a union. Food Worker Justice describes itself on its website thusly:

> together we will[ ] [e]ducate our coworkers about wage increases, fair and stable scheduling laws, and paid sick leave, so that we know our rights and can protect them in our workplaces[;] [f]ight for more improvements in the fast-food industry so fast-food jobs can be good jobs [; and] [u]nite for positive changes in our communities—including affordable housing and transit, just immigration reform, fair policing and criminal justice reform.

Either facially or as applied is the ordinance preempted by the Labor Act? Restaurant Law Center v. City of New York, 360 F. Supp. 3d 192 (S.D.N.Y. 2019).

C.   ENFORCEMENT OF COLLECTIVE AGREEMENTS

Page 1054. Add to Problems for Discussion:

7.   Keystone Visiting Nurse, LLC., employs nurses to provide home health care. The nurses are unionized. Their collective bargaining agreement sets out the compensation per visit; premium pay for work beyond the standard work week; scheduling of work—which "shall not be changed without prior discussion between both parties"; completion of all care and documentation "at the point of care or prior to the end of the employee's shift" with "any variation subject to approval of the clinical manager"; a recitation of management rights including the right to schedule and assign work; and, a grievance-arbitration provision.

A number of nurses have brought a class action against Keystone for the failure to pay overtime for the completion of required patient visit paperwork done after the completion of care and away from the patients' home. They assert this to violate state wage and hour law. That law requires employer knowledge, actual or constructive, that the employee worked time in excess of that scheduled. Keystone has moved to dismiss on the ground that the claims are completely preempted by § 301. How should the court rule? Rueli v. Baystate Health, Inc., 835 F.3d 53 (1st Cir. 2016); Kobold v. Good Samaritan Regional Med. Ctr., 832 F.3d 1024 (9th Cir. 2016).

8.   David Rocker has worked as a bus driver for Suburban Transport, Inc. (STI), for five years. On average, Rocker worked at least eight hours per day, at least five days per week, at a wage of $21.57 per hour. Rocker alleges that STI maintains a time-shaving policy. STI set the schedule for every bus run and, if the actual run time exceeded the planned run time, STI required drivers to fill out a "pink slip" giving the reasons for the delay. STI instructed drivers not to list "unrealistic schedule" as a reason, and instead to attribute delays to "traffic." Pink slips were then forwarded to a supervisor responsible for approving the excess time.

Rocker calculated the "shortages of actual pay" that should have been reflected in his paychecks. He alleges underpayment in the amount of approximately $1,000. Rocker raised the underpayment issue with STI management several times, to no avail. He then discussed the issue with two union stewards, who felt that it would be futile to pursue a grievance.

Rocker files a putative class action claim against STI, alleging the time-shaving scheme violates the state's wage payment and collection law, which requires employers to pay all wages earned during the pay period. The term "wages" is defined as "any compensation owed an employee by an employer pursuant to an employment contract or agreement between the 2 parties, whether the amount is determined on a time, task, piece, or any other basis of calculation." The statute further provides that "to state a claim, [employees] are required to demonstrate that they are owed compensation from defendants pursuant to an employment agreement." The employment contract whose terms Rocker seeks to enforce is the CBA between STI and his union. Rocker's claim relies on the CBA provision requiring that "all employees shall be paid for all time during which they are required by STI to perform any duties." Is this claim preempted by § 301? *See* Singer v. Regional Trans. Auth., 338 F. Supp. 3d 791 (N.D. Ill. 2018).

PART NINE

THE INDIVIDUAL AND THE UNION

I. THE RIGHT TO FAIR REPRESENTATION

C. THE INDIVIDUAL AND HIS GRIEVANCE

Page 1102. Add after Note:

On October 24, 2018, the NLRB General Counsel sent out an instruction to the Regional Offices on the administration of § 8(b)(1)(A) charges of breach of the duty of fair representation involving union assertions of "mere negligence."

> In cases where a union asserts a mere negligence defense based on its having lost track, misplaced or otherwise forgotten about a grievance, whether or not it had committed to pursue it, the union should be required to show the existence of established, reasonable procedures or systems in place to track grievances, without which, the defense should ordinarily fail.
>
> Similarly, a union's failure to communicate decisions related to a grievance or to respond to inquiries for information or documents by the charging party, in the General Counsel's view, constitutes more than mere negligence and, instead, rises to the level of arbitrary conduct unless there is a reasonable excuse or meaningful explanation. This is so irrespective of whether the decisions, alone, would violate the duty of fair representation.

Memorandum GC 19–01 (Oct. 24, 2018) (footnotes omitted).

Page 1104. Add to Problems for Discussion:

6. Selma Rich worked for Buell Foods for twenty-eight years. Buell had had a rule for some years that any employee who passes the cash-out lane without paying for any merchandize in his or her possession will be deemed to have stolen those goods irrespective of intent and will be dismissed. The Food Service Workers Union represents Buell's employees. It was aware of the rule and never objected to it or sought to change it. While at work, Ms. Rich received a cell phone call from her husband that her grandson was ill and that she was needed. She told him she would take her grandson to the hospital as soon as her shift ended, shortly. As she proceeded toward the exit with her coat bag and other articles in a shopping cart she noticed two bags of bird seed on the floor, one opened. She put these in her cart intending, she later said, to put them on the shelf, near the exit, reserved for misplaced goods. She passed the cash register with the cart and was stopped by a store security agent. He reported the incident including her account that in her rush to leave and her concern for her grandson she'd simply forgotten about the birdseed over which she'd placed her coat. After an investigation, Buell notified her and her Union that she was dismissed for theft.

The Union filed a grievance. In the step one meeting, management invoked the above rule. The Union decided not to pursue the grievance any further. Has the Union breached its duty of fair representation? Rupcich v. United Food & Commercial Workers, 833 F.3d 847 (7th Cir. 2016); *see also* Rollins v. Community Hosp. of San Bernadino, 839 F.3d 1181 (9th Cir. 2016). Assume that a few years previously the Union had brought another dismissal for petty theft to arbitration and lost because the arbitrator found the employee had intended to steal the item. Would that make a difference? Would it make a difference that Buell's rule on misappropriation of goods was neither appended to the collective agreement nor circulated to the workforce?

II. UNION SECURITY AND THE ENCOURAGEMENT OF UNION ACTIVITY

A. UNION SECURITY AND THE USE OF UNION DUES

Page 1131. Add at the end of Problem 2:

Days before this Supplement went to press, the Supreme Court, in a 5–4 decision overruled *Abood*, holding that an Illinois law mandating the payment of agency fees by nonconsenting public employees violates the First Amendment. Janus v. American Federation of State, County, and Municipal Employees, Council 31, ___ U.S. ___ 138 S. Ct. 2448, 201 L. Ed. 924 (2018). As a result, neither an agency fee nor other payment to a union may be deducted from public sector employee's pay without the employee's affirmative consent. As the adjoining materials in the Casebook suggest, this decision is likely to have far reaching implications for public sector unionism.

Page 1132. Add at the end of Problem 6:

What if the collective agreement allows employees to revoke their dues deduction authorization only on the anniversary date of their authorizations? *See* section 302(c)(4) of the Act; *cf.* Stewart v. NLRB, 851 F.3d 21 (D.C. Cir. 2017).

B. STATE RIGHT-TO-WORK LAWS

Page 1153. Add at the end of Section B "State Right-to-Work Laws":

The Sixth Circuit reversed the district court in *Hardin County*. It held that the word "state" in section 14(b) included political subdivisions. Accordingly, a county (or city) can legislate to make itself a right-to-work (RTW) zone. UAW v. Hardin County, 842 F.3d 407 (6th Cir. 2016). The holding has been rendered moot for Kentucky as it, and Missouri as well, have become RTW states. Nevertheless, the theory may well be tested in non-right-to-work states. The Village of Lincolnshire, Illinois, had enacted an ordinance making it a "right to work" political subdivision.

The Seventh Circuit held that § 14(b) does not authorize a state to delegate the power to ban agency shops to lower levels of government. Int'l Union of Operating Engineers v. Village of Lincolnshire, 905 F.3d 955 (7th Cir. 2018). New Mexico has done the same by legislation N.M. House Bill 85 (2019).

The economic impact of these RTW laws poses rather difficult problems for labor economists to assess. *See* Benjamin Collins, *Right to Work Laws: Legislative Background and Empirical Research*, CRS Report (Dec. 6, 2012). Elise Gould and Will Kimball, in *"Right-to-Work" States Still Have Lower Wages*, Economic Policy Institute Briefing Paper #395 (April 22, 2015), argue that the key question is whether working in a RTW state lowers the wages of similar nonunion workers when compared with other states. *Id.* at 9. They find little effect of RTW on manufacturing employment growth. They find that high-tech manufacturing's locational motivation is governed by strong educational systems, the presence of research universities, good digital infrastructure and the like, which is more characteristic of non-RTW states: 7.9% of workers in non-RTW states have less than a high school education compared to 9.8% in RTW states. Conversely, 12.9% have education beyond the collegiate level in non-RTW states whereas 10.3% do in RTW states. They conclude that wages in RTW states are 3.1% lower than in non-RTW states after controlling for a comprehensive range of individual demographic and socioeconomic factors as well as state macroeconomic indicators. If unions are able to raise wages significantly above the wages paid by non-unionized employers, thereby increasing purchasing power in the aggregate and the capacity for individual economic improvement, why would a state's political leadership not see unionization as a desirable state of affairs? See Part Ten, *infra*.

PROBLEMS FOR DISCUSSION

1.   A provision in the RTW laws in Georgia and Wisconsin makes dues deduction authorization revocable on 30 days' notice. The former, for example, prohibits any deduction from "wages or other earnings of any employee any fee, assessment, or other sum of money . . . to be paid over to a labor organization except on the written authorization of the employee. Such authorization may be revoked at any time at the request of the employee." O.C.G.A. § 34–6–25(a).

Section 302 of the Taft-Hartley Act forbids an employer from paying or delivering any money to a labor organization. This is subject to a set of exemptions including subsection (c)(4) which allows deductions from wages for union dues:

> *Provided*, That the employer has received from each employee, on whose account such deductions are made, a written assignment which shall not be irrevocable for a period of more than one year, or beyond the termination date of the applicable collective agreement, whichever occurs sooner. . . .

Are the RTW deductions in Georgia and Wisconsin preempted by federal law? You should review the theories of preemption set out in Part Eight. *See* Georgia State AFL-CIO v. Olens, 194 F. Supp. 3d 1322 (N.D. Ga. 2016); *cf.* Int'l Ass'n of Machinists Dist. 10 v. Wisconsin, 194 F. Supp. 3d 856 (W.D. Wis. 2016).

2.   The Wisconsin law provides *inter alia* that:

No person may require, as a condition of obtaining or continuing employment, an individual to do any of the following:

1.   Refrain or resign from membership in, voluntary affiliation with, or voluntary financial support of a labor organization.

2.   Become or remain a member of a labor organization.

3.   Pay any dues, fees, assessments, or other charges or expenses of any kind or amount, or provide anything of value, to a labor organization.

Wis. Stat. § 111.04(3)(a).

Flock's Outdoor Gear, Inc., is a unionized sporting goods company. It has outlets in Kenosha, Wisconsin, and Waukegan, Illinois, about fifteen miles apart. Alan Bates lives in Waukegan and works at Flock's Kenosha outlet. Monika Howe lives in Kenosha and works in Flock's Waukegan outlet. May either or both be required to remit union agency fees under the collective bargaining agreement's union security clause?

3.   Section 14(b) allows state law to prohibit the requiring of union "membership." The Wisconsin RTW law, set out in Question 2, above, prohibits not only the required payment of union dues, fees, and assessments, but also "any charge or expenses of any kind." Is this part of the law preempted by the Labor Act? Int'l Union of Operating Engineers v. Schimel, 210 F. Supp. 3d 1088 (E.D. Wisc. 2016).

III. DISCIPLINE OF UNION MEMBERS AND THE NATIONAL LABOR RELATIONS ACT

Page 1189. Add this following the paragraph set out in the Problem for Discussion:

A Union has adopted a policy governing the manner in which a member may resign: by appearing in person at the Union Hall with a photo identification and a written request; or, if that poses an "undue hardship," by making "other arrangements" to verify his or her identity. The employee charging party lived 200 miles from the Union Hall. He wrote a letter to his Employer stating his intent to resign. The Employer sent the letter to the Union. The Union called the employee to verify his identity and accepted his resignation. Can the General Counsel proceed on this charge to issue a complaint? Does the Union's policy violate § 8(b)(1)(A)? Local 58, IBEW v. NLRB, 888 F.3d 1313 (D.C. Cir. 2018).

PART TEN

THE LABOR ACT TODAY

II. THE CHANGING CONTEXT

C. EMPLOYER POLICIES

Page 1203. At the conclusion of Section C add the following Questions for Discussion:

QUESTIONS FOR DISCUSSION

1.   It has been reported that when the Organization United for Respect of Walmart, known as "OUR Walmart," was formed in 2012, supported and funded by a union, the Company reacted by forming a "Delta Team" that included representatives from the Company's global security, labor relations, and media relations departments. The Company also hired "an intelligence-gathering service . . . contacted the FBI, staffed its labor hotline, ranked stores by labor activity, and kept eyes on employees (and activists) prominent in the group." Susan Berfield, *How Walmart Keeps an Eye on Its Massive Workforce*, www.bloomberg.com/businessweek (Nov. 24, 2015). No doubt the reaction reflected the company's concerns for its ability to anticipate and deal with local protests, especially "flash mobs" gathering in the store during store hours. But does this reaction reflect something more? According to this press account, the Company's "labor relations team uses information from the [labor] hotline and social media monitoring to determine which stores are most at risk of labor unrest. These are dubbed Priority 1 stores, in need of extra training for managers and extra information sessions for employers." Why is the Company seemingly so fearful of having its workers unionize?

2.   It has been reported that, in the ten-year period from 2006 to 2015, the two organizations most aggressive in seeking "right to work" legislation, the National Right to Work Committee and the National Right to Work Legal Defense Foundation, received contributions totaling $105 million and $64.4 million respectively. 192 DLR (2017) at p. 9. What explains the devotion of sums of this size to this effort?

III. THE "REPRESENTATION GAP"

Page 1206. At the end of that section add:

A recent survey of over 4,000 workers produced a set of highly nuanced conclusions about their preferences. Hertel-Fernandez, Kimball, and Kochan, *How U.S. Workers Think About Workplace Democracy: The Structure of Individual Preferences for Labor Representation* (2019). Among its conclusions is the following (references and footnote omitted):

Overall, our results make clear that the primary function of the traditional union, collective bargaining, continues to be highly valued by potential members. Still, other benefits and services, such as the provision of health insurance, retirement benefits, unemployment benefits, and labor market training, are also highly valued by all workers, and this was especially true for workers with lower levels of education. Workers were also supportive of organizations offering legal representation and input to their work routines and into management decisions.

. . . Our results show American workers would support means of achieving industrial democracy at their workplaces that are modeled after those found in systems that provide co-determination, works councils, and more informal engagement in workplace decision-making. They also would value having unions provide valued labor market services throughout their careers as do unions in "Ghent" systems found in several European countries. This in turn is consistent with a growing number of labor law and policy scholars. . .who suggest that American labor law forces unions to conform to a model that is poorly matched to the present economy and workforce with its firm-based organizing and bargaining and the limited influence the law grants unions over corporate practices. The findings we present in this paper suggest another reason that labor law is restricting growth of the labor movement: it currently limits unions from providing many of the benefits and services that workers value.

Labor law is not the only obstacle to further union growth, however. So too are workers' preferences against labor organizations that use strike threats and engage in election campaigns. Despite the fact that both of these strategies have historically been central to union economic and political power. . .workers, on average, were skeptical of joining and financially supporting organizations that deployed these two tactics (at least in the abstract). This was especially true for workers who self-identify as Republicans and those reporting already high levels of influence at work. Although our analysis of organizational bundles indicates that neither characteristic entirely rules out broad-based worker support, it does underscore the difficulty of building large membership associations dedicated to *both* representing workers' narrow workplace concerns *and* engaging in broader movement politics.

IV. LABOR LAW REFORM

Page 1208. Add at the end:

The Labor and Workplace Program at the Harvard Law School initiated a project—"Rebalancing Economic and Political Power: A Clean Slate for the Future of American Labor Law"—looking toward proposals to refashion American labor law with a focus on increasing union density.

ADDENDUM

Page 355. Add after *Levitz Furniture*:

On July 3, 2019, the Board, by the three Member Republican majority, handed down a partial abrogation of *Levitz Furniture*. Johnson Controls, 368 NLRB No. 20 (2019). The facts were these: the Union had a collective bargaining agreement governing a unit 160 production workers effective to May 7, 2015. On April 21, 83 unit members signed a petition that they no longer wanted to be represented. It went on to state that the petitioners

> UNDERSTAND THIS PETITION MAY BE USED TO OBTAIN AN ELECTION SUPERVISED BY THE NATIONAL LABOR RELATIONS BOARD OR TO SUPPORT THE WITHDRAWAL OF RECOGNITION OF THE UNION.

The Company promptly informed the Union that it would withdraw recognition when the collective agreement expired. The Union then circulated unequivocal union designation cards. Sixty-nine of the 160 unit members signed it of whom six had signed the prior petition. On May 6, the Union offered to meet and "share evidence" of its continued support. The Company declined and withdrew recognition.

The majority summarized the result thusly:

> Under extant precedent, the Board determines the union's representative status and the legality of the employer's action by applying a "last in time" rule, under which the union's evidence controls the outcome because it postdates the employer's evidence. As we shall explain, this framework has proven unworkable and does not advance the purposes of the Act. Today, we adopt a new framework that is fairer, promotes greater labor relations stability, and better protects Section 7 rights by creating a new opportunity to determine the employees' wishes concerning representation through the preferred means of a secret ballot, Board-conducted election.
>
> Under well-established precedent, an employer that receives evidence, within a reasonable period of time before its existing collective-bargaining agreement (CBA or contract) expires, that the union representing its employees no longer enjoys majority support may give notice that it will withdraw recognition from the union when the CBA expires, and the employer may also suspend bargaining or refuse to bargain for a successor contract. This is called an "anticipatory" withdrawal of recognition.
>
> When the contract expires, however, an employer that has made a lawful anticipatory withdrawal of recognition still withdraws recognition at its peril. If the union challenges the

withdrawal of recognition in an unfair labor practice case, the employer will have violated Section 8(a)(5) if it fails to establish that the union lacked majority status at the time recognition was actually withdrawn. In making this determination, the Board will rely on evidence that the union reacquired majority status in the interim between anticipatory and actual withdrawal, regardless of whether the employer *knew* that the union had reacquired majority status. As a result, an employer that properly withdraws recognition anticipatorily, based on evidence in its possession showing that the union has long majority status, can unexpectedly find itself on the losing end of an 8(a)(5) charge when it withdraws recognition at contract expiration. Moreover, the remedy for that violation will typically include an affirmative bargaining order, which precludes any challenge to the union's majority status for a reasonable period of time—at least 6 months, as long as 1 year. And if, within this insulated period, the parties reach agreement on a successor contract, the union's majority status will again be irrebuttably presumed for the duration of that contract, up to another 3 years. [Footnotes omitted.]

The majority thought the state of the law to create problems for a company facing these conflicting claims.

The framework we announce today addresses all these concerns and creates a mechanism that settles questions concerning employees' representational preference in the anticipatory withdrawal context through a Board-conducted, secret-ballot election, the preferred means of resolving such questions. In doing so, we overrule *Levitz, supra,* and its progeny insofar as they permit an incumbent union to defeat an employer's withdrawal of recognition in an unfair labor practice proceeding with evidence that it reacquired majority status in the interim between anticipatory and actual withdrawal. Instead, we hold that proof of an incumbent union's actual loss of majority support, if received by an employer within 90 days prior to contract expiration, conclusively rebuts the union's presumptive continuing majority status when the contract expires. However, the union may attempt to reestablish that status by filing a petition for a board election within 45 days from the date the employer gives notice of an anticipatory withdrawal of recognition. [Footnotes omitted.]

Member McFerran's dissent took on the assumptions for and content of the new rule:

The way the majority describes existing law reveals the fatal flaw in the majority's position. The majority announces that it overrule[s] *Levitz* and its progeny insofar as they permit an incumbent union to defeat an employer's withdrawal of recognition in an unfair labor practice proceeding with evidence that it reacquired majority status in the interim between anticipatory and actual withdrawal.

This tendentious framing obscures the long-established principle that an incumbent union always is entitled to a continuing presumption of majority support—conclusive during the term of a collective-bargaining agreement and rebuttable after the agreement expires—which the employer must overcome with objective evidence to justify its withdrawal of recognition from the union. The Board's "anticipatory withdrawal" cases do not involve a union's supposed "reacquisition" of majority support, but rather the employer's inability to meet its burden to demonstrate that the union has actually *lost* majority support at the crucial time: when the employer withdrew recognition after the collective-bargaining agreement expired (and not earlier, when the agreement remained in effect and the employer was not allowed to withdraw recognition).

The majority, in turn, misconceives the issue now before the Board. According to the majority, the "issue presented in this case . . . is how best to determine the wishes of employees concerning representation where the employer has evidence that at least fifty percent of unit employees no longer desire to be represented by the union, and the union possesses evidence that it has reacquired majority status [*sic*]." There is an obvious answer to that question under existing law: The employer should file an election petition with the Board, just as *Levitz* expressly permits. If, rejecting this option, the employer chooses to withdraw recognition from the incumbent union unilaterally, then it properly does so at its peril—for the reasons explained in *Levitz*, namely that the presumption of continued union majority support serves to stabilize collective bargaining and that elections are the preferred method of resolving representation questions. To be sure, under the election procedure permitted by *Levitz*, the incumbent union (because it is the incumbent) remains in place unless and until employees reject the union in a secret-ballot vote. *That* fact seems to be the unspoken reason for the majority's creation of a "new framework" for cases like this one. [Emphasis in original; footnotes omitted.]

PROBLEMS FOR DISCUSSION

1. The majority rests the change in law on the ground that it is fairer, provides greater stability in labor relations, and better protects worker section 7 rights. In what way is the new approach fairer? In what way does it better protect section 7 rights? How does it conduce toward greater stability in labor relations?

2.   Recall that as a result of *Allentown Mack Sales*, casebook page 346, an employer with an objectively grounded good faith doubt of majority status may file a petition for an election to resolve the question. *Levitz Furniture* abandoned a good faith doubt for the withdrawal of recognition: to do that an employer had to have knowledge of the actual loss of majority support. Member McFerran said the Company had good faith doubt on the basis of conflicting claims. The Employer's quandry can is better resolved, says the majority, by the electoral process. If that is so, why should the Employer not be required to file an election petition? What purpose is served by withdrawal of recognition?